THE
STRANGER
WITHIN

Marvin Kistler

SYNERGY
PRESS

Designs and drawings by Marvin Kistler.

Published by
Synergy Press
P. O. Box 414557
St. Petersburg, Fl. 33743-1457
(813) 545-1560

Library of Congress Cataloging in Publication Data
Kistler, Marvin
The Stranger Within

Library of Congress Catalog Card Number 94-92397

ISBN 0-9644784-1-2

Publication date May 1995
$29.95 Softcover

CONTENTS

APPENDIX   A

INTRODUCTION

When you strengthen and develop the emotional coping skills of your inner child, you can accomplish things that have never been done before. You develop the emotional social skills of the child within you, just like you teach the inner self to type, by practicing daily. So after 2 or 3 months, this new emotional behavioral skill can occur automatically as a new habit. This is the same way you teach your inner child to play the piano, or swing a golf club.

There are 12 emotional growth periods between birth and 5 years of age. These growth periods involve specific emotional behaviors involving distinct circuits of the brain that you can train your inner child to acquire with feeling exercises. These emotional drills and workouts will allow you to develop and maintain a sense of emotional balance and equilibrium. The emotional equilibrium you acquire with these behaviors allows you to handle the daily stress of dealing with people.

Teaching emotional social skills to your inner child has never been attempted before. This new technique allows you to develop behavioral skills to control anger, fear, anxiety, depression, etc. After you complete the course of emotional training, you will be able to overcome overwhelming anger, anxiety or fear within minutes. Controlling these devastating emotional states has never been accomplished before without drugs.

When your inner self achieves the adult-child stage of development, you will acquire emotional skills to make you emotionally more mature and increase your emotional stability; and you can develop an inner peace and serenity with yourself.

And finally, there are two emotional states that you choose in your relationships that are exclusive of each other. These two emotional states or systems operate without the awareness of most people. One system causes all the social problems, the other leads to a higher quality of life. When you learn to recognize and use the appropriate emotional system in your relationships, you will achieve a much greater control of your life; and the quality of your life will improve tremendously.

Chapter 1

The Remo

The Inner Child

There is a genie bottled up inside of you. The right words can get him to come out and grant you your desires. He may not have all the magic powers of the genie from Aladin's magic lamp, but if you rub him the right way he will do his best for you.

This allegory shows that when the child within you, who is the great problem solver, reveals himself, you will begin to realize many of your desires and dreams. And you'll become much wiser when you are able to use your whole brain by including the half of the brain represented by the child within you.

Each of us is actually two people confined together in the same body. Each is represented by a distinct personality that is the exact opposite of the other; and each is represented by one of the brain's hemispheres. There is a relationship between these two personalities, via pathways between the hemispheres, that can cause a person to get along with himself and even love himself, or not get along with the self and even hate the self.

The relationship between the two hemispheres of the brain is very similar to the relationship between two people. If there is a problem getting along with the self, there usually will be entanglements and problems when dealing with others.

This relationship depends on communication between the two hemispheres. The hemisphere that operates below your level of awareness is the child within you. You communicate with this emotional half of the brain by being aware of your feelings. The better the communication the better the chances of a positive relationship. This book will allow you to develop higher levels of communication which in turn will improve your relationship with the "child" within you.

The term for the "child" within you is the remo, pronounced r ê • m ō.´ See Figure 1. Although the remo's hemisphere operates below the conscious level, you experience your remo's emotional vitality when you become aware of your feelings.

The remo has been referred to as the subconscious, the preconscious, the unconscious, the conscience, the submerged mind, the subliminal self, the id, the libido, yin and instinct. The remo may also be recognized as the child ego, the alter ego, the imaginary companion, the primitive self, the psychic self, the spiritual self, the guardian spirit, and the fairy godmother. When you hear people say "the devil made me do it," they're talking about their remo. The remo may also be referred to as the parent ego and the superego. Finally the remo is synonymous with what is known as your "heart" and "soul."

These names represent the many diversified aspects that describe the remo. But none of these terms paint the whole picture. None of these references give an adequate portrayal. So the term remo is used to encompass all the terms just referred to and all the characteristics and behaviors known to emanate from the right hemisphere of the brain. The rEMO is EMOtional, thus the term remo(tional) is used.

To recognize and better understand your remo, and your remo's roles and behaviors in your everyday life, there first has to be a delineation of the remo's psychological functions.

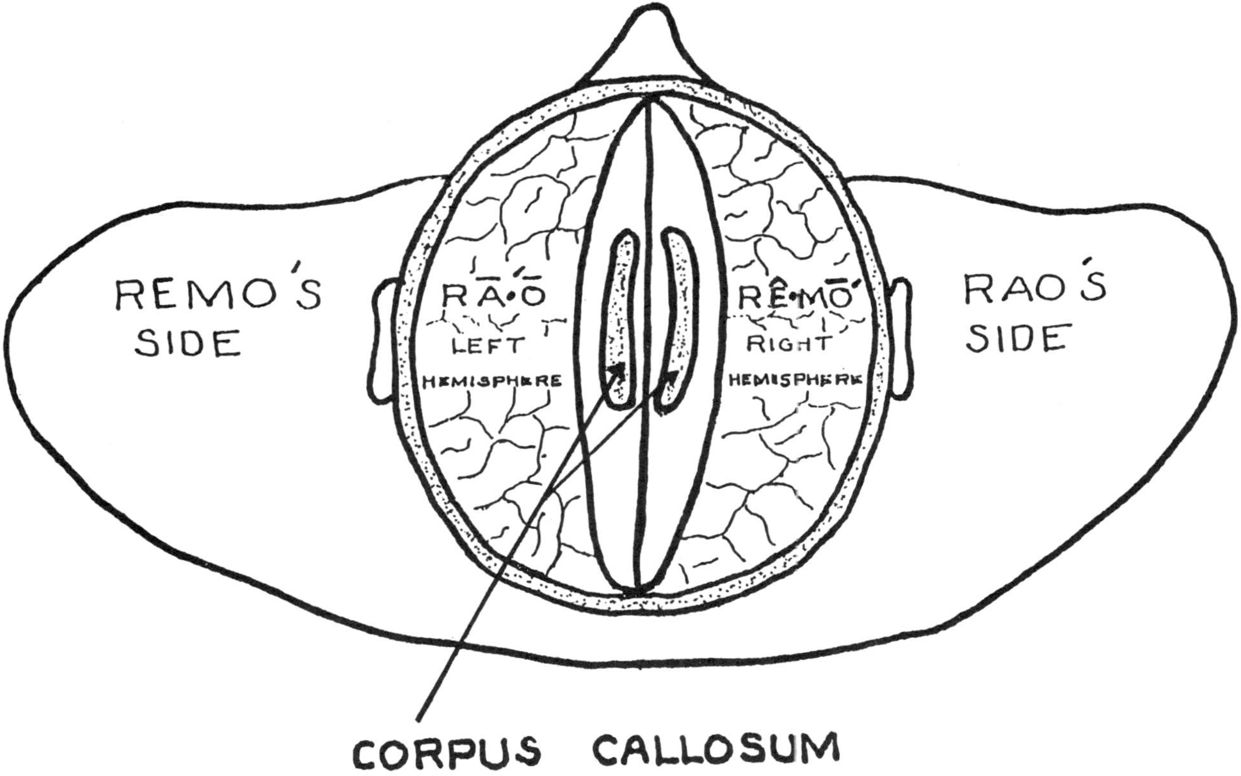
REMO'S
SIDE
RĀ·Ó
LEFT
HEMISPHERE
RÊ·MṒ
RIGHT
HEMISPHERE
RAO'S
SIDE
CORPUS CALLOSUM

FIG. 1

REMO'S PSYCHOLOGICAL CHARACTER

Your remo controls your emotional state of being. When you do not communicate on the same wavelength as your remo, you may experience feelings of anger toward someone for no apparent reason. Or you may feel like a smile or giggle at a most inappropriate time and you don't know why.

The automatic actions of your everyday habits are actually the actions of your remo, operating without your awareness. When you bite your fingernails, you can blame it on your remo. When you go through the motions of bathing and shaving early in the morning, these are tasks your remo can carry out for you when you are still half asleep, so you don't have to think about them. If you itch, your remo will scratch. And if you find yourself suddenly foraging in the refrigerator, that's your remo at work wrecking your diet.

You need to practice some sport or activity, like swinging a golf club, typing, or playing the piano, until the new task becomes automatic. The reason you need to practice is to let your remo learn that behavior, so your remo can take over that function. You know your remo has learned the behavior when you can do it automatically without thinking about it. This enables you to think about some other aspect of the activity.

Your remo also exerts a strong influence over your sexual activity. It is your remo's fantasies and dreams that spur your desire and drive for sex. A person who was abused psychologically or physically as a child will often have a remo which may be aroused sexually by someone abusive. And it is your remo who determines whether your sex partner is of the same sex or not.

Your remo affects your motivation to approach or avoid someone or something. Thus a bug or snake may cause you to recoil uncontrollably, while you may rush to see a loved one or a pet. Or your remo can make you a greedy pig who eats more than you need, or can motivate you to be anorexic.

And your remo is your efficiency expert. Your remo loves to cut corners, to take a short cut, to use abbreviations and would much prefer a picture to a 1000 words.

Your remo is a great problem solver. Your remo loves to figure out puzzles, mysteries, brain teasers, riddles, etc. If you awake in the morning with an answer to a problem that had you baffled, then your remo has been at work figuring out a solution to the problem while you slept. But some times a problem can be so engrossing that your remo can become obsessed.

When your remo's motivation becomes dominant, or when your remo tries to have its own way without your cooperation, then you have the addiction of an obsessive, compulsive response. You can't help yourself or you find it hard to control your actions. As an example, you can observe a person's remo when under hypnosis because the conscious hemisphere is incapacitated. A post-hypnotic suggestion may be given when the remo has been commanded to do something without your conscious involvement. So you may feel compelled or even obsessed to do something you may have no desire to do.

On the other hand, when your remo does not provide you with any motivation, you can experience feelings of being lazy; you just don't feel like doing anything. And when you procrastinate your remo may not be too keen about participating in an activity or seeing someone.

Your remo dominates the large trunk muscles like the arms and legs that influence nonverbal attitudes in postures. Thus when you fold your arms across your chest, turn your back or slouch, that's your remo expressing an emotional feeling about a situation. For instance, when you dread going to see an unpleasant boss you have to be nice to, your remo may hide your feelings by crossing your legs and folding your arms across your chest, as the remo tries to protect your emotional self.

Your remo is concerned with the immediate satisfaction of desires. You may experience this when you have an impulse to

buy something you may not need. This spontaneity and impulsiveness by the remo can be an inspiration to be very creative or
very destructive.

Your remo has an emotional-social need for support and acceptance from the people around you.   When these needs go
unfulfilled, then your remo has an inner world of imagination to
make up for this deficit. This can be expressed through your
remo's ability to dream, daydream or hallucinate.

Most important when your remo has been allowed to mature,
your remo provides you with the social and emotional coping
skills that allow you to deal with people daily in an effective way.
When your remo has emotionally mature, you can easily gain a
sense of self-confidence and self-mastery when interacting with
others.

CHAPTER 2

THE RAO

The rao, (pronounced r$\overline{a}$'•$\overline{o}$), represents the other hemisphere and what you think of as yourself. Your rao is the conscious thinking, discriminating hemisphere that you know as the self. The rao may be recognized by concepts like the ego, the conscious self, the adult ego, and yang. The RAO is RAtiOnal and so the term ra(tional)o is used.

While your remo reacts to a situation emotionally, your rao, as the thinking part of your self, responds in a more business-like way. Your rao likes to evaluate a situation with some skillful response, while controlling the fine motor muscles like the fingers, thumb, lips and tongue.

On a psychological level, the rao is the seat of the intellect. An I.Q. test is a measure of the rao's hemisphere. The rao plans things in a deductive manner, and lays things out in a sequence one after another, organizes them, and puts them into some kind of rational form.

The rao, an east Indian term meaning leader, carries out the executive functions of the self. The rao guides and directs the remo's emotional desires and drives. The rao achieves a goal with determination and by providing conscious efforts. When you consciously want to do something without the cooperation of your remo, your rao will have to strive hard and make an effort. Any achievement will have to be done on the will power of your rao. The intensity of the effort your rao must make is determined by the degree to which your remo is being uncooperative.

Putting on airs by being insincere or phony happens when your conscious rao emotionalizes a response that goes against the remo's wishes. However, when your rao and your remo are in agreement about what to do, the task or the behavior can be carried out effortlessly, even with pleasure.

Your rao can delay immediate pleasures for a later, more appropriate time, or for a greater pleasure, because your rao is governed by an outer reality instead of the internal personal needs that influences your remo so strongly. To understand the differences between your rao and your remo, you need to recognize their stages of development.

EIGHT STAGES OF DEVELOPMENT

INTUITIVE STAGE

Your remo, the child within you, develops during the first five years of life. You can observe the behaviors of the remo when you watch a child under 5. A lot of intuitive learning is going on during this very creative and imaginative age. Emotional coping skills and social skills are developing. The emotional ups and downs of these youngsters can go from great joy, to anguish and despair. The emotional roller coaster ride, along with the spontaneity of this age, can change a child from an angel one minute into a little devil the next. During these first 5 years, the right hemisphere of the brain seems to develop the bottom 3 of the 6 total layers of the neocortex, the grey matter of the brain.

MALLEABLE STAGE

The conscious rao seems to develop the bottom 3 layers of the left neocortex from 5 to 10 years of age. This is a rational sensible age filled with intellectual curiosity, providing the remo has been allowed to develop and mature. During these years children love school, because the rao loves to learn and develop intellectually.

SENSITIVITY STAGE

From birth to 10 years of age, all 3 nervous systems, the sensory, motor (muscle) and autonomic (viscera) are developing. The house cat represents an animal whose sensory system is most dominant. The race horse has a dominant motor system, and the pig has a dominant autonomic system. A dog is the opposite of the cat with both the motor and autonomic systems dominating.

Between the ages of 10 and 20, the third layer of the neocortex involved with the sensory nervous system seems to dominate over the other two systems. The teen's era is a sensitive, absorptive period when things are taken in, assimilated and learned by the various antennae of the sensory system. There is even a thinness in the build of the adolescence physique.

The remo's hemisphere seems to be developing again between the ages of 10 and 15. Because a society oriented towards social status hierarchies has little use for the remo's emotional childlike qualities, most of the remo's abilities are ignored or repressed. Thus the remo's growth periods can be very turbulent and troubled.

These can be times of emotional extremes for the remo, with the highest of highs, with uninhibited shrieks of joy, and very loving feelings and infatuations, to loud quarrels, sulks and the lowest of heartsick lows. Since the school systems are designed for the rao's type of intelligence, then school can be a real drudgery for the remo except for the social aspect of being with friends. The 14 year old with a "know it all" attitude is at the age most likely to run away from home.

SENSUOUS STAGE

Between the age of 15 and 20, the rao's hemisphere seems to be developing. Now the turmoil of the early teens subsides into the calmer and more studious age of "sweet sixteen," as the rao enjoys school again. The developmental transition from the dominance of the remo to the dominance of the rao can be seen in the remarkable change in behaviors seen in ninth graders compared to the eleventh graders. A growing awareness of the real world motivates the rational rao to plan and study for the future.

IMPULSIVE STAGE

The young adult from 20 to 30 years of age seems to develop the 2nd layer of the brain's neocortex, concerned with the "muscle" motor nervous system. This motor division of growth is involved with action, productiveness, accomplishment and the refinements of motor skills. And you can see a muscular hardness and definition in the muscular body of the adult in the 20's.

The remo's dominance is seen again from 20 to 25 years of age, there can be impulsive and emotional overreaction or even unstable behavior at this stage. Both men and women can be more vulnerable to impulsively falling in love and getting married.

PRODUCTIVE STAGE

The rao's dominance is seen again from 25 to 30 years of age, as the cost for car insurance rates decreases, and the criminal activity of those over 25 also decreases. Career and the workplace take on the most importance. Driven by the rao, a person can become a workaholic.

FAMILIAL STAGE

Mature adulthood occurs from 30 to 40 years when the "integrative" top layer of the brain, involved with the "visceral" autonomic nervous system, develops. This is a period when more intricate associations are developing to handle more complex social situations. And this tends to be a time when intimate social relationships become more important in the needs of the individual. Even the viscera organs tend to take on physical growth during this period as the waist spreads and bulges with a softening of the physique.

From 30-35 years of age, the maturing remo is developing strong social needs, especially for the emotional security of a family. Often you may see a strong drive in women to have a child, as her "biological clock" ticks the loudest, and in single men to get married. Artist, stylist and entertainers in the "talent" world see a peak of their abilities occurring around 35. And some are said to become "set" in their ways after 35 years of age.

POLITICAL STAGE

And finally, from 35 to 40 years of age, the rao's left brain is at the height of intellectual development. An individual is now more likely to enjoy and even be involved in social and political activities and even organize these events. The rao may now turn the radio dial from music the remo loves to a controversial talk station. And intellectual endeavors are now reaching a productive peak in the lifetime of the individual.

The stage of life when menopause begins marks the completion of the development of the rao. This may vary anywhere from 40 to 54 years of age in women, and is indicative of the great variability that can occur in different rates of development in different people. Those whose motor system is dominant usually mature the fastest and can burn themselves out sooner, whereas the late bloomer, who usually has a dominant sensory system, matures the slowest. Since men tend to develop the motor system more than women, they tend to mature faster and not live as long as women.

The rao's job is to lead and direct the remo's emotional and motivational drive towards appropriate task during the day. But because of the prevalence of social hierarchies operating throughout our society, this is often reversed. When the remo wants to be dominant and tries to be the leader, all kinds of problems are created.

So you need to understand how the two social systems of status and synergy operate to make you either happy or miserable. A daily battle is waged between status and synergy to determine which will dominate in your relationships. And you need to use this information to enhance the quality of your life.

STATUS AND SYNERGY

The problems that really bother us are the ones we have getting along with each other. These troubles exist because we have adopted a social system that is incompatible with our minds. There are two social systems that operate in our lives. These two social systems, referred to as "status" and "synergy," are in a constant struggle for dominance. The next chapter deals with understanding how social status hierarchies operate and how they corrupt the relationships people have with the self and with each other.

One of the major problems with relationships between people is there has never been an effort made to discriminate between these two systems of organizing human relationships. If your relations with others are oriented towards status hierarchies, then you tend to feel others are better than you, or that you are better than others.

We are so neglectful of the other system that there is no term to describe it. So a term Ruth Benedict (74) referred to as "synergy" will be used. Synergy is operating when you are able to accept and to relate to others on the same equal level, regardless of whether they are handicapped, a VIP, a star, retarded, etc. This is not to deny that there are differences of ability and intelligence between people; rather it is your emotional attitude toward these differences that's important. Thus, when interacting with a child, or with a poor or retarded person, you always have a choice before you. You can get up on your high horse and be patronizing or you can communicate on even ground.

Ruth Benedict (74) found among primitive people that tribes with high synergy were happy and secure with very little crime, anxiety and mental illness. On the other hand, the crime, greed, and fear found in tribes with low synergy (high status), produced miserable people filled with insecurity.

The synergy operating within Japanese businesses has been outstripping the status-oriented American businesses as Japanese workers love their job while American workers often hate theirs.

Once you are able to discriminate between the factors that produce these two opposite environments, you can begin to have more control over your social environment and shape it in the direction you desire. And once you understand how the status system damages the relationship between people and within yourself, you will be able to correct these status conditions that operate internally and externally. This will allow a more healthy relationship to develop between your rao and remo and between you and others. And as you adopt synergy as an integral part of your life, it will dramatically improve the quality of your life beyond your wildest imagination.

To put yourself on good terms with your remo, you need to understand that social hierarchies cause all the problems between the rao and remo and with others. In fact, it will be shown that social status hierarchies are the root of all evil, in regard to the problems among "men" and within "man."

CHAPTER 3

STATUS HIERARCHY

You will need to develop a more effective way of communicating between the two hemispheres of your brain besides being aware of your feelings. This book will teach you several operational steps that will be fairly simple and easy to follow that will allow you to communicate more effectively with your remo. But before developing this ability, it is important that you understand how a status hierarchy can operate to cause problems between the rao and remo.

The rao and remo are like two opposites that are combined in a complementary way to make a whole. The differences can be a source of pleasure or a reason for conflict. As an example, each has a distinct sense of humor that adds a different quality and broadens your involvement with life through pleasure. The rao can dominate to deny the remo's simple childlike pleasures, as being too naive.

For example, your remo may prefer silly lowbrow comedy that kids enjoy, like cartoons. But you, the rao, may look down on this type of amusement as being beneath the sophistication level of your social position.

On the other hand, the remo can influence an anti-intellectual bias that turns away from dry humor that requires reasoning. Thus, the dry ironical humor the rao finds fun and stimulating, the remo may find boring. Or your sardonic humor may even cause the remo to look on the rao as a standoffish intellectual prig. In either case, these conflicts can hamper enjoyment of living and lower the quality of life.

When such attitudes exist there can develop an internal alienation that is just as severe as the alienation between people. The reason people are alienated from each other and the self will be shown to lie in a belief in the values of a status social system. In fact, the degree of alienation between people is the degree that status dominates synergy.

Status creates almost all of the social problems you have with other people. The values of a status system can disrupt the social accord of people so severely that it causes: antisocial behavior and violence; mental and emotional illness; and nonproductivity and poverty.

Your status in a social hierarchy can be divided into two types. First is economic class status. Are you a blue collar worker? Or a white collar worker? Economic class status meets security needs by developing skills in order to accumulate material goods. This is a primary interest of the rao.

But your remo is interested in your social status. Social status is found in what you believe is your standing of respect and esteem in the eyes of those people within the same economic class and those you see from day to day. This is true whether it is a standing among colleagues, who hold a similar position in a business or profession, or a rank among workers. Your rank of respectability can also operate among friends, family and acquaintances.

How you perceive and interpret the feelings of those around you in regard to their acceptance of you is what is important in social status. This may be recognized as a "pecking order" that is established among friends, workers, acquaintances, etc. It also operates within you when the rao thinks or the remo feels you are better or worse than another, or others, in some way.

Many believe that once they rise to the economic status they desire, they will be happy. But the problem is there are still status hierarchies operating within this economic class that can create unhappiness. What was imagined as a secure, peaceful life of "living happily ever after" can turn out to be an attempt to keep up with the Joneses, or living to avoid criticism.

For example, one who has spent a lifetime striving hard to be a doctor can be left with a deficiency in the development of social skills. He may have a low ranking in the social hierarchy operating among the people of his economic position. He may feel he doesn't belong for any of a number of reasons, for example, because he is unskilled in the appropriate social "niceties."

The people who matter to him may not invite him to certain social functions, or they may snub him in other subtle ways. Thus, he can be left with a basic feeling of unhappiness about his life because his social status is more important to his remo than his professional one, and because happiness is determined by the remo's feelings.

The remo likes to be with people on a close emotional level. But the academic degree that is expected to provide the desired acceptance creates conflicts. The facade a professional and technical role entails gives a distant respect, but not the spontaneous warm affective relationship with people that the remo thrives on.

A position in the social hierarchy operating among colleagues depends upon emotional maturity. Those at the top will usually have an emotionally mature remo close to 5 years of age. Those doctors with a remo under 3 year will tend to be emotionally immature, which can prevent the development of effectively acting and social skills. And so those doctors will unhappily reside in the bottom half of their social hierarchy.

So after all the hard work to get where he wanted to go, a doctor may find himself more alienated from people than before. His own economic status puts him above most people while his own economic class may fail to give him the quality of acceptance that he desires. It has been found that doctors as a group have higher rate of suicide, than the general population.(10, 95 & 111)

Of course doctors are under a lot of stress, but doctors who commit suicide because they can't successfully cure their patients show a lack of maturity that a lack of social status creates. So although it may appear that job stress is the cause of their problems, the real curprit is an inability to emotionally cope with all the social stress involved with dealing with people all day long.

So the real problem is the lack of social skills caused by a lack of emotional coping behaviors which result from a lack of emotional maturity. On the other hand, those who have high social status among a lower economic class may be much happier with their lives.

CHAPTER 4

STATUS–SYNERGY CONTINUUM

Both status and synergy are social systems. Each organizes relationships between people, but each lies at opposite ends of a continuum. Both operate together. However, since they lie at opposite ends of a continuum, then one system will operate at the expense of the other. See Fig. 2.

Since status and synergy operate on the same line, there will be a mixture of the two operating with one being more dominant than the other. You will rarely find only status or only synergy operating but various mixtures of the two.

Synergy may be defined as a social state where people and harmless behaviors are accepted. Instead of a pecking order, there is a trust in mutual support and acceptance from the other people involved in a synergetic group. Instead of a sense of alienation, there is a sense of belonging.

Status system has a vertical social structure that has the shape of a pyramid. Those at the top of the pyramid are entitled to acceptance from all those who are below. Those at the bottom are entitled to no acceptance from those above.

STATUS - SYNERGY CONTINUUM

HIGH   HIGH

$$\longleftarrow \hspace{4cm} \longrightarrow$$

STATUS   SYNERGY

Symptoms Of Status   Qualities Of Synergy

Symptoms Of Status	Qualities Of Synergy
1. Vertical Social Shape	1. Horizontal Social Shape
2. Feeling Superior / Inferior	2. Feeling Equal
3. Desire Power To Control Others	3. Acceptance Of All Harmless Behaviors
4. Qualify For Acceptance	4. Mutual Acceptance
5. Use Threat To Force Solution	5. Use Mind To Find Solution
6. Punishment Not Restricted To Harmful Behaviors	6. Punishment Restricted To Harmful Behaviors
7. Mindless Conformity	7. Refreshing Multiformity
8. Oriented Towards Control	8. Oriented Towards Pleasure
9. Forced Cooperation	9. Willing Cooperation
10. Sense Of Alienation	10. Sense Of Belonging

Figure 2

In order to climb to the top in the status system, you need to be tough and keep a "stiff upper lip," while operating with the manipulating wit of the rao's hemisphere. This kind of "never let them see you sweat" approach to life requires you to deny or ignore the remo's feelings.

The natural ambitions and drives found in most people are wasted with a struggle up the status ladder to gain acceptance from others. But one's gain is another's lost. So often a status seeker will use criticism as a weapon against others to advance the self. This creates an environment where people are at odds with each other.

When each man is out for himself, he cannot be for you. Therefore, a conflict of interest is created. If you value the other person's judgment of yourself, then you place your measure of yourself on a precarious source. If you attach much importance to the opinions of others, who are looking out for themselves, then you do so at great risk to your own self-esteem.

On the other hand, synergy has a flat, horizontal social structure, where everybody is accepted and people can interact on even ground. Thus, the mutual acceptance that creates a sense of belonging leads to feelings of security among the families, groups or communities involved in synergy. Conversely, because of the alienation found in the status system, there is a strong need to struggle up the acceptance chain which creates a sense of insecurity in the population.

Status requires conformity to maintain control of the aggression it creates. The harmony synergy creates reduces aggressions and the great need for control. This allows a greater freedom among people to encourage a more stimulating environment of multiformity.

Because of conflicts between people, the status system has to force people to cooperate. While the supportive environment of synergy creates a sense of security and belonging, that will result in a cooperative milieu where pleasure can be found in goal directed behavior.

As you move to the extreme status end of the continuum, the use of physical force becomes more prevalent over the use of reason to solve problems. On the other hand, as you move to the extreme synergy end, reasoning and mental abilities replaces strong arm tactics to find solutions. Synergy requires the use of both halves of the brain; communicating with your remo and developing a synergetic environment go hand in hand. This means you must actively work together with your remo as a team when dealing with social problems.

Status conditions encourage one to operate on an unaspiring low level of mental activity in order to be compliant to the efforts of the leader. It influences a mindless conformity that depends on leaders telling others what to do and think. Thus, a hierarchy results in numerous people making little use of their mental abilities.

And the leaders often show a disdain for the mental abilities of those under them. In a study of two groups of employees who did "equally" good work, the leader of one shared power and decisions with the workers. The leader of the other group used forceful authoritarian techniques, took total control and made all the decisions.

Compared to the leader who shared power, the authoritarian leader devalued his employees by reporting they did not work hard, nor was their work of high quality. They received no credit for what they accomplished. All their good work was attributed to the decisions and orders of the controlling leader.(49) This same characteristic operates in all status systems whether between a man and woman, or within a family, group, community or government.

A status system needs a meek, obedient, compliant and dependent population. It cannot operate effectively with too many chiefs. Too many intelligent people can throw a monkey wrench into a status system and create conflicts and strife with alternative ideas and options to those in power.

Since the status system values leaders who command control and take responsibility for all decisions, it downplays the value of the human mind in the nonleader. Status also requires you to be cut off from the emotional half of the brain. To be in touch or communicate with your feelings can make you too vulnerable for the ruthlessness required for the climbing struggle to the top. So the status system tends to operate on half a brain.

On the other hand, synergy depends upon an internal communication that uses both halves of the brain completely. The power of each individual mind is the essence of synergy. It makes use of your mental abilities to organize life around pleasure and goals.

Social status hierarchies are actually incompatible with the human mind. The human brain has the ability to discriminate, to understand, to know minute differences between people, and to make inferences on these distinctions. It is this ability to form inferences on the multitude of fine differences among people that causes so much injustice and so many problems.

The only reason an immoral system like status can be effective and dominate is because most people are unaware of the two social systems. They do not realize when status is in force or when synergy is functioning. This lack of awareness causes an ignorance about how a social society operates, and causes conflicts between people and within the individual self.

Man is involved in a struggle between two social systems in his everyday life, where there is a clash between using the reasoning ability of the mind versus using fear, physical and emotional threats, control and coercion in his dealings with others.

Even today there are some who believe that destroying neural pathways of the brain, whether with electrical shock treatment or surgery, is the best method of eliminating emotional problems within the disturbed individual. On another plane, many who struggle everyday with the alienating stress and adversity of status find that deadening the brain by using drugs or alcohol can make living more tolerable.

People have to resort to such extreme coping tactics because of their ignorance of the two social systems that operate around them everyday, pulling them apart. They don't realize the choices that are constantly available to them from one moment to the next in their personal relationships.

Among the lower social animals status hierarchies are needed to create order and effective group action, and cull the weak so the fittest will survive. But with humans, the status system is such a contrary antagonist to the human mind that this process is operating in reverse.

Here the status value system is shown to be a fraud. Since the emotional support and acceptance people need are so often withheld, then the family often becomes the only source of emotional security. Thus, it is the lower class poor who procreate and multiply instead of our productive and talented best. The most fit find that the effort it takes to stay on top is too consuming to leave time for a family, while the lowest levels, alienated, unemployed or deprived of constructive activities and emotional support, reproduce prolifically.

JAPANESE

The Japanese have not incorporated synergy in their family and social affairs but they have for the most part in their successful businesses. On the other hand, American industries are organized in status hierarchal fashion.

Japan was once a poor, impoverished nation that was not much better off than many third world countries seen today. But Japan went from poverty to become today's most wealthy and thriving nation in a short period of time. The brilliant economic moves that propelled Japan past all the other nations of the world were not accidental. The third world countries that have tried to adopt democracy have failed because they tried to employ the vertical structure of status hierarchies. But Japan adopted a horizontal social-economic structure of synergy, utilizing the concept of "bottom up" rather than "top down."

Japan's businesses have a flatter synergistic system so that those involved in organizing the business will roll up their shirt sleeves and become involved in the activity on the production line; on the other hand, those down in the trenches are involved in the decisions that concern the company and its products.

The Japanese worker is also trained to take part in almost any aspect of the business. Thus, the Japanese worker is referred to as a "generalist" who finds the variety mentally stimulating and interesting. Conversely, the American counterpart is often referred to as a "specialist" who usually finds doing the same work all the time mentally dull and monotonous. Therefore, the Japanese love their work and willingly work long hours. Many would rather work then take a vacation. Contrarily, the high rate of absenteeism among the American worker who looks forward to the day he can get some time off is indicative of a host of personal and social conflicts.

What usually causes problems in the production and quality of a product are problems between workers, and between workers and their superiors. The severity of the problem between people is caused by the degree that status is dominant over synergy.

In the business world of America, many companies organize their people in a power structure that takes the shape of a pyramid. Thus, if they have one hundred employees, each one of those employees could be on a different level. Even those who have the same position or title are often ranked in a vertical manner by superiors. This creates the condition where there is a continuous shifting and fighting for positions of status. To gain status and a sense of superiority, political maneuvers are needed for the in-fighting among those of the same rank, while trickery and subterfuge are used to control subordinates.

The Japanese with their synergetic system have effectively reduced most of the bad effects of status and created a co-operative environment in which it is enjoyable to work. That is why American businesses can only compete with Japan's industry to the degree that they can replace status with synergy.

The next chapter will introduce you to the development of the emotional behaviors of the 12 growth periods that your remo went through as a child. As you practice these behaviors, and the remo develops a repertoire of emotional behaviors, it will allow your remo to mature emotionally. Your coping skills to deal with people will improve as you mature emotionally, because you will be able to develop excellent social skills.

Many people have a remo who was stopped in development, especially during the terrible twos. The rebellious nature of the two year old is incompatible with the status values of obedience and discipline. Those behaviors must be punished so parents can maintain control. By going back to the different psychic ages of a child, you can work through the problems of those ages to give you a second chance to grow and mature emotionally. As you practice the behaviors of each period, they can eventually become automatic behaviors for your remo, so that you will be able to handle any social or emotional situation with confidence and ease.

The purpose of developing behaviors of the emotional growth periods is to develop the neglected half of the brain. And you do that by practicing an emotional behavior until it becomes automatic, just like you would practice typing, playing the piano or swinging a golf club. But now you will be developing your emotional and acting abilities, which is the natural forte and domain of the remo. As the remo, the child within you acquires these behaviors, you will be able to mature emotionally, and develop a trust in yourself and your instincts.

CHAPTER 5

DEVELOPING THE REMO

Everything in nature wants to develop its capacities. If a man has always been blind or without legs, he is not necessarily unhappy because he cannot see or cannot walk, as that is not within his potential. On the other hand, the individual whose remo has been stopped from realizing full emotional maturity can be subject to quite a bit of internal unhappiness. This internal incompleteness is often expressed as a need to "find the self." It can create such unhappiness that people will quit successful careers to "find the self."

The most important thing in your life is to realize your full potential, especially in your ability to deal with people effectively. Interacting with people socially everyday of your waking life can be a difficult activity unless you have the social skills to cope with people. The foundation for those skills and the level of proficiency will be determined by the level of your emotional maturity. So to realize your full emotional potential or maturity in order to deal with people effectively can be one of the most powerful drive that can motivate people to change.

And one of the purposes of this book is to help you realize your full emotional self. You can do this by developing a repertoire of emotional behaviors that occurs between birth and 5 years of age, that will allow your remo to mature emotionally, so that you can have trust in your spontaneous reactions.

The remo, the child within you, will identify with the behaviors of children between the age of 1 and 5 years. The remo has to be childlike, because the young must be raised with empathy and compassion. The age your remo identifies with will tend to be the age of your remo. You can ask your remo to let a number between 1 and 5 "pop" or "flash" into your head. This number represents the age your remo presently identifies with.

THE REMO'S GROWTH POTENTIAL

The remo's growth possibilities correspond with neural pathways that can be developed in the brain. The remo's behaviors are limited to the neural synaptic connections that are possible. The brain does not produce new cells, but it can develop and strengthen new synaptic pathways.(122)

Synaptic plasticity provides the mechanical means for the development of new emotional behaviors, so that new combinations of pathways can get started along a neuron's axons, dendrites synaptic boutons and collaterals. What all this means is that pathways develop to convey new information along nerve fibers. The "incoming" aspect is when you see or hear something, and the "outgoing" aspect is when you react in a new way to this information.

Emotional growth is also possible along new neural routes. Long neurons have growth cones at their tips that shove and open new paths through glia membranes. This permits the extension of the nerve fiber tip to make contact with neural pathways that lie ahead.(93)

The neocortex of animals in enriched environmental conditions has been found to be measurably thicker than that of animals in impoverished conditions.(8) It was also found that the neocortex of the animals had thickened in the stimulating environment, because of the increased dendrite branching of the cells and the increased length of the neural fibers, even though the number of cells actually decreased. The level of chemical transmitters was also found to be significantly higher in the enriched conditions.(7)

New behaviors create electrical potentials that seek equilibrium by creating new pathways. Learning creates this difference in electrical potential that guides the gradual growth process involved in new pathway formation. This can occur in anyone regardless of age, unless short term memory is lost, as in Alzheimer's disease.

Thus, when you learn to type, your rao is consciously thinking about which keys to strike, while your remo is learning this new skill. As you practice typing, nerve fibers create new neural pathways in the remo's half of your brain. And when you strike the keys automatically without thinking about them, then the new pathways are completed and are permanently in place. The remo can take over the job of typing.

This is exactly the same process you will go through when you learn to develop a new emotional behavior. As you practice the behavior, you create a highly charged area in the brain that causes nerve fiber tips to grow and expand into new pathways. When the circuit has been completed your remo will have learned a new emotional, social behavior, that it can express on its own without any thought from your rao. And in addition, your remo will have emotionally matured in the process.

How long this takes will be very similar to the length of time it takes you to become a good typist. For you to type automatically depends on how much and how often you practice. How long it takes for your remo to change depends on how well you set up a good and effective daily routine of practice, or how frequently you practice the emotional behaviors. Also, you want to come up with as many variations on the main behavioral response in many different situations as you can by using your imagination.

However, emotional behaviors are more the natural domain of the remo than mastering physical skills, so the time it takes to develop your remo's emotional potential should be shorter. The remo's maturing process requires developing neural pathways that correspond with the development of the remo's emotional behaviors. Learning new behaviors and learning so many new ideas can be overwhelming. But the rewards are worth the effort.

Many spend thousands of dollars to attend college classes, for many months of the year, to learn things they may never use again. But the effort expended in learning new emotional behaviors will be skills you can use, practically every day for the rest of your life. And yet the expense is only the cost of this book.

And the time it takes will be much less. Specifically, the time it takes to change will be the length of time it takes new pathways to consolidate into new habits; then you will be acting automatically without having to think about it. You will have made yourself what you want to be.

On the other hand, the relearning of behaviors whose circuits have been lying dormant from disuse can easily be reactivated and re-established.

The period between birth and one year of age is called the infant stage. The first behavior you will develop or strengthen of the remo's twelve periods of development and growth as a child will be referred to as the "vegetative" response.

CHAPTER 6

SYNCHRONAL
PERIOD
BIRTH TO 3 MONTHS
THE INFANT STAGE

VEGETATIVE RESPONSE

Between birth and five years of age, the remo's development seems to be divided into 12 distinct growth periods, involving 12 distinct neural circuits that operate below the grey matter of the brain. These 12 growth periods seem to occur again in the remo's teen years from 10 to 15, again from 20 to 25, and again from 30 to 35 years of age, approximately.

Each of these 5 year periods uses the same subcortical limbric circuits of the brain. At the end of each critical growth period a neural circuit is "locked-into" its connections in the neocortex. These are located in the third, second, and first layers of the brain's neocortex for each of the five year period, respectively.

These 12 circuits and growth periods also seem to occur in the rao's hemisphere from 5 to 10, 15 to 20, 25 to 30 and 35 to 40 years of age, approximately.

The circuits of each growth period from the first to the 12th can be found in animals in the same order that corresponds with the lines of evolutionary ascent.

When you practice the behaviors that you need to develop, they can eventually become strong automatic behaviors of your remo. Your remo will mature emotionally so that you can have trust in your remo's ability to handle difficult emotional and social situations.

The "vegetative" responses that occur in the first 3 months of life can help to alleviate anxiety and other stressful feelings. The "vegetative" responses run on a continuum from a state of relaxation to a deep sleep.

Generally, the "vegetative" response influences oral activity around the region of the mouth, so that the lips, tongue and jaws take on a loose slack appearance. When the lips contract, they draw up thin; but when relaxed, they protrude, thicken and hang loose. The jaw slackens, drops and relaxes, permitting the corners of the mouth to come closer together. The tongue thickens, enlarges, and may even protrude slightly in some.

The eyes lose their sparkle and take on a dull untempered quality. Your breathing should become deep and rhythmical. If tense and stressed out, you want to transfer this negative energy and tension to the diaphragm located in the bread basket of your stomach. You should flare your nostrils as you contract your midriff, so that you inhale and exhale in deep forceful rhythmic breaths through your nose only. And sniff the air so you draw the air past the deep back part of your throat with a force that pushes the air into the sinus cavities to cause you to activate the olfactory region of the brain. If your teeth are clenched you want to transfer that excess tension to a positive, useful source in your diaphagm so you can breathe deeply and relax your lower jaw.

Anxiety induced by stress sometimes creates a choking sensation. What is actually experienced when tension is felt in the back of the throat is a contraction of the tongue muscles. Tight tongue muscles can be relaxed by gently letting the tongue protrude slightly, e.g. by wetting the lips with the tongue. You can also try alternately contracting the tongue muscles by making it as small as possible, and relaxing the tongue by making it as large as possible.

A gentle suckling motion, e.g., as when you kiss, will also help to relax the tongue muscles. Just as an infant sucks on a pacifier, you can create the same sucking sensation by enlarging the tongue so it fills the mouth. The suckling behavior also causes you to breathe in deeply and slowly to help you restore a slow relaxing rhythm. However, if out in public, you can keep your lips gently together, while your upper and lower jaws are apart and relaxed, to create a suction on an enlarged tongue. This should be a light, gentle, sucking action. If it is strong and intense you can cause the tongue muscles in the back of the throat to contract to create a hard swallowing reflex or gulp.

And if alone, there is nothing wrong with sucking your thumb when you find the stress is overwhelming. It can be effective at restoring your relaxing rhythms and deep breathing. This is a behavior status oriented people condemn. They have to punish it vigorously, and make up the old wives tale that your teeth will buck out. But the sucking action is more likely to pull teeth back in as not.

The stress from emotional displeasures can cause the restorative function of the "vegetative" responses to go awry, because the oscillating rhythm that help you relax are often impaired under the stress felt in our status environment.

Although the "vegetative" response creates a listless feeling of inertia, it is an energy response of the para-sympathetic division of the autonomic (viscera) nervous system. On the other hand, active excitable behaviors use energy from the sympathetic division.

The energy of the "vegetative" response may be experienced best when you are extremely sleepy or tired, and when awaking in the early morning before your sleep is out. The heaviness of the "vegetative" response has what may be described as a "buzz" or "rumbling" feeling that can overcome you. This seems to represent the synchronized "alpha" and "theta" brain waves, produced by the firing of brain cells, as read from an electroencephalogram.

When brain cells fire at a random or irregular rate, they are called beta waves. Beta waves make you feel excited. "Vegetative" responses can synchronize beta waves to control over reactions or unwanted excitation. It synchronizes cellular firing to create a sense of well-being and generate a relaxed casual feeling of self-contentment.

You should pay close attention to these "vegetative" feelings when you first wake up. Or when you wake up in the middle of the night, you should make an effort to study and note this feeling when all your brain cells fire together in unison. If you memorize this feeling it becomes easier and easier to recall and emulate later. You can recall these to help you cope or modify an unpleasant excitable state you are experiencing.

You may also notice a suction created within the mouth can elicit this synchronized "buzz," especially when used together with recalling these early morning feelings. With a few minutes practice throughout the day, your remo will more readily use these recuperative behaviors in difficult social situations.

The essence of the "vegetative" response is these slower alpha waves or rhythms. To re-establish your alpha rhythms, you should start out by taking a deep breath which is relaxing. Just hold it a couple of seconds and then let it all out. If you are really nervous, breathe out as if you are gently blowing out candles on a birthday cake. Relax by creating or imagining the heavy feeling you experience when arising from sleep; or the feeling that you are sinking into a chair.

The "vegetative" responses allow you to maintain a dependable regularity of biological functions, such as rhythmical breathing, going to sleep easily, awakening at approximately the same time every day, and bladder and bowel regularity.

These biological rhythms can be disrupted when too much stress is coupled with the personal alienation of a status social system. When rhythms are disrupted, then even a minimum amount of effort can produce tiredness and fatigue.

The "vegetative" responses can provide some control over excessive excitation, adverse stress, and displeasures, such as anger and anxiety. This allows you to pull back on the reins, slow down, and take it easy for a while.

A "vegetative" response may require a temporarily mindless state of being. In a world like ours, this simple act can be a very challenging behavior to re-establish. You may feel dumb engaging in "vegetative" behaviors, because you may feel it presents a dull, stupid appearance. However, being critical of such harmless but necessary behaviors is a status value condition that you want to be rid of. The "vegetative" responses are essential to your psychological well-being, your biological rhythms, and your ability to sleep and relax.

Each growth period of the remo's emotional development can increase self-control and self-mastery. Each emotional growth period can advance social relationships to a more complex and stimulating level. However, the "vegetative" response is the most important, as it is the foundation for the development of the behaviors of the other periods.

The "vegetative" response is important from a social aspect because it encourages an acceptance of the self. It also operates to sustain relationships with others, because it indicates that you feel good, and feel at ease in the company of others. "Vegetative" feelings allow comfortable relaxation and quell the tensions or uneasiness that can develop between people.

You should try to practice this response as often as you can throughout the day and night, as this response will be the basis on which you establish a state of equilibrium for all the other emotional growth periods. Think ahead of all the possible difficult, stressful and tense social situations in which you might find yourself. Then practice this response to that situation in your imagination, so you can better establish this response when you find yourself in a real stressful situation.

DRY MOUTH

Stress also tends to produce a dry mouth. The stress you experience when interviewing for a job, when you have an important date with the opposite sex or with business people and when you have to speak before others can all cause the embarrassing condition of a dry mouth that interferes with your effectiveness.

However, you can overcome this speaking difficulty by activating the "vegetative" response, which can be very effective at producing copious amounts of salivary juices. The gentle suctioning action within your mouth is effective at making your mouth water. Although your mouth is closed you want your teeth to be apart and your lower jaw to be as relaxed as possible. You want to take deep rhythmic breaths drawing air past flared nostrils so that you can feel the air rush silently past the deep back part of your throat.

SNORING

Those who snore and who have a problem with sleep apnea can use the "vegetative" response to cure this problem. Stressful social situations that occur during the day cause some to react with an inhibited tension that can suspend breathing momentarily or cause shallow breathing. As long as the rao is awake, the intake of air will be sufficient to sustain the individual. But when sleeping at night the remo's bad habit of inhibited emotional responses to social stress and inhibited breathing during the day are relived during dreams to create the threatening condition of apnea which causes snoring.

To stop snoring you need to practice the following exercise using the "vegetative" response with your imagination. You need to recall stressful situations, and react by transferring tension within the body to the diaphragm in order to take deep rhythmical breaths. If you have a wristwatch that chimes on the hour, you should use that as a signal to flare out your nostrils while taking deep breaths. You want to transfer the negative energy of tension in your jaw, neck and shoulder muscles to be used as a positive source in your diaphragm muscles to breathe deeply.

By rehearsing this response to stress throughout the day, you'll find when you are actually in such a situation that you have the ability to breathe and relax. By continuing to practice this response after a month or so, your remo will have "locked-in" this response as an automatic behavior, which then can be transferred to the remo's nightly dreams about daily activities. The additional behaviors you develop during the "juvenile" and "adult-child" stages will provide social coping skills that will permit you to relax even more. Then the snoring problem will cease to exist.

TMJ

Those people who suffer with TMJ (temporomandibular joint syndrome), often grind their teeth at night. The reason for this is that they have learned to clench their teeth during the day in response to stress. They should begin now to transfer that tension from their clamped jaw to the diaphragm in the pit of the stomach, while relaxing the oral region of the mouth with the "vegetative" response. The lips should pucker and protrude slightly while the jaw drops and loosens. However, to overcome TMJ will probably require the additional behaviors that occur during the "juvenile and adult-child" stages of emotional growth, but this is the first essential step.

MORNING FATIGUE

Awakening tired and fatigued in the morning stems from the same bad habits of restrained breathing when reacting to stress through the day, instead of using your natural emotional abilities of breathing naturally while relaxing the mouth region. To help you establish the habit of deep breathing during stressful periods, you need to go back to your basic instinct of sniffing the air. By flaring your nostrils to smell the air you are effectively using your diaphragm breathing muscles. Review past situations that bothers you, and while using imagery, practice transferring the negative tension to your diaphragm muscles by sniffing the air so you can breathe effectively.

While mastering this breathing technique, you'll develop a greater control of your diaphragm that will allow you to speak more assertively and forcibly when dealing with stressful social situation.

Whether you snore, have TMJ or wake up tired, it's very important that you practice the breathing exercise of the "vegetative" response for approximately five minutes upon retiring. And you want to give instructions to your remo to continue employing those breathing techniques of transferring tension to the diaphragm while you sleep.

SYNCHRONAL CIRCUIT

This is the first of twelve periods of growth. The subcortical areas interact with the fourth, fifth and sixth layers of the remo's neocortex. By the end of each age period the "wiring" of the neural circuit seems to solidify or "lock-in" in a permanent mode. These seem to lay down the major "highways" of the brain's neural pathways, although smaller "country roads" and "byways" that branch off can always be developed at later times.(93 & 122)

For the sake of brevity, the term "synchronal" circuit will be use to refer to the medial preoptic, anterior and posterior hypothalamus, olfactory bulb, medial and lateral olfactory stria, olfactory tubercle and gyrus, and anterior perforated substance regions. (Fig. 3) These

FIG 3 SYNCHRONAL CIRCUIT (0-3 MONTHS)

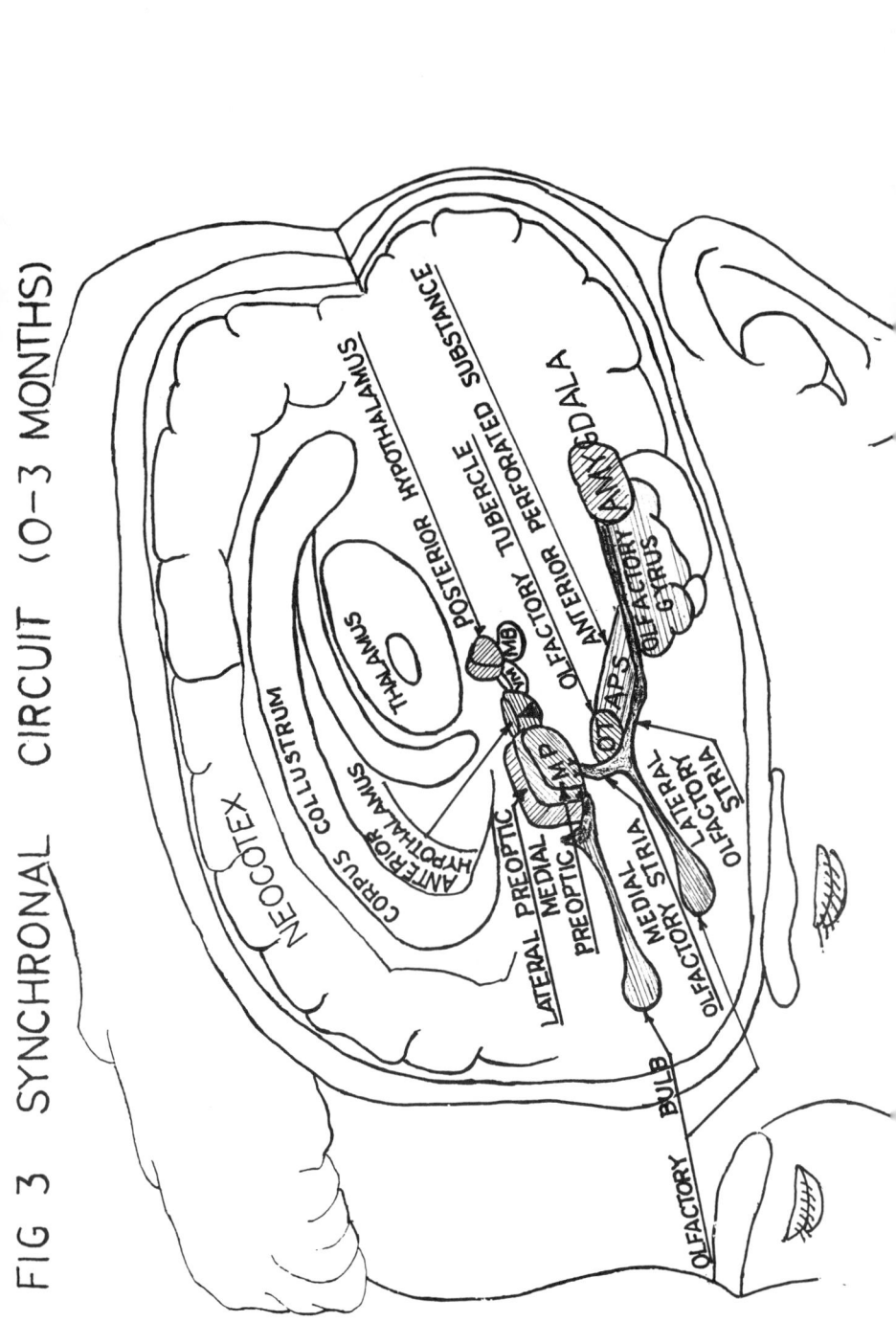

areas are grouped together to represent the "synchronal" region where "vegetative" response behaviors originate.

The "synchronal" region seems to be developing in relation to the three lowest layers of the neocortex. The nerve fibers in this area of the neocortex seem to be developing and solidifying until 3 months of age.

The "synchronal" region initiates rhythmical alpha waves by firing the cells of the brain in a synchronizing pattern.(112) This synchronizing area acts in a preservative function of sleeping, drinking, eating and eliminating. A restorative function also operates here to revitalize the body from the cellular breakdown, caused by the excitatory tension states of fast high frequency beta wave rhythms of the sympathetic division.

The olfactory region influences gross motor oral activities of tongue movement, swallowing, mastication, salivation and vocalization. Olfactory stimulation produced para-sympathetic reactions such as inhibition and acceleration of intestinal peristalsis, increased gastric motility, pilo(hair) erection, salivation, urination and defecation. It also produced an arrest of spontaneous movement to impair consciousness with tired or sleepy feelings.(106)

The connections of the olfactory region with the neocortex are very extensive even in animals with no smell (olfactory) function such as dolphins. So the olfactory region also has an emotional function that acts on the viscera to influence bodily attitudes, disposition and affective moods, by producing gross visceral approach and avoidance reactions.(46)

The anterior and posterior hypothalamus are involved in approach and avoidance behavior related to nutrition of oral activities, such as sucking and feeding, along with the olfactory function of discriminating desirable and noxious odors.

The anterior hypothalamus, as the nuclear control center for the para-sympathetic nervous system, (38) forms the rudimental basis for sexual behaviors.(25)

The preoptic area and anterior hypothalamus seem to be not only the point of origin for synchronized brain waves, but are also considered to be the sleep center at a higher level of functioning and control. When this area was destroyed, animals were not able to sleep.(81)

The preoptic area is a part of the hypothalamus that regulates endocrine and visceral activity by functionally tying together the olfactory area with the hypothalamus. (71)

Stimulation of the preoptic region can produce anger,(32) urination, defecation,(47) and behavioral sleep.(112)

Stimulation of the preoptic area creates synchronized brain wave patterns that produces inactivity, lassitude, drowsiness, and often sleep.(3)

The preoptic area has the ability to terminate appetite by inhibiting desires experienced as satiety. It does this by changing the excitatory appetite to slow synchronizing rhythms.(112)

CHAPTER 7

DIFFERENCES BETWEEN THE RAO & REMO

BIOLOGICAL LEVEL

Structurally, at a biological level the remo seems to emanate from a nuclear group in the brain known as the hypothalamus. (See Fig. 4) With the hypothalamus as the central organizing seat of subcortical nerve centers, the remo operates the brain's right hemisphere in the right-handed person in order to control the opposite left side. Thus, a person will hold a baby on the remo's left side, since carrying a baby on the rao's right side has an unnatural feel about it.

Moving to the opposite flank, the rao seems to be structurally centered at the thalamus. The 12 growth circuits in the rao's hemisphere seems to originate and be orgainized around the

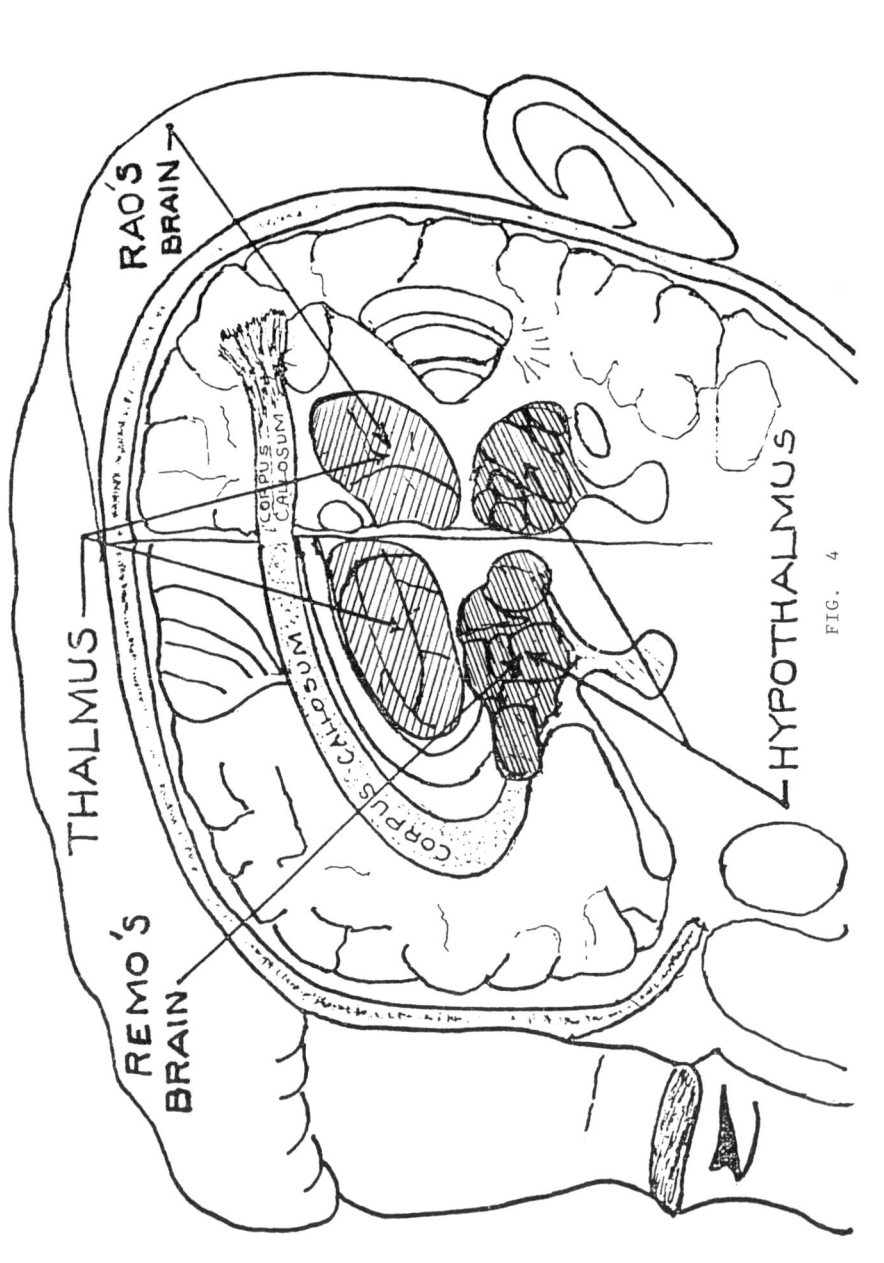

FIG. 4

thalamus. The rao's thalamus seems to influence the opposite right side of the body.

The remo is able to operate and carry on below your level of awareness.(109) The remo can size up a situation, come up with a solution, solve a puzzle or know intuitively how to react or move without the rao's knowledge.

The remo can achieve the awareness of consciousness by communicating impulses to the rao across nerve pathways that connect the two hemispheres. This bundle of nerves is called the corpus callosum (Fig. 4).

R. W. Sperry(108) stopped constant epileptic seizures by cutting the corpus callosum. After disconnecting the two halves of the brain, these patients would not respond to stimulation on the left side of their body.(35)

The left side was numb, and they would complain they couldn't feel anything with the left side.(108) During tests, they would watch their left hand move a pointer spelling out letters of words, answering questions restricted to the remo's right hemisphere. Their left hand would move seemingly on its own, as if it was possessed, or had a mind of its own, causing the patient to be perplexed and confounded

The right hand literally didn't know what the left hand was doing. If an object was placed in his left hand unseen by the patient, he would deny its presence even though it was manipulated with the fingers of the left hand.(35) Those with split brains could carry on two different tasks simultaneously. And they were able to complete both tasks as fast as a normal person could complete one task. The double task created too much confusion for a normal person to achieve any success.(37)

Each hemisphere had its own separate knowledge, perceptions and learning experiences. And each hemisphere had a separate memory from the other, which made recall inaccessible to the other half.(108)

In experiments, these patients with a divided brain were often like two separate people within one body each with different concepts and wills. Some patients had ethics, values and attitudes in one hemisphere different or opposite than the other hemisphere. This could produce internal conflicts.

As an example, one of Sperry's patients was asked to arrange some wooden blocks to match a certain pattern. The rao tried using the right hand but failed. Since this type of task is one of the remo's strong points, the remo tried to help but the rao slapped the remo's left hand away. But the remo continued to try to help anyway, so finally the willful rao had to sit on the remo's left hand to keep it from interfering, even though that was the hand that could get the job done. And another patient after buttoning up a shirt to go out socializing realized the left hand was unbuttoning the shirt to indicate a conflict, a disagreement he was no longer able to communicate and resolve via the nerve pathway called the corpus callosum.

DIFFERENT ABILITIES

Because of these experiments carried out on the patients with a divided brain, different abilities were found residing in each hemisphere. The creative right brain of the remo provides originality, while the rao's left brain has a practical nature to apply this originality. So the remo provides the creative talent to paint a beautiful picture, but it's the rao who gets down to the business of selling it.

The right brain of the remo is able to deal with many different factors simultaneously. The creative remo can play the many different roles of an actor, or in a negative way, create the many people involved in a multiple personality. The remo provides a creative diversity and multiformity. When you get to know your playful and contrary remo you may find your remo hates conformity.

Your remo can size up a situation instantly. When you get premonitions about future events, these intuitions come from your remo. Your remo's immediate comprehension and intuitiveness can give you insight into a situation.

The remo, the "generalist," sees the forest instead of the trees; the rao, the "specialist," provides the concentrated attention needed for fine details, and is more concerned with the trees. The rao's less instinctual thinking process is analytical and slower, but more certain and accurate with calculations that can be very computer-like. And the rao provides more specific skills, such as those found in reading, writing and speaking.

What this all means is the rao's brain provides the intelligence as measured on an I Q test, while the remo's brain provides, problem solving abilities, comprehensive overview, insight and creativity; and when the rao and remo communicate effectively they can combine to provide the wisdom of a sage. The reason you don't see more wise men is because most men don't know how to effectively use all of their brain power by communicating with their remo.

Playing chess and music composition are the domain of the remo's right hemisphere. Great chess masters and musical geniuses like Bach or Beethoven had enhanced brain development in the remo's right hemisphere.(43) The remo is able to learn and retain vast vocabularies of positions or patterns needed for chess or music.

The remo can see many aspects simultaneously, integrating irrelevant material into some kind of whole as seen in dreams. The remo likes to take many parts and put them together, rather like putting pieces of a puzzle together, or combining bits of information to solve a problem in order to make some kind of "holistic" sense.

Since the right hemisphere is able to process a multitude of sensory input simultaneously, the remo can be both very inventive and very inappropriate. The remo, the nonconformist who can be expected to do the unexpected, can create behaviors that appear original, mischievous or deviant.

However, this originality along with the emotional subjective state of the remo makes creativity and play natural vehicles for expression. The remo's right brain controls the left hand, and this has been found to be the hand that has the ability to draw and sketch in split-brain patients; while the rao's right hand was still good at writing, it could no longer draw or copy shapes; nor did the right hand of the rao have the ability to sketch three dimensional objects in space, such as perspective drawings.(35) You'll notice almost all great artists are left handed.

It seems that the left hand of the remo should be developed and used to do creative work, such as art and drawing. Our ignorance about ourselves has created a one-sidedness in man, but it appears that a specific ambidexterity should be the more normal condition for man.

COMMUNICATION

Man is not only one-sided in his manual dexterity and one-sided when interacting in a social system of status, but he is also one-sided in the use of his brain. When you learn how to use and develop the remo's neglected half of the brain you will increase your wisdom and intelligence. But before you can do that you need to learn ways to communicate better with your remo. In the next chapter you will be given a communicative activity to do with your remo. You will be taken through six different levels of communication, each step at a higher level. Most people communicate with their remo at the lowest level by being aware of their feelings.

Two people have a more harmonious relationship the more they communicate effectively with each other. So too, the more your rao and remo are able to communicate effectively, the better off you will be. People with emotional/mental problems and people who do not get along with themselves, usually don't even interact at the lowest level of communication which is being aware of their feelings.

It has been found that children who had an imaginary companion, were more secure and emotionally stable than children without imaginary companions.(105 & 124) They were less aggressive, more cooperative, smiled more, had a greater ability to concentrate, were seldom bored, watched half as much TV and were not interested in violent cartoons as were other children. Their language was richer and more advanced. But just as important, these children felt their imaginary playmates were true companions who were steadfast and loyal.

Their good emotional health is an example of how communicating between the rao and the remo can make for a richer and fuller life and can vastly improve the quality of your life. Communicating with your remo at higher levels would be our natural state of being if it was not for the status hierarchies operating in our society. The degree of our estrangement from our remo is a direct function of the degree that social status hierarchies are dominating.

CHAPTER 8

INNER SELF

You have an exciting world inside yourself that has been left virtually unexplored. This begins a challenging adventure which will take you on eye-opening excursions into the far side of the mind and present astonishing pathways into this frontier. Your journey on this voyage will have connections between the two hemispheres of the brain. But the only people you are going to meet will be yourself.

You interact with your remo by being aware of your feelings. Six operational steps will disclose stages that can put you on more sophisticated levels of inner communication. Each stage will take you to a higher level of interaction, until you achieve a communication breakthrough with your remo at the sixth and final stage.

A beautiful way to interact will unfold as you discover exciting ways to improve the quality of your life. When you achieve a communication breakthrough, you will be amazed at how much more intelligent and wiser you will become.

They say when making a decision that "two heads are better than one." Nowhere is this more true than with a ready access to the hidden half your brain. The very talented and brilliant people have much easier access to their remo, than most people. They are able to utilize much more of their whole brain, instead of only using half their brain as so many do.

Your communications between your rao and remo will develop a very enjoyable, loving relationship within yourself. Your ability to communicate is a function of synergy. The degree that you can adopt values of synergy will be the degree that you can advance to higher levels of communication with your remo. And conversely, developing synergy between the rao and remo and with others depends on more advanced inner communications. In addition, if you want the remo to develop and mature, you need these higher levels of internal communication.

You should be aware of conflicts between the rao and remo. Conflicts can arise when one tries to do the job of the other. Conflicts can be seen on the golf course, where you may often see this internal war after a bad shot, as some will angrily berate themselves.

While practicing, it is your rao's job to learn how to perfect a golf shot by thinking and experimenting on how to correct the flaws in a swing. But when your practice is over, and the game is to be played, it is your remo who is the shot or play maker. When your rao tries to think too much about how to make a shot, the rao's mental effort actually interferes with your remo's natural ability to execute a shot.

Very few people play up to their potential, because they don't understand their self and how they function. So when it's game time, they perform like the split brain patient in a previous example who would sit on his remo's hand even though that was the hand that could get the job done.

On the other hand, the responsibility of your rao is to lead or guide your remo. Your rao's decisions through out the day direct your remo's emotional motivational engine to interact socially with others, to work, to study, to read, etc. And when there is a problem, you can call on your remo to find a solution.

The most serious conflicts arise when your remo takes on the responsibility of the rao and tries to be the leader. When your remo wants to make the decisions, you will have a lot of emotional turmoil. When your remo tries to dominate, then relations with others can be fraught with difficulties.

The only way to correct this problem is to communicate with your remo. In this case, your rao has to take charge and direct the remo to cooperate at each of the upcoming communication steps. When your rao takes command, your remo will obey and go along with your rao.

When you can communicate with your remo while practicing the values of synergy, it will allow your rao and your remo to work together as a team. By communicating on higher levels, you can get to know your remo and better understand yourself. This will also improve the quality of your life. Your exchanges with your remo can fill your times alone with pleasure and energizing mental activity. And you can enjoy and love yourself, while having fun with your "mate," your remo.

OPEN RECEPTIVITY

You need to be receptive with an open-minded attitude to overcome the communication barrier created by the myths and fears of our status society. As you communicate in a more intimate way with your remo, your conflicts will fade away and you'll enjoy yourself more and more. And you'll find when your start developing your remo's emotional coping skills, you're going to have a lot of fun with your remo. You will eventually get to the point where you can have trust and confidence in your natural impulses, i.e. the impulses of the remo.

Communicating with your remo will require some effort on your part. Everything hinges on your rao's desire to want to get to know your remo. An individual's remo has always known about the rao, but for most people the conscious rao has had no idea about the intricate existence of the remo. The remo's complex behaviors that operated below awareness were labeled and passed off as automatic reactions or habits.

The remo tends to operate much more from inertia, so that the way things are and have been will tend to continue that way. So the desire needed for the effort to break the communication barrier has to come from the conscious desires of the rao. You cannot depend on your remo to come forth voluntarily to achieve this endeavor. You will have to be determined and "will" it to happen.

And finally the most important reason you want to communicate is because your rao is the leader who guides and directs your remo's emotional motivational drives. But the degree to which you are out of touch with your remo will usually be the degree that this will be reversed. So when you have a topsy turvy inner relationship, with your remo in command and determining your actions, then you will tend to have an emotionally unstable life filled with all kinds of personal problems.

ADVENT OF ADVENTURE

Your first operational step is to establish a signal code. This involves putting together a pendulum with a thread and needle, or you can use a string tied to a small object, such as a ring, safety pin, etc. Let the object hang about six inches below your thumb and finger. Rest your elbow on a table with your wrist bent so that your forearm is vertical, parallel with the thread and needle.

You will ask your remo questions that require a yes or no response. An answer of "yes" will be observed when the needle swings in and out, towards you and away from you, just as you would nod your head in agreement. "No" is signaled when the needle swings from side to side, moving in a parallel direction with your shoulders, just as you would turn your head as if to say "no." A rotation of the needle in a circle will signal a response that the remo doesn't know or doesn't want to answer. You can ask your remo which direction, clockwise or counter-clockwise, represents which response. You will need to stare at the needle or ring until you become immersed in a state of absorbed concentration.

When asking a question, you need to make yourself very receptive to feelings by staring intently at the object in a dreamy sort of way. When you centralize your attention you are reducing distractions around you, and your energy is concentrated for use by your remo.

Remember this is a mental interaction between your two hemispheres, so it is important that you don't ask questions out loud. This internal process uses your ability to ask questions silently within your own private thoughts.

Your remo will make these responses with your large trunk muscles in the upper arm and shoulder, so your small muscles of the hand and fingers should remain relaxed and motionless. These responses will all occur below the level of awareness, so you will act as an observer of your movements without any conscious control.

If you are surprised when you experience this, then you should start becoming more familiar with yourself and with your ability to function below the level of awareness. The more understanding and knowledge you can gain about yourself and how you function, the better off you are going to be in every way.

CHAPTER 9

EXPLORATION

When communicating, it's fun to emotionally arouse your remo. Your remo grooves on emotional excitement and appreciates any awareness you give to feelings. You can get an emotional rise by being very loving toward your remo, or a negative one by trying to put over a phoniness. For example, when you have to be nice to some mean spirited boss or leader, the remo dislikes.

So the questions you ask will need to be of an emotional arousing nature, questions about your spouse or sweetheart, your friends or enemies, your boss, relatives or family, your work or hobbies, questions about some pleasant or unpleasant past happening or some future happening.

You can ask questions about your dreams to start understanding what they mean. Often in a dream, the rao and the remo will be symbolized differently, e.g. a plane or ship may symbolize your remo while your rao may be represented by the pilot or helmsman. A review of the emotional or significant situations that happened during the day is usually what your remo will dream about. You can ask questions about some emotional event that occurred between fellow workers on the job or between friends during some social occasion.

You can ask your remo about certain specific body postures or movements and whether they convey certain attitudes or feelings about someone who was with you. Especially rousing are questions about your mother and father, about things good and bad they have done. Questions about your childhood days. Your remo can remember things not available to the conscious recall of your rao.

Your inquiring interaction with your remo results from a division that exists within you. Awareness of the self and feelings require this split within you. If you were undivided you could not observe your own mental and emotional reactions. You could not be critical, embarrassed, or pleased with your own feelings.

The rao and remo are a duality that complement each other. Their bipolar capacities create a charged atmosphere of creative living. However, like an "opened capacitor," a communication gap can keep the remo in an emotional state of charged tension and prevent the flow of "juices" that can "energize" your life.

CULTURAL MYTHS

The communication breakthrough is something for you to have fun with. Your two halves want to be able to enjoy each other, to love each other and to be able to have fun with each other. You want this to become a natural part of your daily living when you are alone. In addition, the higher the communicative level you can achieve with your remo, the greater are your chances for good emotional health, which in turn will often greatly improve your physical health.

On the other hand, when you move in the opposite direction away from communicating to deny or ignore the remo's feelings you can develop a host of emotional problems and even mental illness, depending on the maturity of your remo. When there is both a communication barrier and the rejecting stresses of a social hierarchy they can combine to create a nervous breakdown of your behavioral defenses. A person with an infant-child remo

(1-2 years old) can be susceptible to a psychosis, or a child remo (2-3 years old) to a neurosis.

But if you learn to communicate with your remo, the rao can regain the proper leadership role of advising, guiding and directing the remo away from emotional trouble and turmoil. If the rao doesn't take command because of the communication barrier, the remo can overwhelm the self and be the dominate controlling force. A job the remo is not suited to handle. When the rao loses control, then self-control is lost.

The most unhealthy divisions between the rao and the remo are created by a lack of communication. It produces an inner alienation. The degree that there is a lack of awareness of the remo, is the degree that emotional illnesses can exist. The emotionally ill individual is almost always so alienated from the remo prior to the illness that there wasn't even any awareness of feelings.

We wallow in many myths not only about the self but about mental illness. A schizophrenic, who suddenly realizes there is another personality within the self, namely the remo, who has always been there obscure and beyond awareness, causes a state of panic.(4) Our culture has ingrained so many false beliefs in us about mental illness, that a patient's sudden awareness of the remo suggests that he is going insane. This new personality begins to think in an unfamiliar way which he believes, from what he has heard, is a sign of madness. And he is petrified. This fear can overcome and incapacitate the rao's ability to think and be in control.

The final result of this ignorance is the eventual discovery of the remo under the worst set of conditions possible and at the worst possible time, when feelings are terrifying. And instead of the individual feeling at home with the remo on more peaceful and loving grounds, which may have prevented this misfortune to begin with, the remo is revealed as a terrible avenging spirit.

Even though the remo comes forward to assert itself when full of hate and fear, this communication is still the most natural step toward health that can resolve internal conflicts. In other words, there are no conditions, no matter how terrible you may feel about yourself, under which you cannot communicate with your remo.

Nature creates this condition so the rao is forced to acknowledge the remo as the source to be dealt with if recovery is a possibility. And those who become locked into mental illness, even for a lifetime are those who cannot lower the communication barrier and make contact with their remo. The emotionally broken spirit of the individual has to be regenerated and healed by being in touch with the remo to create an internal environment of acceptance and mutual support.

So the corrective circumstances are produced by nature as a measure of last resort. First, the conditions of a psychosis create a psychological withdrawal to allow an escape from the adverse status conditions. Second, resources are concentrate to allow the individual to go into his own mind to make repairs of this inner domain. Third, the most fertile conditions are produced when a clear cut division is created internally between the rao and the remo. And last, the individual is allowed to become acquainted with his inner self and get to know his remo.

As an example, a mentally disturbed man developed an imaginary companion during psychoanalysis. This relationship with his imaginary mate (his remo) was instrumental in restoring emotional health and resolving personal problems.(34) By communicating with his remo he was able to develop confidence in himself and have normal mature relationships with others.

If you're the worst that you can be, you're going to be better off to the degree you can communicate with your remo. If you're the best that you can be, you're still going to be better off to the degree you can communicate with your remo. This is nature's way of calling man back to himself. And this is nature's way for man to get to know and answer his own needs. The communication barrier is the reason that people have problems getting along with the self. This lack of communication is the main reason the remo is so often under developed. It is the reason for the lack of wisdom and intelligence in people. It is the reason most people do not have good social skills. It is the reason people do not mature emotionally. And it is the reason the status system dominates our social system.

If we keep following the social-psychological myths in our culture, instead of communicating with the remo in an effective cooperative way, then we shall remain in the emotional dark ages of knowledge about ourselves. And we will continue to have sick individuals and a sick society. A measuring device for the sickness of a society is a gauge that can measure the degree that status dominates over synergy.

CHAPTER 10

MIGHT
MAKES RIGHT

Status hierarchies overcome the dangers of anarchy by forcing cooperation with laws, and with a conformity that requires respect for authority. It forces cooperation with pressure, and the threats of punishment via criticism, disapproval, rejection, coercion, fines and imprisonment.

But punishment is taken out of its proper context to control harmful behavior and is used inappropriately to threaten and force people to cooperate. This weakens punishment's essential role to control harmful behaviors.

When punishment is used to control harmless behaviors, it creates all the injustice and lack of fairness so common in a status system, which in turn encourages more antisocial behavior. Thus, a status system shapes and develops an antisocial and violent people because punishment is diluted, and loses its effectiveness to control harmful behaviors.

The use of punishment for victimless crimes increases the harmful acts of authority. This increases the power of those in control to make status more entrenched as a system. So to the degree these types of laws increase, the power of the state increases, until a democracy can become progressively more similar to a totalitarian state.

NON-VERBAL SIGNALS

The use of coercion that the state uses to enforce cooperation on its people can also operate between two people. When one tries to control another to achieve some cooperation, an inequality is created that results in a dominance over another. An example of this dominant-submissive interaction based on inequality is a masochistic-sadistic relationship, that is much more common than you think.

But the operation of status is not always so obvious. There are many intuitive signs of one's personal status that take place on a non-verbal level. Who among us hasn't been deterred from speaking in a social situation due to a sneer, a raised eyebrow, whispers behind the back, a cold shoulder or eyes rolled upward? In addition, more subtle signals suggest condescension, inferiority, rejection or avoidance from people that the remo is adept at picking up, but which the rao may often be oblivious to.

The radar of deaf people to pick up these non-verbal cues makes them a victim of this non-verbal abuse from others. As a result the deaf are a relatively unhappy group with more emotion-al problems, as compared with the blind, who are spared by virtue of their handicap this non-verbal mistreatment from others.(53, 76, 92 & 127) Because of the unnatural conditions of a status hierarchy, one is better off emotionally being blind than deaf, as non-verbal assaults make their oblivion a protective shelter for happiness.

The insensitivity that results from retardation also cuts down on the negative feedback so rampant in a status system. Retarded boys were observed to be happier than normal boys both in the classroom and on the playground.(16)

This is another indication of how the human brain is incompatible with a social hierarchy. The lower the intelligence the more effective status can be. The status system is most effective in wild social animals. And the status system is more effective at creating order and harmony among geese than monkeys for the same reason.

When Eve ate the forbidden fruit of wisdom, she condemned Adam and the rest of humankind, because wisdom in human minds is not compatible with the authoritarian power needed for control under status.

The point is you want to free yourself from the pain and displeasure of a status environment and status oriented people. And you want to replace them with attitudes oriented towards pleasure by developing values of synergy. The next chapter illustrates the second growth period which is a positive emotional behavior that's completely dependent on pleasure.

CHAPTER 11

APPROACH
PERIOD
3 - 6 MONTHS

APPROACH RESPONSE

The "approach" response develops in the second growth stage. The "approach" area of the brain is an especially strong pleasure area.(87 & 128) Although there are pleasure areas in the "vegetative" synchronal region (86) of the brain, they are not nearly as strong. The "approach" and "vegetative" responses combine to find great pleasure in sustenance. Now there develops an approach or "looking" to pleasure, as a healthy baby coos, smiles or laughs easily.(40)

The ability to relax yourself during the first 3 month period with the "vegetative" response provides the most important behavior to reduce the stresses of a harsh status environment. The second most important defense to fight the stress of our alienating status system is to use a positive outlook on life, that pleasurable reactions provide during this "approach" period.

The "approach" response is an important behavior that helps you to be oriented towards pleasure. When you are positive and upbeat, good things are going to happen. To increase the quality of your life, your communications with your remo should be filled with fun and enjoyment.

It is helpful to be around a child under five to entertain and play with so you can watch a pure remo in action. In the same way you elicit pleasure and fun from a young tot or even a baby, you can also elicit pleasure from your own remo.

Just as your own remo needs your rao's support and smiling face, so family members, friends, and acquaintances also have remos who need support and friendly acknowledgment. When you pass someone who looks a little down, why not smile, speak, or even compliment them to cheer them up, just as you would do with your own remo. Just as you would try to make a 4 month old baby smile, you can get your own remo or the remo of someone around you to smile. Only by getting to know how vulnerable your own remo is can you ever come to realize how much support and comfort is really needed by the remos of other people.

When you give your remo a hug, or a wink and a grin in your mind's eye, you are giving your remo some pleasure, and saying, "Hey! things are not all that bad." This orientation towards pleasure helps to shift out of the displeasurable circuits in the brain into the pleasurable pathways. This can help you negate the negative apprehensions in life so you can develop a more constructive, positive approach. If you practice this attitude several times a day, your remo will soon start showing this positive attitude on its own.

You activated the para-sympathetic division of the autonomic nervous system when you relaxed your lips with the vegetative response, but for the "approach" response you want to excite the sympathetic division. You do that by contracting the lips, drawing the lips up thin, so the upper and lower teeth are exposed in a smile. When you smile you can reroute the negative energy of displeasure into the pleasurable circuits of the brain.

You want to activate the pleasure pathways in your brain as often as you can throughout the day. When you start communicating with your remo, you should always try to have fun with yourself. You can kid yourself if you like or try to find humor in a situation. The more you become oriented towards pleasure, the less likely you are to slip back into the displeasurable circuits of the brain.

When out shopping you should have fun with the clerk, and they enjoy the fun and humor of being kidded. Young kids you come in contact with causually are usually a kick, and up for a little fun. When driving you should let your remo dance to your favorite music in your mind's eye. And you may want to move around a little to the beat of the music yourself.

APPROACH CIRCUIT

The "approach" circuit refers to the corticomedial amygdala and the lateral olfactory stria and stria terminalis pathways which have connections to the medial preoptic region and the anterior hypothalamus. (See Fig. 5) The corticomedial amygdala has been found to be an especially strong pleasure and reward center in electrical stimulation studies. (87 & 128) These feelings of pleasure are very similar to the emotional pleasure experienced in eating, especially when hungry. (86 & 73)

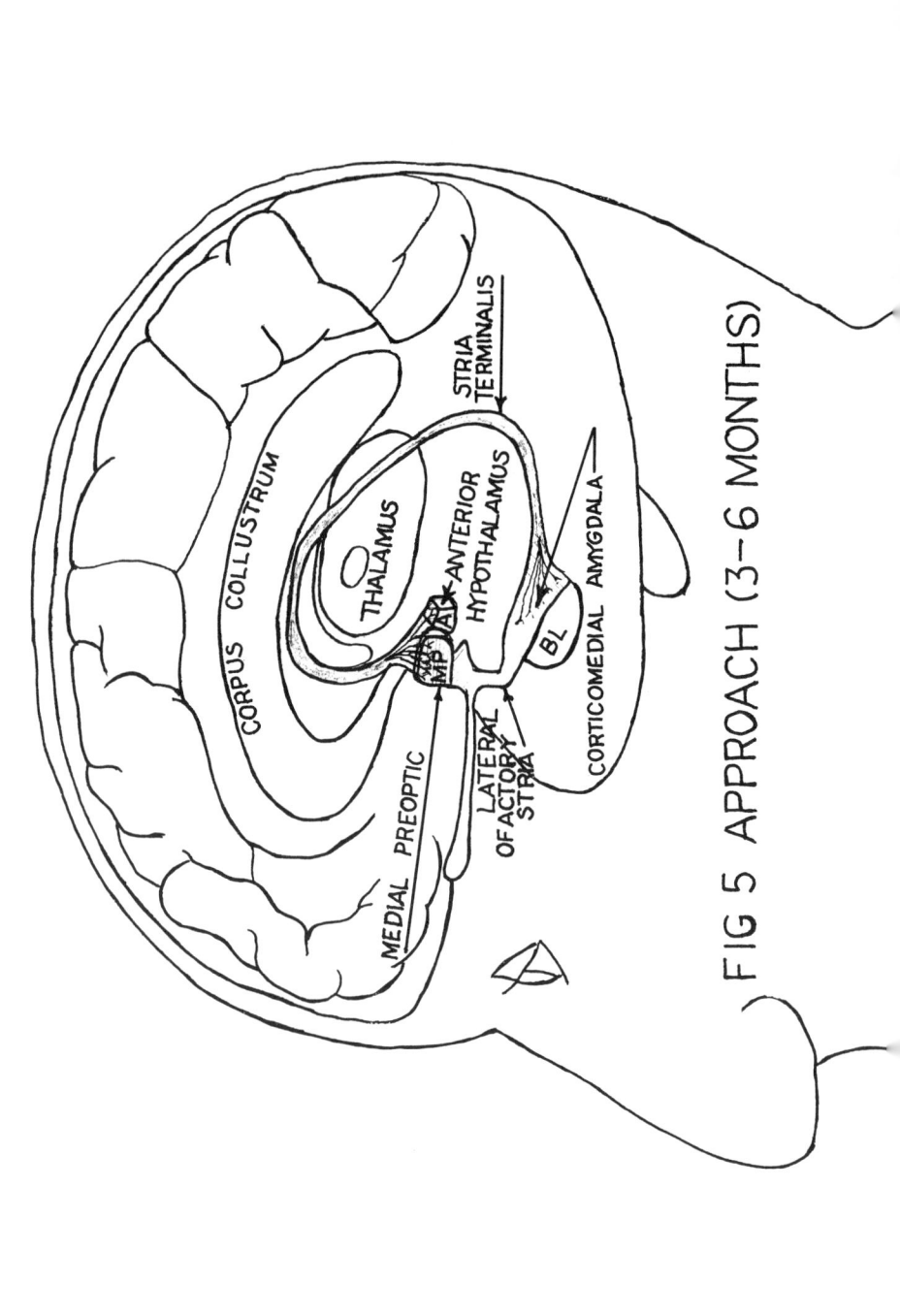

FIG 5 APPROACH (3–6 MONTHS)

CHAPTER 12

GAMES

The "approach" growth period is the essence of synergy. To activate the "approach" circuit you need to be oriented towards pleasure. Our brain is wired with circuits that can produce pleasurable behaviors. We are made to approach pleasure and avoid displeasure. But status reverses this natural order of the way our brain is wired by approaching displeasure.

A status system relies on the displeasures of fear and punishment to enforce discipline and obedience to motivate and control people so that they will conform and get along with each other. But this sabotages concurrence. Being oriented towards status, means being oriented toward control, and thus displeasure to produce an alienated unnatural environment.

When you're enjoying yourself, you're into synergy. But if you're into status you need influence and control to move up the social hierarchy to increase your acceptance and respect. And the more people contained in this hierarchy the more conflicts and troubles there will be.

The displeasures and problems inherent in a status social system increase as the number of people increases. Two people can get along better than three. Four get along better than three only when they can split into two subgroups.

At the workplace or anywhere a group of people get together, usually the upper limits for cordial behaviors is about ten.(18) Any more have to split in factions or cliques because of the strength of the social status hierarchies that operates among them.

However, even with an exchange between two people, a status system can still disrupt that chance of co-equality.   When you are talking with another person, there sometimes exists an underlying jockeying for position.   A feeling of dominance or submissiveness can shift back and forth, as criticalness, a feeling of power or control, or a lack of energy can affect the relationship.

An inequality can develop, because of our well-developed, fine-tuned intellectual ability to perceive, analyze, and critically pick apart the faults in dress, manner, speaking skills, level of energy, intelligence, confidence, and endless list of how you may somehow be different than others. And the inferences that can be drawn on these differences, can be used against you for purposes of dominance and control. You can even be criticized for being too perfect, too good or too kind. This is a prime example why the status system is incompatible with the human brain.

So what may result from this exchange is that each may come away vaguely feeling somehow the better or worse. This may be experienced as a feeling of confidence or a lack of confidence, rather than any conscious thought. However, a guarded vigilance can gradually build up that is more conducive to caution or wariness then cooperation.

DOMINANCE

One method status seekers use to boost their status, is by using scapegoats such as the "slow," whose esteem and worth they can credibly attack. This show of force demonstrates their potential dangerous power to intimidate, so others will give them their due respect or "else." If you don't accede to their influential control, then you may be jeopardizing your own esteem within the group, as a lack of deference can target you as the next game.

All the harmful games, put-ons, come-ons, etc., that people play on one another have the common purpose of gaining status. The higher their status, the more acceptance they are entitled to. This often depends upon using aggressiveness and power to dominate others.

Dominance games operate among people usually without their awareness. As an example, first a hook is used by the "con" in the initial encounter with some kind of compliment. The compliment puts the "mark" at ease and disarms any defenses. The person is now vulnerable to offensive tactics that can bring the "mark" under the manipulative domination and control of the "con."

This may be accomplished by pointing out how the "mark" may differ in some way from others. Dress, possessions, manners, speech, all may have unique differences from other people that can be used against the "mark" in dominance games. Here the object of the power game for the player is to be critical of the person in a tactful way so the "mark" is not aware of being criticized. The discrimination of differences gradually erodes the "mark's" confidence and creates discomfort. Now the "mark" needs to go on the defense to justify what has been done, to explain likes and dislikes, and to account for personal tendencies in some way, etc.

The whole tone has now subtly shifted so that the "con" is now riding a superior confidence over the other. This allows the "con" to be stronger, to be more effective, or have more control. And that sets up the "mark" to conform, or to follow the directions or whims of the "con."

BACK - OFFS

The offensive strategy, whether applied to weaknesses or differences, needs to have back-offs to save face. Back-offs are often needed when vague terms like "weird" or "strange" are used. The obscure meaning of these terms can infer anything from a little difference to something so bizarre as to be unacceptable or repulsive. These terms allow the communication gap to be sufficiently widened so that you are left only to muse or wonder at their intended meaning.

This allows them to imply the worst with a judgment about some harmless behavior to establish their superior status. But if called down for having harmful intent, they can back out gracefully by indicating it was only an innocent, passing comment and nothing was intended by it. Or back-offs can be used aggressively as another "put down" with "I was just kidding, don't be so sensitive," or "What's the matter with you, can't you take a joke?"

These games appear harmless on the surface, until you understand that the power to control others is based on the ability to threaten the status and therefore the acceptance of another. This can harm with discriminating inferences or judgments that embarrass, belittle or criticize. Status games produce a kind of emotional aggression or violence that is much worse than physical violence, because physical wounds heal while emotional ones can live painfully on in the memory.

What is so harmful is that not only do such games undermine the good will and bond between people, but desires are created to retaliate for loss esteem, and show that you are not to be taken lightly or walked over. In the next communication step, you may want to ask how the remo feels about someone you know who gossips or someone who has criticized you or another.

CHAPTER 13

THE MUSE

The second communication step is to demonstrate the ability of the remo to draw conclusions and make decisions, independent of your awareness, as your remo is able to think without any dependence on your conscious thinking rao. You will discover that your remo is capable of very intricate behaviors below your level of awareness.

Depending on your emotional maturity, there are many complex behaviors of which your remo is capable. Some individuals have remos who can spell, think, solve problems, form complex sentences and create very original ideas, and all below the level of awareness. Actually, there probably are many things your remo can do that you may not be aware of, and that even your remo may have no idea about. Your remo is the undeveloped part of the self. This is because the pain and displeasure the status system inflicts on your feelings leads to an avoidance or denial of your emotional remo's vulnerable nature.

Your remo has certain responsibilities that are distinct from those of your rao, which you want to recognize. So you will want to establish an identity for your remo by having your remo choose a special nickname.

This second step involves the use of an Ouija board or a close facsimile with which you can ask questions. For the material, if you don't have an Ouija board you need to produce some squares that represent each letter of the alphabet, say from a Scrabble set, or write them on small post-it notes. You may also want to write out a "yes" or "no" response. Then line them up in alphabetical order on a smooth table, like a coffee table. The pointer can be a plastic or metallic object that can slide, e.g. a large serving spoon. By placing both hands on the pointer so the arms hang down and are relaxed, your remo will spell out the nickname desired by making movements with your large muscles in the upper arm.

Your rao can keep your mind occupied by being immersed with a dreamy, vacant stare, or by humming, singing a song, or by casually watching a TV program, casting an occasional glance to see how it is going. These motor movements, that take place without your conscious control, show how your remo carries on the ordinary repetitive business of living automatically so that your rao can more effectively handle the complexities of life without being overwhelmed with everyday routines.

The mystical force that guided the pointer, magically across the Ouija board, spelling out prophecies of future events and messages from the spirits, was of course your intuitive remo. For fun you may want to ask your remo questions about the future, lottery numbers, etc.

It is important that you keep an open mind and be receptive, to gain some understanding about the unknown qualities within yourself. Your remo can do many things to help you or hinder you. You can communicate with your remo and become the best of friends, or snub your remo so that conflicts left unresolved can fester. Your remo will surely become an aid and comfort to support you, when you learn to communicate.

KNOW THYSELF

When you ask your remo questions, the main objective should be one of pleasure with a complete acceptance of the self as you are. When you come to know your remo, the child within you, you will start to get a protective concern for yourself.

When you can learn to relax your critical facilities and sophisticated attitudes, then you may discover that the remo enjoys the comics, the cartoons, or the shows that kids love on TV. When you can allow inner sentiments to be expressed, then you are not only giving your remo attention, but you are showing some consideration for your remo's feelings and pleasures.

Those with little internal conflict may perceive the desires and beliefs of their remo to be easily and sensibly realized. On the other hand, those with a rebellious or immature remo may uncover distorted, unreasonable desires, or inaccurate mythical beliefs that their rao may be completely unaware of. For example, you may believe you are liberal on the matter of sex, only to discover you are merely a liberal thinker, while your remo's head may be in a "Victorian swill!"

The resolution of internal conflicts within yourself occurs just as it does between people. It is primarily a matter of communication with a discussion about differences. These conflicts may be overcome by the interaction of your rao with your remo, of reason with feelings. A process of mutual understanding, bargaining and adjustment is made until a compromised agreement is reached.

And as you develop the ability to discern the differences between status and synergy, you'll find almost all your conflict will involve a belief by your remo in the status value system. And that is only because that was the way your remo was raised.

We have ignored and avoided the remo to create an emotional immaturity within ourselves. We should be more receptive and aware of the remo's many nuances and abilities. For example, there are two types of realities, an inner reality and an outer reality.

REALITIES

The rao has a reality that exists in the outer world. In contrast, the remo has an internal reality with its own language of imagination and feelings. It is a language which expresses a craving for acceptance, self-importance, security and novelty, all embellished by the chromatic scales of emotion.

This inner realm is a natural training ground of the remo for personal growth, and is our correct and proper place of refuge, especially when all other forms of escape are denied in an adverse environment.

You can see this internal reality in your dreams. After you achieve a communicative intimacy with the remo, you will be able to better understand what your dreams really means. You can go over your dreams, and possibly resolve some of your anxieties, frustrations or conflicts which may cause you to awaken in a bad mood in the morning.

Daydreaming also enters the realm of this inner reality. Daydreaming is a spontaneous form of self-hypnosis. When feelings accompany imagery, there is witnessed a reality from within which is based on the real feelings you are experiencing. The reality is in terms of the emotions you experience, while imagination expands the dimensional space of this inner world. Your feelings then act as a variable with imagination, so that the greater the intensity of the feelings, the more real the imagery will seem.

This inner realm of the remo can be easily entered by the rao by creating the receptiveness found in wonder, or by some form of intense concentration such as experienced in staring with a blank look, or when you are absorbed in watching a movie, or immersed in reading a book.

As you become a more intimate friend with your remo, you will begin to know this inner reality and see how it plays a vital role as a source for motivation. Your private inner reality also serves as a source to orchestrate the outer reality, so that you can rehearse in your mind the behaviors you want to develop.

CHAPTER 14

PAINS AND PLEASURES

PUNISHMENT

The motivational system that operates within the remo's inner reality is the desire to approach pleasure and avoid pain. Punishment should only be used to control harmful behavior. However, a belief in discipline or obedience requires a belief in using punishment for harmless behaviors. The use of punishment to correct harmless behavior is one of the cruelties we perpetrate on each other, in deference to our unspoken belief in status values. When you use punishment to achieve discipline, obedience, control or to correct harmless behavior, you fray and unravel the cooperative fabric that holds people together.

Punishment belittles and lowers your rank in the social hierarchy operating. The lower the rank, the less acceptable you are. Usually the immediate meaning of punishment to your remo is that your self is not acceptable. Disapproval can be a crushing total rejection, or it can create feelings that you are not acceptable momentarily, depending on the maturity of your remo.

When the remo is raised with criticism, then the remo learns to condemn. When the remo condemns the self it punishes the self. Punishment may be experienced as some form of anger, or depression. Anger, like punishment, is maladaptive and futile, and is an expression of one's frustration or failure. It accomplishes nothing.

But the energy from anger, if not discharged in aggression, can be turned inwardly as self-punishment to impair your emotional or autonomic functioning, with disorders like depression or physical illness. Hostility and chronic anger have been found to be so damaging to the body that they can lead to an early death as quickly as cigarette smoking, obesity and a high-fat diet.(94)

Aggressive action can neutralize anger, whether turned toward an object, goal or people. When anger is changed into some kind of aggressive action, it can be either constructive or destructive. When anger is expressed as some form of punishment, either towards the self or others, it is usually destructive.

Unless applied to harmful behavior, punishment is maladaptive and futile, and is a confession of failure. Punishment's only reason for being is to control harm either by suppressing actions or by creating an avoidance reaction. The belief in punishment, as a motivating tool, is one of the worst values of a status system, and has led to a widespread misuse of this powerful controlling mechanism.

When over 90% of American parents believe that spanking children is a proper form of punishment, (115) then a lot of adults don't have a clue about the human condition, neither internally nor externally. Corporal punishment will usually fail either sooner or later. No one denies that limits on behavior need to be set. But there can be many fun and amusing ways of enforcing those limits without using punishment, especially after you start using both halves of your brain by communicating with your remo.

However, physical punishment is an excellent method to develop hate and resentment in the remo. Or the remo may prefer pain to being ignored and may seek punishment as a means of gaining attention.

Spanking can actually delay the development of the remo's conscience. The remo has to feel guilty about something to develop a conscience. But the use brute force over reason creates a lack of communication. The child's remo can believe that the punishment was unfair because there was no harmful behavior that deserved punishment.

When a child hurts another intentionally, then the remo is likely to feel the punishment is justified. However, if the remo is not made to understand exactly what it did that was harmful when punished, the child may feel it was paid for with the physical pain of a spanking. Now since the slate is clean, there is freedom to misbehave again. Thus in later years, the remo, as the "parent ego" of the self, adopts this punishing attitude of correcting behaviors, whether harmful or not.

Self-criticism usually originates from the remo. People who experience self-criticisms are often people who were raised as a child under an authoritarian parent who ruled with a righteous iron hand to control the spouse and family members. When punishment is used with intimidation and fear to achieve obedience, control and enforce rules, then this status value system is usually assimilated and adopted by the remo.

Thus, when you show some weakness, when you are not at your best or when you fail at some task, your remo will inflict your rao with punishment. Your remo will express self-criticism, emotionally, as punishment. Your rao will perceive this self-criticism as depression, tension, bad feelings, a stiff neck, a bad mood, anger or a headache.

The hardest thing for someone raised in a status environment to realize is that punishment is not something that can motivate the desire needed for personal growth or development. Self-punishment lowers morale. It can reduce any chance of overcoming weaknesses, because it not only lowers esteem but inhibits behavior and takes away the very confidence most needed. And when inhibited performance becomes uptight and ineffective.

On the other hand, most mistakes and problems can best be overcome when the rao and remo can huddle together as a team using a more positive approach. This way a problem can be attacked from different angles with an internal spirit of cooperation instead of submitting to an internal chastisement when the remo brings out the whip.

PLEASURE

A status hierarchy perverts pleasure. Many derive pleasure in delivering the put downs that belittle and hurt others. This can be seen any evening on almost any situation comedy found on TV. Thus pleasure can becomes associated with the harm inflicted on others. These very unnatural conditions where pleasure is found in the put downs of another exist because empathy is a drawback under status.

Pleasure is the key motivating force for personal development, both psychologically and biologically. Most of the pleasure areas of the brain are involved with goal-directed activity. Most people are not aware of how much their happiness in life and their quality of life is intricately bound with the number and the quality of goals they set for themselves.

When you don't have anything to do or you don't have something you want to achieve, after a time you lose your feeling for a purpose in life. The distress and even increased death rate caused by unemployment (28) have a lot to do with the void of inactivity. Thus when you are deprived of goal directed behaviors you are robbed of pleasure, and sometimes even the motive to live, especially when this is coupled with living in the unsupportive status social system.

Approximately five percent of the brain's pleasure areas are of the intense type involved in eating and sex. Neural pathways involved with goal directed behavior permeate the rest of the less intense pleasure areas of the brain. The real pleasures of life can be achieved by doing the things you want to do. And the greater the number of these goals that you have, the greater will be your enjoyment of life.

The point of all of this is that if you're into status, you're into displeasure. If you believe in pleasure and enjoying life, then you should believe in the values of synergy as a way of life. People who have strong status values believe in suffering with pain. Pain, so they believe, builds strength of character. When this type is a nurse or doctor, she will hold back pain medication from those suffering because of these status beliefs.

You are constantly making choices between status and synergy throughout the day. When you choose synergy, you'll find yourself residing in the pleasure pathways and circuits in the brain. On the status side, when you try to control the behavior of others and you are not successful, you almost always activate the displeasurable circuits in the brain with judgments of disapproval and criticism, or feelings of anger or resentment that can lead to spite, pouting or revengeful feelings.

Pleasure and synergy are especially needed to develop the emotional behaviors of your remo. The more behaviors you can teach your remo, the more reliable, the more trustworthy and stronger you will make yourself. The "expectancy" response is the next growth period that occurs between 21 and 24 months during the infant-child stage. And the "expectancy" response is the next emotional growth period that you need to develop to achieve an emotional maturity that will allow you to cope with the social problems of dealing with people.

Those interested in the growth behaviors that occur in the periods between 6 and 21 months, can refer to Appendix A. For example, those who need to develop the visual or auditory aspect of the imagination, should read and practice the behaviors of the "imagery" period.

CHAPTER 15

EXPECTANCY
PERIOD
21 - 24 MONTHS

INFANT-CHILD STAGE

EXPECTANCY RESPONSE

The "expectancy" response is a circuit of the sensory nervous system and can be witnessed in an "orienting reflex" of a house cat when it directs all its senses and concentration towards some sound. The anticipation of the "expectancy" response provides a state of readiness. This is a therapeutic behavioral defense to ease problems of stress and help your remo handle difficult social situations more handily.

By using your ability to anticipate, the "expectancy" response creates a state of readiness, by orienting your senses towards a greater awareness of your surroundings, especially when used in conjunction with a positive orientation towards pleasure.

The anticipatory energy produced by the "expectancy" circuit has the purpose of increasing one's awareness of the environment. In a state of low arousal, stimulation of sensory cells was found to create excessive excitation that was overwhelming. And this was because a lack of awareness created a state that was unable to handle the stimulation. While in a keen state of awareness and attention, this same stimulation could be handled in stride with little noticeable excitatory effect.(230)

Being observant and paying attention to the details in the environment, makes use of your energy of anticipation in an effective way. When you fail to use your natural abilities and behaviors by withdrawing, being "spacey" or being too laid back, you have an excess of energy available that has no where to go except into the displeasurable circuits of the brain. So if you can't fight! Or flee! The energy can quickly flow into the anxiety and fear circuits of the brain.

When you don't make proper use of your anticipatory ability, the excess energy over-stimulates you, while in a state of mind that cannot effectively handle it. And that's when displeasures such as irritability, agitation, anxiety and fear can result. The excess energy that creates excitation doesn't have to be displeasurable, it just has to be controlled and redirected into pleasurable channels or neural circuits by you.

But being laid back or retiring can be very maladaptive. The anticipation of the "expectancy" response, with attention and awareness of your surrounding is an emotional behavior that can use energy in an adaptive way. If you're uptight about entering a new situation, and you try to be "cool" by being ultra relaxed and indifferent, then the lack of awareness, the lack of anticipation, inattentiveness or withdrawal from the environment will actually backfire on you.

The ability of a status environmental to create displeasurable conditions can multiply negative energy. Thus playing the role of a wallflower because you're apprehensive and you want to blend into the surroundings and be unnoticed, can cause you to become inhibited, shy and easily startled, to create agitation, anxiety and fear.

When under new or stressful social circumstances, the "expectancy" response allows you to be on the attack in a more assertive role. You want to open your eyes wide to be alert to details in your environment, you want to sniff the air, listen for sounds, etc. You want to use as many of your senses as you can. And the alert readiness of the "expectancy" response that allows you to be more aware of your surroundings, should be used with an orientation towards pleasure. A state of pleasure can handle stress and excess energy with much greater ease.

ATTENTION TO DETAILS

The "expectancy" response can also strengthen the characteristic or trait known as an "attention to details." If this is a weak point you need to strengthen for you place of employment, studying for a test, or just in your daily life, then you especially need to practice this behavior through out the day. You need to practice and strengthen this behavior whether with people or when alone studying or doing your work on the job. And if you want to be a safe driver, this is a behavior you should always practice while driving a car.

This behavior is an aspect of the sensory nervous system where you take things in with your senses. You want to pay attention to the little things you hear and see. And the more you can anticipate these details of life the more they will make an impression on your senses.

AWARENESS

The information in this section was obtained from Gesell and Ilg.(40) At 21 months the infant-child comes into a new awareness of people again, and with it comes a fear of strangers. His new awareness of people is reducing the prolonged busyness of the 18-21 month period. Instead of being so reckless, he is becoming somewhat more sedate and wary in his play. His walks three months earlier went "hither and yon" impulsively, but now he goes to a place knowingly and with remembrance, and with more awareness on his part.

The future is starting to have meaning, as he is able to sit at the table and wait for juice. And he is able to respond appropriately to "in a minute." A concept of space is developing so that he can point or pull a person to show things. He clings to routines and likes to have patterns repeated. He may even have definite demands as to how mother shall speak and act.

This begins a period of sleeping difficulties which may continue to 3 years of age. Sleep is more disturbed now and there is more night waking. Difficulties occur not only on going to sleep and during sleep, but also on waking. After going to bed instead of going to sleep he may repeatedly call his mother back for numerous demands that whimically come to mind. There is difficulty in taking a nap also just as it is with night sleeping.

He has a poor command of words, but he has much to say, so in frustration he "bawls" or throws a tantrum in an unreasonable manner. However, his intense crying is usually because he can't verbalize his wishes which are often for the repetition of certain things. He responds less quickly to requests, and is apt to do the opposite of what is asked of him, e.g. he may run in the opposite direction when it is time to go home. He may stand rigid and frozen when told to do something. His inability to verbalize increases his tendency to "freeze" into inactivity.

Earlier toilet training may have a relapse associated with diarrhea. If he has a sudden bowel movement in his pants, he may be unable to move and may stand screaming in distress and continue screaming while being changed. He likes to undress completely when alone and run about naked. It is a common sight to see a 21 month old without any clothes on.

Since the child at this age is sensitive to peripheral stimuli, distractions may interrupt or terminate his meal. And when feeding himself, he eats better alone with his mother moving about close by but not paying attention to him.

He is more conscious of his acts as they are related to the adult's approval and disapproval, as he is both more responsive to and more demanding of adults. He may refuse to return to solitary play after his mother comes to him. His adjustment to nursery school weakens and wavers, as he may approach other children and hug them too tightly with a bear hug.

He is not only more aware of people than formerly, but also knows what belongs to different people. He likes to have his own place for his things. The enjoyment he derives from putting things back in place indicates the categorization and organization going on.

EXPECTANCY CIRCUIT

The dorsomedial thalamus has two way connections with the basolateral amygdala and with the orbitofrontal neocortex lobe. (see fig. 6) The dorsomedial thalamus acts as an intermediate control to combine the emotional impulses of the basolateral amygdala with the ability of the frontal area to categorize and to generalize in a more refined manner, in order to respond to the external situation in accord with internal needs. The frontal lobe augments the emotional-motivational states of the basolateral amygdala with strong anticipatory energy, referred to as "expectancy waves."(125)

The crude relevancy of the basolateral amygdala has now been more refined into the more effective discrimination and generalization ability of the frontal cortex. In other words, the basolateral amygdala provides the emotional arousal and general direction, while the frontal area increases this energy with greater relevancy, and discrimination, and provides the persistency which memory permits. This is a non-verbal communication area that allows one to adapt by learning from mistakes in order to avoid them in the future.

The attentive process of the "orienting reflex" operates with greater awareness now as the frontal lobe along

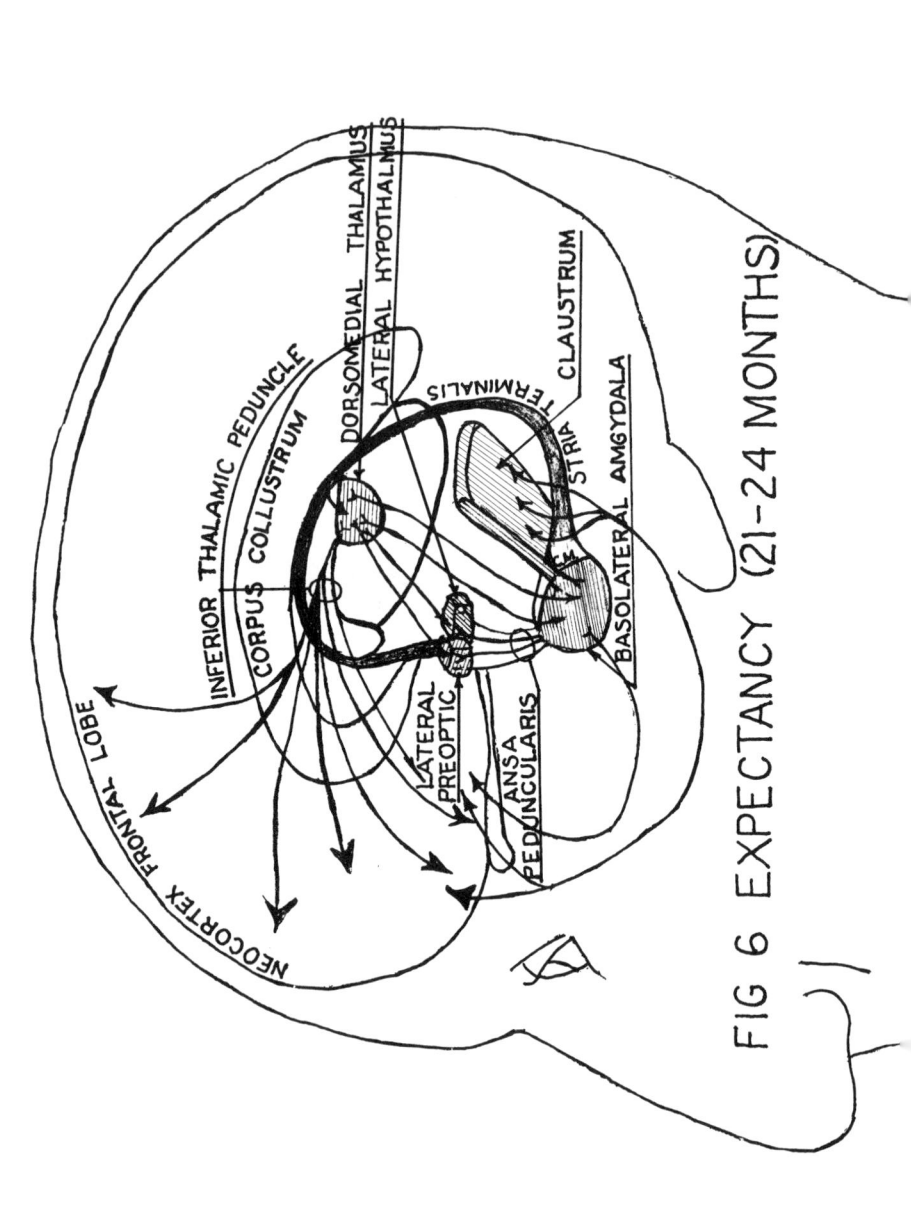

FIG 6 EXPECTANCY (21-24 MONTHS)

with the basolateral amygdala play a preparatory role in regard to cognition.(107) Optimal alerting facilitates perceptual readiness to minimize the surprise for the individual, and limits the need for searching by letting the senses do the work of muscles.(14)

For events to be comprehended and labeled, they require a selective attention to the specific aspect of a stimulus. This selective attention is related to expectancy as well as other variables, such as anxiety.(65) If you know what is to happen you will be prepared to focus your attention, and to perceive and record the events more accurately.

The reticular formation is the energy source that provides the impetus for this sensory modality, as stimulation of the reticular formation facilitates sensory sensitivity and discrimination.(49, 64 & 42)

However, as excitatory impulses increase in the area, avoidance and withdrawal behavior produce introversion, because the dorsomedial thalamus, like the basolateral amygdala, is a punishing area where stimulation creates fear and escape reactions. But the dorsomedial operates the frontal area on a higher level of motor control to express and augment the fear originating from the basolateral amygdala, rather than create the fear itself.(50)

CHAPTER 16

STATUS: FALSE GOD

PERFORMANCE AND STATUS

Many believe that the competition, pressure and stress that status hierarchies create deserves the credit for the development of performance skills. A status culture is a performance culture, and can produce good performance skills. But many people can be good performers when given the proper acceptance and support needed to develop skills.

A status society is only a performance culture to the extent that it supports the performance abilities of those at the top of the heap, because they are the ones whose effectiveness is disrupted the least by the emotional harm from disapproval and subtle rejections.

The support that acceptance provides is parceled out to those who are winners; acceptance is given to those in the upper levels of a status system. Or so it seems. But even here the rewards of status are a fraud that doesn't deliver.

When the ultimate achievements of success and status are finally realized, the "winners" are often faced with depression, drug abuse, life threatening pursuits such as driving cars at dangerous speeds or suicide. Thus, the Betty Ford Clinic, and other clinics are filled with various famous and successful people addicted to whatever could get them through the day.

After striving for many years to achieve success or fame, disillusion may occur when the successful sit back to enjoy their laurels. They experience disappointment because the discrimination wasn't made between the rewards of status and the rewards of pleasurable goal-directed activities.

It all starts with a status system that uses punishment to force children to be obedient. As a result there are many who suffer from insecurity or a lack of confidence, because of the effectiveness of punishment to suppress growth and stop the remo from reaching emotional maturity. And the outcome of all the problems an immature remo creates cannot be corrected by fortune and fame.

To the remo punishment can mean rejection and without supportive acceptance, the remo may gradually give up. During the remo's growth years, the energy needed to deal with rejection and bad feelings will cause mental and emotional development to be pushed aside. This is what punishment is best at accomplishing. Punishment is extremely capable of suppressing behaviors, performance and growth.

CONDITIONAL ACCEPTANCE

The rewards of status are a sham because they are based on conditional acceptance. This means that your acceptance by others is dependent on being successful. That is, your approval will be forthcoming as long as you can perform at a certain level of competence, or as long as you do what is right and what is expected of you.

Whether this is the attitude of those around you or not is unimportant. Once your remo has been hooked by this status motivational belief system, there is little release from this internal stress, until you can get inside yourself to change your remo.

When striving for status there is no let up. No matter how successful you may be, success is always temporary. Each day you have to prove yourself again. This can gradually undermine confidence, subjecting you to the same anxieties and dejections as those who have yet to prove themselves.

In addition, the acceptance that results from success is often not based on the natural self, but is attributed to the facade created when you were "up" for a successful performance. Thus you are more susceptible to develop a cognitive dissonance of the image held by others and what you know is yourself. So you can remain uncomfortably guarded about yourself, behind the facade, uncertain because you may not be able to live up to the public image. You may feel the need to show how exceptional you are in order to deserve the acceptance of others.

Also, many foster magical beliefs that their shortcomings and weaknesses will suddenly disappear once they're on top with success, only to find they are still the same frail human being with all the same vulnerabilities as before.

In addition, the acceptance achieved at the expense of others, is not free from resentment, envy and jealousy of others. This is not usually expressed but is felt as tension and uneasiness, when the successful may get respect but feel estrangement from others. They are admired, but they may often be alone. They don't really feel they belong nor receive the intimate social stimulation the remo needs so much. This emanates from equality which is a state that allows you to be happy. It is the only state which allows the remo to be as he or she naturally is.

Generally, status subtly places people into higher or lower social positions in a hierarchy of greater or lesser acceptance. But each level alienates people from those on another level, so that those at the top level and those at the bottom level are usually the most alienated of all.

The next chapter will be your third communication step, and the last of the more difficult steps to achieve. It is used to understand the complex abilities that the remo is capable of demonstrating.

CHAPTER 17

THE AUTOMATIC REMO

For this communication step you want your remo to write on some paper using a soft pencil or pen. This process is referred to as automatic writing. Hold the pencil in the hand you normally write with, although the remo will tend to use the large muscles in your arm and shoulder more than the fingers of your writing hand. You may want to place a tray on your lap to write on, so the elbow is raised above the surface to let your arm swing free.

Dr. Anita Muhl(79) found that subjects who performed this automatic writing could be divide this way. There were those who could only write while their conscious awareness (namely their rao) was occupied and stimulated by reading a book or a magazine. This group was divided into two subgroups, those who could only write well when they had no idea what their hand was doing and those who had ideas corresponding to the ideas being written. Other subjects could only write while they were relaxed with their attention fixed on some object. These were subdivided into those who had no idea of the material written, and those who had similar ideas to those written.

It seems for some that attending to what is going on will tend to inhibit the remo's ability to perform. Also some will tend to have an irresistible urge to have some conscious control over these movements. So to overcome this tendency you may have to have your mind absorbed with extraneous thoughts, with a vacant, dreamy stare or by distracting your mind by reading, counting, reciting some verse or watching TV.

When performing automatic writing you may find that your remo may volunteer information to write about. The remo will enjoy creative writing the most. You should try to encourage this originality in your remo. If this is not successful, then you need to ask emotionally energizing questions to get the remo to respond. Questions about animals, pets, snakes or bugs, about someone you care about or someone you dislike a lot, like a relative or a past friend.

Dr. Muhl found that some subjects had to go through as many as a "dozen futile trials" before success could be achieved. This may be due to a lack of motivation on the part of the remo, or because this is a new learning experience for the remo.

When you successfully perform automatic writing, there is no feeling of difficulty that you have accomplished something, and there is no sense of effort that comes when you have to concentrate on what you are doing. You may find that your remo tends to run the words together or use numbers and letters to represent words, such as, 2b4u. The remo may also like to write vulgar expressions you don't normally use when speaking.(100) Actually, this may motivate the remo to write more energetically.

If automatic writing shocks you, or makes you feel uneasy, it shouldn't. This ability of the remo is a natural part of you. These movements will seem disconnected from yourself, so that it will seem that it is your "arm" and not "you" that is doing the writing.

Instead of being disturbed about what the remo can do, you should enjoy this discovery about yourself. The ignorance about the self shows that with all our technological achievements, we are still in the "Dark Ages" as far as understanding both our inner self, and how to provide for our emotional well-being.

We have one body, but we are not singular wholes! As long as we continue to fool ourselves that we are, we will continue on with our rationalizations to find reasons to support unexplained actions and motivations. Conscious awareness is not a complete experience, it's only part of a complex phenomenon.

Dreams are an unconscious act that apparently bears a resemblance to automatic writing. Dr. Schneck(100) has found that automatic writing has obvious similarities that are consistent with dreams. Thus, how you dream will determine by and large how your remo will write. If your dreams contain well-integrated stories with intricate plots, your automatic writing will also follow that scheme. Conflicts found in dreams will also be shown in automatic writing. Dr. Muhl(80) found that automatic writing was invaluable in getting at unconscious processes, such as conflicts, and also in recalling early forgotten childhood impressions.

Dr. Muhl(80) concluded that latent talents can be realized through automatic writing and become a part of the conscious activity. Muhl(79) was surprised at the unexpected variety of material written. Also when the subjects discovered their talents which they were in complete ignorance about, they were amazed. Their automatic writing demonstrated ability in writing poetry or stories, composing music, artistic drawings and designing.

Your first attempts at automatic writing may produce hard to read scrawls, but as you improve with practice, and allow your remo to develop the physical skill of writing, you may discover you have some hidden talent within you.

CONFLICTS

Many people are ignorant about the internal conflicts that can exist between the rao and the remo. Conflicts are inevitable as a part of status life. Communication can resolve the differences between two people so that compromises can be worked out. The same thing applies to the conflicts within an individual, so that different needs and desires between the rao and the remo can be compromised and resolved.

Pierre Janet(48) gave an example of a twenty-year-old girl with a personal conflict who was out of touch with herself. Her remo wanted to get away from a stressful home situation, but her rao wanted to endure the existing conditions. So she escaped in a fugue. A fugue is a spree in which all memory is lost about the things that took place. The girl was unable to tell why she went away or where she went. But with automatic writing her remo explained what happened during the fugue. Her remo wrote the following account.

"I left home because mamma accuses me of having a lover and it is not true. I cannot live with her any longer. I sold my jewels to pay my railroad fare. I took a train..."

Her remo was able to indulge in every complex behaviors, and relate the entire fugue with precision in automatic writing, although her rao was not able to recall anything about it.

TOOKIES

Muhl,(80) showed another type of internal alienation that can create conflicts and problems, with a patient whose name was Elizabeth, but whose remo in automatic writing had the nickname of Tookie.

"...The sad part of it was that while Tookie knew "Lizbeth" as she called her, "Lizbeth" had no knowledge of Tookie's existence and that is where so much of the conflict in the patient's life began."

"Tookie was an imp-she loved everybody and everything; she adored the flowers, the birds, the sky, the clouds, and the breezes; they were all living things to her; her garden was peopled with fairies and curious creatures galore and she was forever having the most glorious adventure with them."

As for her rao Tookie wrote, "Lizbeth was horrid and prim, her wouldn't speak to the flowers or anything." "The fact that "Lizbeth" was prim wasn't nearly so much of a crime to Tookie, as the fact that she so thoroughly ignored the great-out-of doors. However, Tookie seemed to derive some satisfaction from the fact that "Lizbeth" invariably got punished for Tookie's misdemeanors, as she would always manage to submerge herself before the chastisement was administered; this was the phenomenon responsible for the conviction which grew in the parents that Elizabeth was a very untruthful child, and it was also the cause of the conflict in Elizabeth for being unjustly punished for something she hadn't done."

Tookie tended to blame anything or anyone for her actions. Tookie wrote a story, verified by her mother, of when Elizabeth came home covered with mud, but which Tookie blames her feet in the following bit of automatic writing:

> "I was looking very neat
> so I told my little feet
> to walk me down the street.
> I didn't even speak to the little worms
> though I did make them squirm,
> then we came to a puddle that was new
> and wondered how we'd ever get through.
> I thought we ought to go home
> but my feet they wanted to roam,
> course I couldn't go home alone.
> But time I spoke,
> I'm such a old slowpoke,
> they wouldn't heed,
> well there really wasn't much need
> 'cause we fell flat in the mud,
> what a thud!
> I picked us up and we went back,
> making everywhere a track."

Tookie also wrote of her dislike of her rao, Elizabeth, and "wanted to be rid of her."

"Lizbeth doesn't know about the flowers.
She picks them and that kills them.
She never saw a fairy,
they run when she comes.
She is horrid.
I heard someone say so, I know it.
Why one day some one gave her
2 tiny white mice with pink eyes.
She let them go.
I found them and hid them in a dresser drawer
and they eat up a dress of my mothers
wasn't very pretty anyway."

And another example of how Tookie felt towards Elizabeth.

"I am Tookie and I am very small
about as tall as 3-1/2 of my daddy's feet.
I hate to be good
maybe if I had a magic hood I could.
But sh, sh, I had rather be bad.
Is that not sad.
I have a white mice which are very nice
2 dears the kind with horns,
but brothers I do not want another,
but only 1 mother and 1 daddy
now is that not odd.
Oh yes, Lizbeth, you see is the other me
I don't care for her.
Her is a snob.
Her never speaks to the flowers or anything.
Her is very prim.
Her never wants to get dirty

and her never wants to climb trees or hunt for fleas.

Always says don't,

but I just stop up my ears,

I wish I could leave her to home

and go off alone.

Mebbe the devil will take her 2 that bad place

dare not say where, 'cause Lizbeth might hear."

This example shows why it is important for you to communicate with your remo. If Elizabeth could have interacted more with Tookie, her remo, she could have resolved most of her problems. She could have expressed her socially unacceptable impulses in more constructive ways with her talent for creative writing. The problems between Tookie and Elizabeth were caused not only by a lack of communication, but by her remo, Tookie, who wanted to lead and direct her rao, Elizabeth. It was the job of Elizabeth to lead, but when this role was reversed a multitude of problems were created, especially in the punitive, familial status environment she lived in.

If she had been nurtured by a family who believes in the values of synergy these problems could have been avoided in the first place. The status system produces almost all the conflicts between people, between the rao and the remo and between people in their community, their job and their government.

CHAPTER 18

MOTOR SYSTEM DISORDERS

Social status hierarchies produce all of the following: crimes and violence by those who act out their personal troubles and hostilities in antisocial behavior; hopelessness and apathy that leads to poverty; and mental and emotional illness. It does this by creating conditions of insecurity, anxiety and fear.

It seems that these unwholesome effects are produced by the same rejecting conditions of status, depending on the temperament of the pathological individual. When the motor hormones and motor nervous system are more predominant, one tends to be physically violent and destructive. When the "viscera," autonomic nervous system is most dominant, it can encourage a helpless vegetative state of being that can lead to a physical and/or mental poverty. And when the "sensitivity" of the sensory hormones and sensory nervous system are predominant, mental/emotional disorders may result.

Except in humans these pathologies are rarely seen in the animal kingdom. Humans are the only social animals that cannot get along with each other. We are supposed to be the superior animal. Yet these pathologies can create an emotional life of anxiety, mistrust, fear and destruction that can be much worse than the emotional life of lower social animals.

Animals can live in harmony with nature. However, if you put them in a bad unnatural environment, you can make them vicious, neurotic or apathetic. Specifically, you can produce a pathological condition in any animal by punishing their natural way of behaving.

It is important that you understand that there is nothing wrong with you or anybody else, but there is something terribly wrong with the environment around us. This is because man has chosen to live in a social environment that is incompatible with the neural "wiring" of the brain's emotional circuitry. People may turn out to be "no good," but people are really "good" by nature.

It is only when you raise them in an alienating environment by superimposing a status hierarchy meant for lower animals that you produce the pathological conditions of a sick society that presently exist.

HOSTILITY

All criminals suffer from a superior/inferior complex that a status culture inflicts. The rejecting conditions of status can lead to an aversion of the self and a malice towards others to produce antisocial behaviors. As a result, life can have so little meaning that a sense of recklessness with life can come close to a readiness to die. Many at the bottom rung of the status ladder or those who feel rejected and worthless, believe their lives are wasted. They are ready to destroy and wreck the lives of others and their own.

When the remo doesn't develop emotional coping skills, because of a lack of acceptance growing up, the remo usually blames the rao among others in later years. Blame can grow from discontent to disapproval, dislike, and then hate. These bad feelings created by a status environment can operate without one's awareness of the remo's attitude. And these bad feelings can be directed inwardly at the self when the sensory system is dominate. Or they can target others when the motor system dominates.

As one grows up and becomes caught up in the day to day stress of a dog-eat-dog status atmosphere, these bad feelings can be projected out and targeted onto anyone who is different. Someone's race, color or religion can be subjected to hate or hostility that is so far out of proportion that it is irrational.

Thus, explosive antisocial behavior, violence and insanity grow from the little seed of inequality that social status hierarchies cultivate to grow into a poisoned weed that society must cut down and eliminate.

Hateful feelings can find some release in the aggressive competitiveness that flourishes throughout our society. In a study of competitiveness among children,(79) it was found that they were irrationally competitive in the sense that they were willing to work hard to make sacrifices that would reduce the rewards of other children.

They were also "sadistically rivalrous" as they would take toys away from the other children 78% of the time, even though they were not allowed to keep the toys for themselves. Some would even show their delight in the displeasure they had created with such statements as, "Ha! Ha! Now you won't get a toy!"

The important result of the study was that irrational competitiveness increased with age, so that ten year olds showed poorer adjustment by reducing their own reward in order to reduce the reward of a peer as compared to five year olds.

This is indicative of the incompatibility of the human brain with the principles of status. As a person's brain reaches a more mature development with increased intelligence, the ten year old children raised in a status oriented society were more concerned with pursuing personal ends and blocking opponents. This interfered with their capacity for cooperative problem solving, even though cooperativeness would have been more adaptive in getting the prizes they wanted.

Status encourages this aggressive competitiveness in the young because this is the model they see to emulate. The young intuitively know that there is competition to be accepted. And competition requires moves up the status acceptance chain with limited room at the top. Compassion or sympathy robs one of the ability to rise and dominate others. Thus a concern for others can be a handicap.

Those who can be aggressively unconcerned about their fellowman will have the greatest potential to come out on top, while "nice guys finish last." This creates the conditions where people are not only indifferent to "man's inhumanity to man," but encourage and develop it as a model for emulation.

The appetite for violence, so rampant under status, is given some vicarious release through movies concerned with death and destruction. Thus, the degree that violent movies are popular in a society is an indication of the degree that social hierarchies are flourishing.

Although your rao may be aware that the violence in movies is make believe, to your remo's inner world of imagination the violence can be very real, especially to the remo that hasn't been allowed to mature. (This immaturity is more common than you could possibly believe, because of the many status oriented families.) Thus, a remo filled with hostility, who can watch the bloodshed and slaughter of others, can realize a feeling of gratification as the remo vicariously fulfills a common desire, fantasy or need created by a status culture.

VIOLENCE AND SEX

Aggressive violence and affectionate sex are antagonistic opposites. Bloodshed in movies is approved of because it can satisfy a basic need for violence in a status system, while sexual activity in movies is looked on as being bad and evil.

People of a status orientation believe that watching two people making sexual love is many times worse than watching the detailed slaughter of a dozen people. This is because of the conditions sex creates. Sexual activity usually requires a relationship of care, concern, equality, and mutual support before sex can be successful for both partners.

The endorsement of sexual activity produces the opposite conditions needed for a status system. The drive to increase status impairs sex relationships. A sexually intimate and caring relationship with another can make one vulnerable, and shake the aggressive confidence needed for success in a ruthless social hierarchal system. Thus, physical relationships are used primarily to satisfy appetites, rather than to fulfill emotional intimacy needs. And sexual activity will tend to be unsuccessful, uneventful, rejected with disgust, or else used as a means to an end.

Finally, although status is the primary cause of antisocial acts, a secondary cause is a lack of communication with the remo. Almost all violent criminals have a topsy turvy world internally. Instead of the rao guiding and making the executive decisions, the remo tends to get the upper hand to determine their actions. Once the remo starts to be boss, the person's behaviors will only get worse. Sometimes when the remo takes over during a violent crime, the rao may have no recollection of what happened. The most effective way to reduce antisocial behaviors, besides incorporating synergy, is by communicating at higher levels with the remo, so that the rao can regain command and direction of the self.

CHAPTER 19

AUTONOMIC SYSTEM DISORDERS

POVERTY

A status hierarchy is not organized for the social well being of its members, but is set up to control people. The leaders of a status system are able to maintain their dominance mainly by suppressing any actions that would weaken their control and power. People with alternative choices and ideas to those in power may often be looked on as instigators, forming ideas to provoke trouble. So actions that would strengthen and motivate the individual have to be suppressed in order to create a dependence that allows one to be easily led. Thus a status system does not permit the "cream" to come to the top, as much as it "whips others into shape" to limit them from realizing their potential.

A status system creates a nonsupportive atmosphere. So a struggle is created where others not only have to strive for acceptance, but also have to save their own emotional and economical necks. Thus, when each man is out for himself, he absolves responsibility for his fellowman. What results is a sink-

or-swim attitude that causes many to just quit. They give up, feeling, "What's the use?"

These status conditions of alienation can gradually break down confidence and a belief in the self, as many become "burnouts" and then "dropouts" of one kind or another. Once the mind starts a negative set of expectations, it restricts more and more what can be done.

A hopelessness is created that can result in apathy and poverty. So a status system can produce the conditions where many people are wasted or made indigent. People who lose faith in their selves often find a substitute in authority, and place their faith in this authoritative state. Thus, a segment of the population, often feels that others do not care about them, and they stand alone. Since they can't turn to others and they've turned away from the self, they turn to some form of authority to rely on.

Again social status hierarchies are the culprit. They feel alone in the world cut off from other people and cut off from the self. The status system causes a loss of incentive that otherwise would allow the individual to be effective and productive. The lack of acceptance that operates in a nonsupportive atmosphere engenders a low self-esteem among people which causes them not to care about themselves or others.

Two variables, the presence of status hierarchies and a lack of cooperativeness, create this impoverished condition of the mind and body. These interact with each other in different strengths in different groups to indicate how status hierarchies lead to poverty. Generally, where strong status hierarchies operate with little cooperativeness, the lowest ghetto poverty is produced, like those found in many of the third world countries. On the other hand, where you have a great amount of cooperativeness with relatively weaker status hierarchies operating, you can produce the greatest prosperity, like within certain Japan's businesses.

India is a poor and underdeveloped country with little cooperativeness and a status system so strong and impregnable, that they have no chance of rising out of the poverty of a third world country. No amount of enforced cooperation that does not change the class structure can ever overcome the strength of this status system and permit prosperity.

Since status hierarchies deprive people of the acceptance they need, they are forced to produce large families so they feel a sense of belonging. This will always be the case. Emotional support and security can provide the comfort people need to survive physical hardships, but physical comforts cannot alleviate emotional problems and alienation. People have to secure their emotional well being first; a family can possibly provide this. A family can provide some of the emotional support needed as a basis to obtain those things needed for people's physical well being.

Although a family unit provides the emotional security its individuals need, it causes an overpopulation that further aggravates their poverty. As long as the status system dominates, a large family is the only choice available, because the emotional support of being accepted as part of a group is the natural priority of human needs.

SENSITIVITY

The major factor in the subnormal mental ability often found in the poor is due to the impoverishment created by status. The intellectual ability involved in learning depends on the sensitivity of the sensory nervous system. The absorption and assimilation of information through the senses depends on sensory cell receptors or receptiveness. The more sensitive you are, the more acutely keen your radar is attuned, the more awareness and the more information there will be to will make an indelible impression on sensory cells.

However, developing this sensitivity can make a child raised in strident status conditions very vulnerable to displeasure. Thus, there is a need to harden one's self and one's senses for some protection from the impinging stimuli of emotional harm found in a status environment. This is the very opposite condition that is needed to enrich life.

The displeasures experienced early in life tend to make one tough or callous in order to be less sensitive to sensory stimulation. Thus to survive in a status environment one learns early on not to care about too much. This encourages the harder qualities that can arrest the development of sensitivity and intelligence.

In the end, status hierarchies will often result in economic, social, physical and mental poverty, as they do not provide the emotional support and acceptance needed for people to cooperate, prosper and grow.

CHAPTER 20

SENSORY SYSTEM DISORDERS

EMOTIONAL / MENTAL ILLNESS

A status system creates insecurity, mistrust, anxiety and fear that cause mental and emotional illness. A status society measures its individuals against each other. This tendency to judge and be judged exposes your personal shortcomings. If there is a lack of support and acceptance from those in the social environment, then feelings of inferiority can develop into feelings of self-contempt and worthlessness, that can readily turn into a hatred of the self.

A social status hierarchy uses one of the greatest psychological punishments possible, which is a personal rejection of those with inferior status. This non-acceptance is the catalyst that ignites burning hate, anger and fear, and plants the seeds for emotional disorders.

One problem experienced is an emotional alienation that causes a withdrawal from others. A social status culture produces people who are not only alienated from others, but are empty inside, alienated from their self, even among those who can claim to have a masterful self.(21)

Another problem is that the threat of a loss of status is much more threatening than the advantages from a possible gain of status. Thus the more you are in the company of others, the more you can jeopardize the security of your own position, by ineptness, by mistakes, or by increasing the chance you might expose your weaknesses and shortcomings.

This causes people to avoid each other, and to withdraw into the safety of their homes. Suburbia often has a ghost-like absence of people as most stay within the shelter of their homes. This avoids the apprehensions of the possible consequences of not appearing to be at one's best.

Another avoidance technique people use is to become so busy doing things that they have no time for other people. Some will clean their house daily, or do other trivial chores. Workers, businessmen and professionals will work round the clock to avoid meaningful relationships fraught with risk.

Many feel that intimacies with others are dangerous burdens. They try to remain mysterious, withdrawn, believing the less people know them, the less people can burden them with great expectations, or judge and rank them to some lower category.

Many adjust to status conditions by keeping on the move. This way no one gets a chance to punish them by getting to know them, using their weaknesses to put them down. When they start becoming involved or too close, then they move on.

Some jobs offer an excellent sanctum from a status society, like a forest ranger, traveling salesman, academic researcher, etc. Others find a pet, like a dog can provide a supportive refuge and the unconditional acceptance needed. And others escape from the slings and arrows of a status culture in a mental institution.

Some can escape for a while, but there is no way to avoid the fact that we are very much dependent on each other. To be independent of others is strictly a rationalization of a rao that is oblivious to the needs of the remo.

In order to alleviate anxieties and fears, your dependency on others needs to be directed towards cultivating relationships with synergistic people, i.e., those who are tolerant and accepting, and avoid status seekers. But first "you" have to shift and move towards synergy and away from status values. To do this you have to change the attitude and values of your remo. Your remo's beliefs are not set in stone. But to change your remo requires you to be able to communicate.

The greater the communication between the rao and the remo, the greater the degree that synergy can be cultivated. Those who have ethics that embrace status values will have an extremely difficult time communicating with the remo.

Even through a person's genes may make them susceptible to emotional and mental illness, it is a hostile status atmosphere that activates his defective gene. Status conditions can cause terrible stressful emotions to release or deplete hormones and create chemical imbalances. The status system is the real culprit of mental illness, because the individual, when deeply troubled, feels alone in the world, cutoff from people and cut off from the self.

The self-criticism that originates from the remo, will be expressed emotionally, as punishment. When you show some weakness, when you are not at your best or when you fail at some task, your remo will inflict your rao with punishment.

Worst of all this process is the scenario behind almost every case of depression or suicide, except where there are physical losses, such as losing a loved one. Many people are out of touch with their remo, and when they are depressed, they have no idea that it is their remo inflicting punishment on their self. But to the degree that you believe in the status value system, will often be the degree you will suffer from depression. The degree to which you have feelings of inferiority or superiority will be the degree that you are caught up in the status system of beliefs.

But the real damage a status system does is to children from birth to five years of age. A young child can handle a tremendous amount of pleasurable stimulation without being overwhelm. And the potential to learn is far greater than what is occurring now.

But when displeasure is used such as disapproval or criticism, then their young minds are overwhelmed with terrible feelings that can negate future efforts. You have to set limits on behaviors, but to use punishment to enforce those limits is ridiculous, as there are many enjoyable ways to enforce limits.

But our use of punishment in deference to status ideals of discipline, obedience and control can so overwhelm the young infant-child, that the remo can actually stop developing emotionally. And if a remo is stopped in development before two years of age, and has an emotional breakdown in later years, it seems to be susceptible to a psychosis. If the remo is between two and three, then a breakdown may result in a neurosis. When the remo is stopped between three and four, the remo is able to control most irrational fear and anxiety, but is susceptible to antisocial behaviors, in response to the injustices of a status system. But when the remo is able to achieve a full emotional maturity at the adult-child stage of five years of age, then fear will be restricted to the rational type, such as a fear of losing life or limb.

CHAPTER 21
RAISING
THE REMO

Prior to the 1940's, the belief in harsh punishment to achieve discipline, obedience and control created a lot of emotional cripples. However, with the advent of the synergetic techniques of Spock (108) and Gesell and Ilg (40) in the 1940's, a much greater percentage were able to realize a stable emotional maturity.

But the problem is there are still a large number of status oriented people, who still believe in using punishment to control their kids. Straus conducted studies with 6002 couples, detailed in his book, "Beating the Devil Out of Them," and found that 90% of American parents believe spanking children is a proper form of punishment.(115) And many of the status authoritarian minded actually curse Spock, thinking him a villain who has caused most of society's ills.

One problem was that, a lot of the parents who tried to apply Spock's ideas, were emotionally immature themselves. And because they didn't understand the concept of synergy, they didn't know how to interact with their child on an equal level. So when a child achieved a greater emotional maturity than the parents, the status hierarchy operating within the family was turned upside down.

Many felt threatened by the emotional dominance of the child, so that raising a child was just too much for them. And the child was just turned loose to run wild without setting any limits on behaviors. This can be emotionally damaging to a child, as he doesn't learn to control his behavior or develop a concern and empathy for others.

When raising a child you "have" to set limits on behaviors even if they're artificial, but to use punishment to enforce these limits is the height of absurdity. There can be 101 fun filled ways of enforcing limits without using punishment, especially when you've achieved a communication breakthrough with your remo, the great problem solver.

In addition, the degree to which status ideals are eliminated from the child-parent relationship is the degree that harmony creates a sense of cooperation, and when a child is much more likely to go along with the limits you set.

On the other hand, you "do" want to use punishment when a child harms another. Now you are using punishment for what it was meant. If a child is mean to a brother or sister, or insulting to an adult, you definitely want to come down hard on the child verbally, but never physically.

When parents believe in the status value system, they can create a little "monster." They may punish the child with spankings to achieve discipline and enforce obedience and gain control, but when they do hurtful things, or say hateful things to a brother or sister, or some other child, they look the other way. They may even gloat and think, "My kid has some spunk, he's going to be a real "go-getter."

What you have here in effect, is a very bad moral system. Because what you have, is the values of a status social system. So unknowingly parents insidiously create a negative child, who grows up to be an adult, that often enjoys the dark side of the mind, thriving on books and movies related to violence, horror or evil.

CAUSE AND EFFECT

There are 12 critical growth periods with 12 subcortical neural circuits in the brain. One or more of these emotional circuits, may not have developed sufficiently. This may result in emotional deficiencies in behaviors. Physical illness, temporary family stresses, such as crises, squabbles, moving to a new environment, or temporary separation of the child from the parents, could result in a lack of emotional development of certain specific behaviors.

Our basic nature is geared toward pleasure. We can handle a great amount of stimulation when we are in a state of pleasure. But it doesn't take very much displeasure to overwhelm the very young. Since emotional displeasure is so overpowering, it can impair growth and development. So for growth to occur in your remo you need to create a pleasurable synergetic environment.

Status ideals of achieving discipline, obedience and control using punishment are the main cause of the remo's under-developed circuits of behavior. When disapproval is used to teach behaviors to a child under four, he is not able to understand why he is criticized and punished. But he does experience feelings of rejection, inferiority, helplessness, insecurity, anger and/or fear.

Because the remo can take punishment to mean a rejection of the self, it can be an emotionally devastating event, even life threatening to the sensitive child. Punishment early in life produces feelings of inferiority and insecurity that not only can last a life time, but also result in the suppression of emotional behaviors needed for growth and development.

Thus, children who "should be seen and not heard," dare not develop new potential behaviors because their remo doesn't know what behaviors are to be permitted. Behaviors needed for growth and development can mean a kind of defiance to the parents. If actions are inhibited and their remo remains "quiet and good," their remo will not get the scoldings that are often felt as rejection. This results in the suppression of emotional growth behaviors.

Because emotional security is the first order of business for the remo, it makes the undertaking of new behaviors needed for growth a dangerous affair. When disapproval is used on any new behaviors, e.g. a child's defiance to assert independence, it puts the stakes too high, making ventures into new behaviors a risky business. Thus, a retreat back to the tried and true gives the emotional protection and safety the remo can count on. Growth is discouraged.

On the other hand, the energetic child, who is less sensitive, but who doesn't understand the punishment, strikes back against the feelings of rejection and gets angry. This starts a disrespect or even hatred of the parent. This leads to a disobedience and parental disapproval cycle that can snowball.

Once the use of punishment such as disapproval is established by a family's status value system, then the dye is cast. The parent can be the winner in this status game only when the spirit of the child has been subdued. The parent wins a Pyrrhic victory when the remo stops wanting to learn and develop. On the other hand, a child will disobey a parent out of respect for his own needs, not because of any disrespect for the parent. His own biological rhythms tell him when his visceral system is ready to eat, and he may refuse a mother's request.

Unfortunately parents who were raised in an emotionally unsupportive family environment of status, start depending too much on the child for their own acceptance, and may feel threatened by this active resistance. Some may interpret this as willful disobedience and disrespect, while others may even feel it as personal rejection, depending on the emotional maturity of the parent.

Thus, the family passes on its status environmental deficiencies from one generation to the next, passing on an emotional immaturity that is not an hereditary defect, but an environmental defect that believes in the values of a status social system.

Also, the effects of disapproval can go unnoticed and gradually build up to undermine the child's security. Once a child feels on shaky ground, doubt can take away confidence, that leaves a vulnerability to traumatic experiences the remo normally would be able to handle. When this occurs, it doesn't take much of an unusual event to produce a traumatic situation. Perhaps just an attack by a sibling, or a temporary separation from the mother can be the final blow that produces an anxiety state.

When a new sibling is born into a family, a child in doubt about his emotional support will feel a need to compete more than ever for the security needed so badly. Jealousy develops and creates such terrible emotions that the remo may reject the parents with hate, thereby stopping any further emotional development.

Many will discover that the age of their remo is the same as the difference in years between their own age and the age of their next younger sibling. Thus, it is very important that parents who want a second child should wait until the first child reaches 5 years old.

A large sample of homeless youths, two-thirds of whom came from families of four or more, were found to be more neurotic and hostile than others. Although rootless, very few of these street people cared to keep in touch with their parents.(30)

ALIENATION

When the remo's growth has been stopped before the age of two, a person can develop a strong emotional dependency on other people as an adult. But since people are alienated from each other in a status culture, one has no option but to turn to some authority for guidance, direction and belief.

This authority can have such power over an immature remo that the rao is left helpless in its ability to lead the remo. So instead of the remo being dependent on the rao for guidance, the remo looks to, and believes, in some higher authoritative master or belief system. As a result, what the rao thinks or believes doesn't count if it's in conflict with the authoritative dogma.

As long as the rao agrees with these beliefs, there is no problem. But if the rao disagrees with some aspect of the dogma, then the remo will usually win this conflict. The remo wins because the remo is cloaked in obsurity. In this case the only way the rao can regain control and be the director of the remo is by communicating so that the remo is unveiled and revealed.

The gullibility of an immature remo makes the adult very susceptible to authoritarian persuasions that can easily convert him into the "true believer" that the authoritarians crave. Those in an authoritative position can enjoy considerable influence and power to the degree the population is under-developed or immature. Thus, there can be an unconscious sinister knowledge that using harsh punishment to raise the young creates a meek, compliant and obedient population, which is very dependent on those in positions of high status for guidance.

In fact, for a status system to work effectively, you need to have a population with immature remos. This is the reason that the authoritative "right" hates Spock. As the emotional maturity of the people increases, the lack of justice and the lack of fairness of a status system will not be allowed to operate usefully without a rebellion found in nonconformity, disrespect for authority, drugs, anti-social behaviors and violence.

RAO'S GUIDANCE

The maturity of the individual is definitely related to the subsequent growth periods of the rao. When the rao stops growing, it is a definite act of will. The person says, "To hell with it." If he really means it, then he quits and becomes a "drop out." For example, if the rao stops trying around 15 or 16 years of age, because of the bad social conditions found in the punitive status oriented public school systems, then the rao will tend to voluntarily be immature, i.e. act like a teenager as an adult.

The stronger or more developed the rao, the more effective a person will be at developing the remo. For example, people who are good at convincing others will have a much easier time persuading their remo. The glib rao has a much easier time of persuading the remo to see the brighter side of an issue, to distract the remo's negative thoughts to something different, and to talk the remo into a belief of a more desirable behavior.

The rao's guidance is best accomplished with suggestions rather than commands. And suggestive thoughts are a kind of self-hypnosis. Incomplete suggestions in the back of the mind can relay all the meaning necessary to bring on strong motivation to do something by your remo.

If you can, reduce the desired attitude or goal so that it is encapsulated into just a feeling. This symbolized feeling would have the same meaning to the remo as a well constructed sentence. The reason this is so effective is because this is often the method your remo will use to convey suggestions to your rao.

The rao should guide and develop the remo, as you would raise a child. Parents should develop their remo fully to the age of 5 before planning to conceive a child. If you have trouble getting along with your remo, or if you have problems developing and getting your remo to cooperate, then you are going to have "double" trouble raising a child.

CHAPTER 22

CARE PERIOD

2 TO 2-1/2 YEARS

CHILD STAGE

CARE RESPONSE

The period from 2 to 3 years of age is referred to as the "child" stage of development. The "care" response integrates the behaviors of the sensory nervous system and the autonomic nervous system. It ties together all the behaviors of the prior growth periods. The "care" circuit combines the past growth behaviors into more complex emotional expressions and versatility. The muscles of facial expression now come into full play with a more complex range of emotions, expressed with a new emotional agility.

This is an emotional mobility rather than the acting or performance mobility that develops in the next two stages. For the remo to assert itself it needs a repertoire of emotional responses that are expressive of its needs and desires. And the integrating "care" circuit provides the means to achieve this responsive versatility needed to realize the remo aspirations.

Character develops now. All the previous behaviors are integrated to achieve a personal integrity. You want to be true to the self and your personal beliefs. This integration achieves a high level of conscientiousness to make the remo more susceptible to guilt and shame.

This integration also influences a single mindedness of purpose. A one track mind provides the stick-to-itiveness of persistence so essential for the problem solving abilities of the remo. All efforts are concentrated on the central problem at hand to provide insight. The problem solving ability of the remo may be experienced when daydreaming intrudes into your activities.(41)

The emotions of desire and caring are essential for learning to take place. And a deeper understanding and insight into life develops now to provide a belief in one's inner resources to deal with problems. This is not a confidence in one's performance behavior, but rather a faith in an inner capacity to find solutions to problems. This provides the drive for insight or wisdom that wants to get underneath, and understand what makes things work. This is a step beyond the rote learning needed to recall facts for classroom tests.

LOVE

The ability to love can be developed both for the self and for others now. Prior to this "care" period for feelings of love to be elicited, the remo needed to worship and adore a superior person, especially one with authority, such as a parent or fatherly type, a hero or famous person, God, etc. Here love takes on a submissive quality, so that it is primarily a relationship of dependency that can alleviate the feelings of helplessness to which an infant-child remo is so susceptible. Thus love depends on an external source to create loving feelings, rather than an internal ability that the integration of the "care" circuit can provide.

When you love or care you give meaningful importance to your object of desire. And love is one of the most important of all human emotions, because the whole subcortical limbic nervous system that has been developed up to this time is activated in a pleasurable way. Specifically, the excitement of the "expectancy" response is integrated with the pleasure of the "approach and imagery" circuits. Love tempers the excitement of the sensory nervous system with the relaxation of the autonomic nervous system by adding a "vegetative" response. They combine together to provide a kind of controlled excitation.

Love integrates the relaxation of the "vegetative" response with the excitement of "caring" to make it a relaxing stimulant. Love is one of the healthiest emotional responses available to humans, but without the support and acceptance of a synergetic environment, it can make you too vulnerable in a status system. Thus, the many warnings against love, such as "Fools rush in where angels fear to tread."

The best way to develop the integrative "care" pathways is to learn how to love. Some believe the only way they are going to be able to love is to depend on someone else to elicit loving feelings from them. However, once you can persuade your remo about the importance of loving, the ability to love can be developed between your rao and your remo. And the optimal way of developing the "care" circuit is learning to love yourself.

A love of the self expands and engulfs those around you, so with the remo's ability to generalize feelings, a love of the self can easily expand into a love of others and a love of nature. When you learn to love yourself within an environment of synergy, it is like creating a constant fountain within yourself. The only thing that can dry up this loving spring is a status environment.

However, a healthy love between the rao and the remo is based on an unconditional acceptance of the self. This requires a self-acceptance and love with a full awareness of your faults and inadequacies. It is from this state of synergy that you have a firm basis upon which to grow and mature.

You develop loving feelings by calling up pleasurable "vegetative" responses, while having a caring concern for the self. All types of love involve the para-sympathetic system with good warm viscera feelings. When you successfully create warm loving feelings for the self, you will experience a "buzz on" as your alpha brain waves are activated even through you are in a semi-excited or stimulated feeling state.

If your sensory nervous system is dominant, you will like a touching, sensual erotic love; if your autonomic (viscera) nervous system is dominate, you will like a mooneyed intimate, affectionate love; or if your motor (muscle) nervous system is dominant, you will like a teasing, playful adventurous love.

The pleasures of eating food and feeling love are closely related. Practice going hungry and then indulge yourself with food to enjoy the full intensity of the pleasurable feelings experienced as tension is released. The same can be said about sexual activity. The relaxing stimulation and pleasure of affectionate sex makes the subcortical circuitry come alive as the whole range of emotional scales can be played. Then a sharp awareness on your part makes mental impressions of the emotional experience. Your memories of these feelings permit them to be recalled and practiced later, so emotional learning can occur.

The integrative "care" pathways are there; they just have to be stimulated and activated by you. And the more often you are able to call up loving feelings for yourself, the more you are going to be able to love others. If you can't have a loving relationship with yourself, you are not going to be able to have a truly loving relationship with others.

When you clench your teeth while engaging in the warm feelings of the "care" response, you can easily energize the displeasurable pathways of the brain. This redirects the energy to activate the "avoidance" circuit (see Appendix A), and create a type of fight response, but usually what you will get is a rousing confrontational reaction in yourself and others.

On the other hand, clamped jaws when combined with the "care" response can activate the displeasurable aspects of the "discrimination" circuit (see Appendix A) to create a "red neck" intolerance of the people and behaviors around you. Also, it tends to fixate your autonomic nervous system so that you lose the mobility and flexibility to adapt to a social or emotional situation effectively.

When pleasure predominates, you can approach people. You will be able to get along with people, because the approach characteristics of pleasure provides the basis for enjoying people. If displeasure is dominant, then you lose this ability to enjoy people. Displeasure can activate the "avoidance" circuit. This discomfort can causes you to seek solace with yourself, which may be the response of choice anyway, as people create the status conditions that caused the problems to begin with.

Everything's all right, as long as the individual is using one's full potential by being oriented towards pleasure with alert, affective awareness, and expressive spontaneity, or when feeling displeasure with a fight or flight response. But if these circuits are not being used properly, then the energy from these various regions is not being controlled and has nowhere to go except into the displeasurable pathways of the brain to overwhelm the individual with anxiety at it greatest intensity.

Humor is a good defensive control for this level of development to guard against anxiety. Humor acts to reduce anxiety by bringing pleasurable pathways into action. When you start to feel bad, angry or upset, humor can rechannel this negative energy to pleasurable areas that are better able to handle these uncomfortable feelings. For example, when you're happy, you can enjoy bright lights, loud music and loud conversations, but if you're unhappy these same things can be overwhelming.

Seriousness is pervaded with caring or meaningfulness, and comes into full bloom with the integration of behaviors in the "care" period. Seriousness is a mixture of pleasure and displeasure. On the other hand, being overly serious is a result of so much meaningfulness that a flexibility is lost; so that even trivialities can take on too much personal significance.

Humor can reduce this seriousness for the remo. The "child" remo tends to take things too seriously, which can easily cause over reactions that can move into the displeasurable pathways of the brain. At these times the rao needs to distract the remo's attention to something else just as you would a child. Being oriented towards pleasure, gives you other avenues of responses so you can divert the remo thoughts to something else. And humor lowers the "stakes" and allows the remo to save face by expressing concerns in a pleasurable way.

In other words, in a displeasurable situation, humor allows you to redirect excessive energies into the pleasurable pathways where it can be more easily handled. Being witty, clowning around, looking for the comical, and having fun with puns are humorous approaches that are pleasurably oriented.

READINESS RESPONSE

The anticipatory energy of the "expectancy" response creates a state of readiness, by orienting your senses towards a greater awareness. The alert, quickness and agility of the "expectancy" response can be integrated with the relaxed "vegetative" response involving the lower jaw, mouth, tongue and lips.

Being accident prone is often caused by a lack of alert preparedness. By practicing the "readiness" response you can reduce mishaps and personal injuries. Anytime you're driving a car you should practice the "readiness" response. This allows you to be attentive and prepared for dangerous contingencies while driving. Older people especially need to activate this "readiness" response when driving. It can also revitalize their lives and make them feel young and energized.

INTEGRATING BEHAVIORS

The more curiosity, desires and goals you can create in your remo, the more you are going to develop and strengthen the "care" response. You want to practice the emotional growth behaviors when among people in a non-threatening synergetic environment.

The anticipatory energy developed in the "expectancy" period will provide a readiness to respond to allow the remo to be more flexible. The "expectancy" response orientes your senses towards a greater awareness of your surroundings

When you walk into a new, challenging or different situation, you don't want to fixate on only one response, as the remo has up to this stage of development, but all the circuity responses you have at your disposal should be kept alive with different behavioral options. For instance, the alert, attentive readiness of the "expectancy" response can be integrated with the relaxed "vegetative" response so the lower lip hangs loose to expose the lower teeth, the lower jaw slackens, the tongue thickens, as you sniff the air taking deep rhytmical breaths.

You can practice periodically alternating the various behaviors. For example, you can elicit the "approach" response to cheer up other people around you, just as you would cheer up your own remo, then switch to the "vegetative" response, to re-establish rhythmical breathing, then next you can pep things up with the "expectancy" response. By practicing these various behaviors as often as you can, and practice switching back and forth between behaviors, they eventually can become automatic behaviors your remo can take over and initiate on his own.

You want to integrate all of these behaviors as one response. For example, the "approach" and "vegetative" responses can be integrated when oriented towards pleasure by contracting the upper lip while the lower lip drops in a smile. When the upper lip draws up thin, the lower jaw can drop and relax and the tongue enlarges in a "semi-vegetative" response with relaxed natural breathing. You have integrated these two behaviors when they can occur as one response. This integrative response energizes both the excitement of the sympathetic system in the "approach" response, and the para-sympathetic system with a relaxed state via in the "vegetative" response.

Next you want to combine the autonomic and sensory nervous systems by integrating the "vegetative, approach and expectancy" responses. So an alert, attentive readiness can be integrated with a relaxed lower jaw, mouth and tongue, while contracting the upper lip in a sort of smile, that allows the lower jaw to drop and relax.

The easiest and quickest way to learn this integrative response is with a love of the self, between your rao and your remo. You want to get an alpha "buzz on" with warm tingling feelings in your face and chest areas. When interacting with others a love of the self can give you an inner peace so you can feel at home in almost any social situation.

You need to practice all of these behaviors as often as possible until they occur as one response. And you want to be oriented towards pleasure, and if possible with feeling of love towards the self. When you can perform all these responses as one behavior, you have successfully integrated them. You want to integrate all the circuits together with feelings of love for the self first, and then if possible for another or others.

The "child" stage from 2 to 3 is when care and anxiety is reaching a peak. The "care" circuit that produces these vulnerable states can be experienced again in the remo at 12, 22, and 32 years of age, and the rao's hemisphere experiences similar periods of vulnerability at 7, 17, 27 and 37 years of age approximately. You should be aware of these periods of vulnerability, so you know what's going on within your self and allow you to be better prepared for these emotional periods.

THE TERRIBLE TWOS

The information in this section was obtained from Gesell and Ilg.(40) This is the period when words are undergoing rapid expansion. The child talks to herself, repeats words and names things with a compelling urge in order to exercise her new vocal ability. With a new interest in verbal interactions, she now enjoys listening to her mother's conversation and contributes a few comments of her own. And her developing ability to walk and talk creates a problem, because others tend to overestimate her capacity and expect too much of her.

The child from 2 to 2-1/2 years needs a negative stubbornness to protect himself against overstimulating situations.(33) He may protest against everything more as a sign of his vulnerability, rather than a rebelliousness indicative of a bad nature, or wish to instigate trouble. This hard outer shell he creates protects the softness inside.

Although he mostly enjoys playing alone, he likes to affectionately approach other children to hug, kiss and tenderly pat them. And this is the time when affection for the parents is shown. A real display of affection towards his mother is especially strong at bedtime. This affection may spread to other adults. Even his voice has affective tones. And he may take affectionate care of his toys. In nursery play, children of this age laugh together "with eddies and bursts of contagious humor."

Her sensitivity is beginning to interfere with her sleep. Leaving the door open slightly when going to bed with a night light can relieve some of the child's anxiety of the door acting as a barrier separating her from her mother. She may get out of bed many times because of loneliness. Or she may feel the sensations to urinate many times, even though she won't be able to urinate.

The two year old child prefers a relationship with one adult, as two people create too many difficulties. When with a group of people he may possessively demand all of his mother's time and attention.

His strong demands around home are in marked contrast to the compliance and meekness away from home. His increasing sensitivity to people causes him to be shy with strangers, and he may hide behind his mother's skirt. The two year old is more cautious and conservative than before. He is comfortable with the familiar, whereas the new or strange may baffle or disturb him.

He understands the property rights of others now, and so he is not getting into so many things, but he wants to own as many things as he can. He may be under the impression that just a claim of ownership establishes something as his own, since that's what the adults appear to do.

He does not like to share, and tends to hoard what is his. Instead of letting someone else play with his things he prefers to find substitutes for others to use.

The fights over play material seldom allows cooperative play to develop. He prefers to intently watch what others are doing rather than participate. And he still prefers solitary play in this pre-cooperative stage. He is happiest in his play with books, music and a soft animal toy.

The child at this stage has a genuine interest in the mother-baby relationship, and becomes engrossed in doll play or imitating feminine household activities. The father is the favorite now although he will want his mother if he is in trouble or tired.

The child has to organize his experience through touching, handling, hoarding, fleeing and pursuing. He goes briefly from one activity to another as he did at 18 months, but these short spells of activity are more organized. And the process of organization goes on with the variations on each repetition.

CARE CIRCUIT

The "care" circuit refers to the diagonal band, the medial olfactory stria, the intralamina nuclei of the thalamus, the septal area (paraolfactory or Brocal area), and the subcallosal gyrus.

The "care" region is an integrating circuit where the septal area, as the main integrating unit tie together the remo's past eight periods of development. To facilitate the integration of these diverse regions, the septal has the pathways, structural ability and location to especially coordinate these many circuits simultaneously. (See Fig. 7)

For example, the caudate nucleus, the putamen, and the claustrum send fibers to the frontal area to influence the integration of inhibitory motor response in the septal. The diagonal band connects the putamen, the globus pallidus, and the corticomedial amygdala to the septal, While the basolateral amygdala sends fibers by way of the ventral amygdalofugal tract to join the diagonal band and the septal. The dorsomedial thalamus sends fibers to the septal via the inferior thalamic peduncle to integrate discrimination/generalization functions and avoidance responses.

All of these areas combine to create a powerful inhibitory effect on autonomic and somatomotor responses. This integration allows a greater capacity to suppress learned responses that are inappropriate and thus to enhance problem solving ability.

The para-olfactory or septal area is an important speech area; and it is at this time that speech begins to blossom, jargon is discarded, and the child begins to speak in sentences. (55)

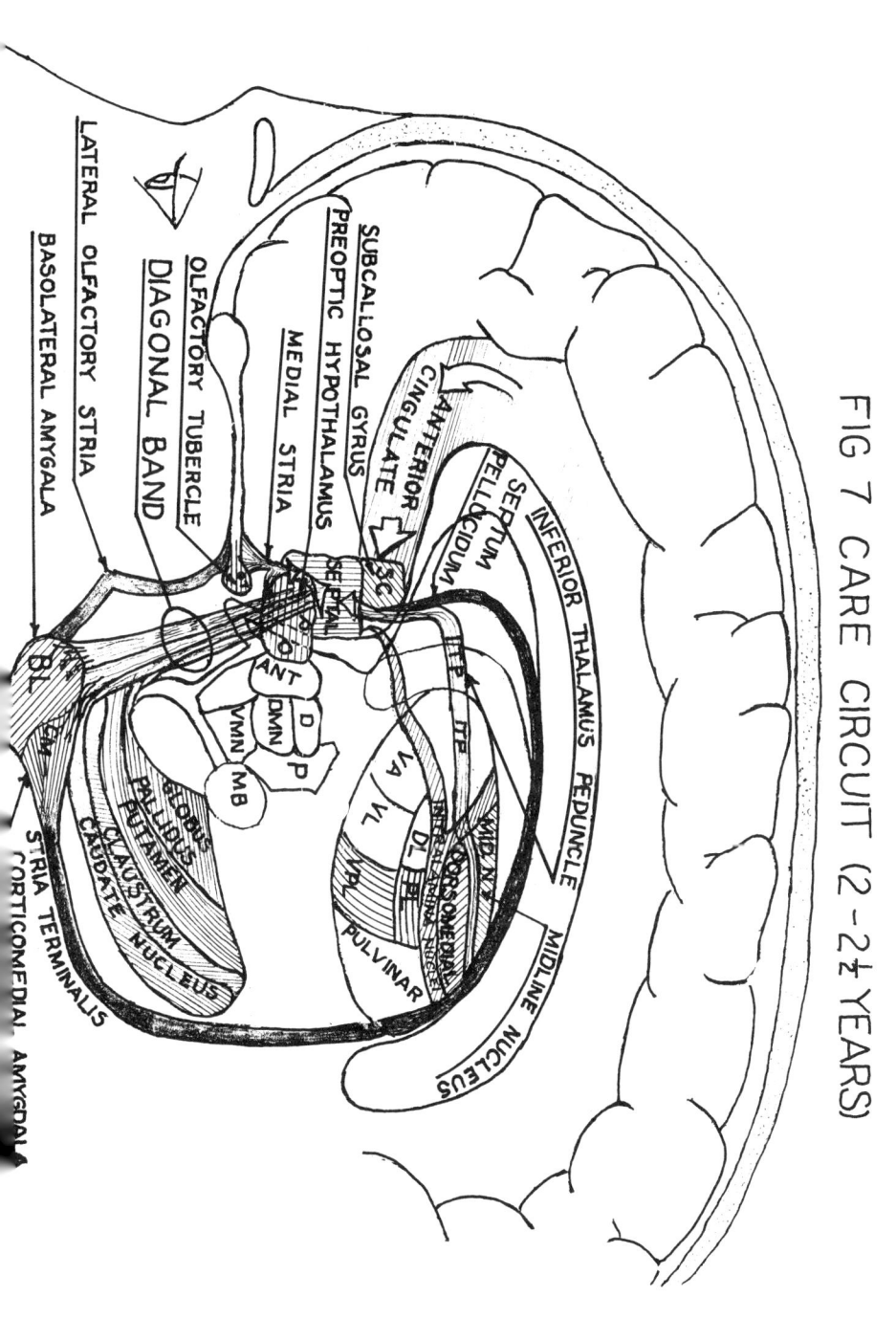

FIG 7 CARE CIRCUIT (2-2½ YEARS)

Association fibers, association nuclei of the thalamus that integrate thalamic activity, the inferior thalamic peduncle, and the intralamina nuclei of the thalamus that receives sensory input, project fibers to the obital frontal cortex and the septal, to coordinate thalamic activity with the septal region.

Further integration occurs within the septal area as the anterior cingulate gyrus becomes continuous with the subcallosal and septal areas; the medial stria from the olfactory area integrates this area with the septal; the stria terminalis hooks up the septal with the corticomedial amygdala; and finally the preoptic area of the hypothalamus becomes continuous with the septal to provide intimate connections with the hypothalamus.

These areas are united at the septal to integrate emotional affect with anticipation and imagination as energy sources that create more intense highs and lows in pleasure and displeasure.

The "care" area, concentrated in the septal, acts as an energy booster by coordinating these past various circuits together, and utilizing their diverse energies in a more adaptive and more effective manner.

Although the septal has punishing sites, it primarily combines other displeasurable areas, and integrates them with other behaviors, e.g. anticipation. As a result, this is the period when anxiety is reaching its peak of intensity. Reward centers can also be found within the "care" circuitry, especially in the septal, to make this a strong pleasurable area.(87)

CHAPTER 23

CONTROLS

If status hierarchies were allowed to operate unimpeded among humans, confusion, insecurity, helplessness and violence would result in total anarchy. So conformity, laws and authoritarian power have to be imposed on a status system to bring order, to gain control, and to compel some kind of cooperation among people.

Those in authority need to be able to control people. To do this they want to possess as much political strength, influence and power as possible. They need power to influence the attitudes of others and have them do things they think are best. They have to be interested in power first, as their primary objective.

One technique of accumulating power and influence is to employ experts who will provide agreeable opinions. Experts are usually servants of power. Their source of prestige and advancement, is based on supporting and proving a certain set of beliefs that helps those in power. The first order of the day is not truth and knowledge. It is developing arguments and persuasions for the interests that give them, and those they serve, influence and power. So the opinion of experts should always be viewed from the standpoint of whose interest does the expert's opinion serve.

A democracy uses laws to govern people. All societies need laws to deal with harmful aggression. These are beneficial. However, the degree to which its laws do not deal with harmful aggression is the degree to which a democracy moves towards being a dictatorial government. Then the laws become the manipulative arm of a few to command the many. An example are laws that deal with victimless crimes. These laws can distribute power to control people, and provide special privileges, so that it works in favor of those well situated in a status system and works against others who are not.

Laws against gambling are an example of laws that don't discriminate and deal with harmful behavior. The prohibition laws against alcohol, back in the 1920's, showed that with increased regulations, more crimes are committed. Another example is drugs. If people don't care about themselves and want to use drugs to escape, it is because of a hostile and rejecting environment. It is no solution to blame them for what was caused by the unaccepting status conditions.

As laws, together with law enforcement, move out of the realm of dealing with harmful aggression, they actually increase a society's harmful aggression. And the more that law enforcement has to expand, the more it is a confession of society's failure to govern its people. Each new law is an admission of the state's inability to get people to cooperate. Force must make up for its failure.

When there are people who dislike the law, who do not respect the officers of law, and who admire or sympathize, with those who go against the law, then the law loses its effectiveness. Eventually it becomes a less protective force for them. When representatives of the law punish those who have not hurt others, some segments of the population will resent those who are suppose to protect them. Thus, an insecure environment can result where people do not feel safe and protected. The way the Mafia leaders are admired, respected and even idolized among some law-abiding citizens is an example of how some law breakers get more respect than law enforcers.

The enforcers of laws can make choices as to what they want to expend their time enforcing. Unless there is pressure applied, there is a preference to enforce the victimless crime laws, as it is safer, or at least not so life-threatening. Law enforcement avoids the ghetto areas of real harmful crime. In a status society where people have to look out for their own welfare first, who can blame them? Law enforcement will naturally concentrate on throwing people in jail for things that don't really hurt others, like possession of marijuana, prostitution, numbers, pornography, etc.

These actions are justified with the reasoning that minor offenses may lead to major offenses. Potential for harm may call for precautionary behavior, where as harmful aggressive crimes call for laws. Instead, these minor offenses are used to justify the continued establishment of power.

Recently, there have been synergetic efforts made at law enforcement in certain areas. Instead of police officers being cut off from the people, ensconced in their patrol cars, they are walking their beat, dealing with people one on one, on more even ground. And they are encouraged to use reason to talk out a bad situation first, before using force to end a conflict.

STATUS CYCLE

When authority can influence people to give them more power, their appetite for power can be hard to satisfy. And power is usually increased at the expense of people's rights. The accumulating cycle of power and belief in authority encourages people to jump on the bandwagon to fight crime. There is usually a plea to increase the power of those in authority, so they can "get tough" with criminals. The result tends to create a snowball effect. To fight crime, you need to pass more laws, hire more police, elect more judges, build more jails and prisons, etc. It has all been tried before and it never has worked and never will work, except in a police state. Thus a status system feeds off itself so that the people and their leaders are trapped in a vicious status cycle, which can insidiously move towards an authoritarian state.

As laws (especially those that deal with victimless crime) increase, crimes increase. The seeds of contention and defiance that grow from personal disapproval and rejection prevalent in a status culture can create a disrespect for society and therefore for its laws.

This leads to aggression, which in turn leads to more laws, together with greater restrictions on behavior. Punishment either by laws or disapproval, because of its innate injustice and unfairness, sabotages cooperativeness to produce a deterioration in the economy. This builds up resentment further, to result in more retaliatory aggression. The punishments for these transgressions then start the status cycle of aggression, laws-conformity, and punishment all over again.

People are trapped in this cycle because they are trying to maintain and control a status system. This amassing of power can only be stopped by understanding how synergy operates to elicit cooperation among its members. In other words, the best way to fight crime is to fight against the status system. This is done by restricting punishment to harmful behaviors, so that we can get along, cooperate and work together in a supportive environment.

And those in authority in a status culture use methods to impair the ability of its members to reason effectively. They delight in sound bites that short circuit critical thinking, that take the simple road with slogans such as "might makes right," or "we will crush and stamp out crime."

The real violent criminals laugh and think it's all a big joke, as the jails fill with drug abusers who they can use as pawns to control and dominate in their prison kingdom, if they do have to go to jail. It's a joke because there is no real punishment of prisoners. They are given all kinds of privileges and special considerations with TVs, sport and recreational facilities, libraries and law books to harass anyone they don't like. But that's the topsy turvy world of a status social system, as macho authoritarian types bluff, threaten and posture to gain power and control, but deliver a weak ineffectual government.

A child who repeatedly breaks the law under ten years of age, forebodes a career criminal, because of the rao's involvement. However, juvenile delinquents can be rehabilitated if they can be put through a training program where they must communicate with their remo at the highest, sixth level in an environment of synergy; but they must also learn the behaviors that can allow them to mature emotionally so they can gain more self-control if they want to be released early. The same scenario would hold true for older criminals in a prison system.

The people who usually break the law often have a remo who did not develop a very effective conscience. However, they are capable of feeling the humiliation of shame when in the presence of others. The concept of public shame as put forth by John Braithwaite(12) is an approach that could provide solutions. His system of "reintegrative shaming" is a preventive strategy that uses a community controlled criminal justice system that publicly shames really harmful behavior, and uses methods such as frowns, shunning, gossip, public confrontation and humiliation.

Newspapers and television should show pictures of those who harm others, especially when the remo's conscience is going through refinement between the ages of 10-15 and 20-25. However, in our society criminals are shielded from shaming and protected from feelings of disgrace as they are sheltered away from public view.

When a person's remo has been made to feel ashamed of some harm that was inflicted on another, the remo will tend to punish the rao who is suppose to guide and lead the self away from these situations.

On the other hand when the remo punishes the self because of some stupid remark or blunder, then the remo is using the status value of punishing harmless behavior. To teach your remo a new set of values is one of many important reasons you want to be able to communicate with your remo at higher levels.

CHAPTER 24
VISIONS

For the fourth communication step you want your remo to create a vision of itself. Ask your remo to create an image of how it feels about its self, using the visual imagery of the mind. You do not want to make any effort to create this visual image. Your remo needs to be free of your influence. If there are too many distractions interfering with your remo's freedom to create an image, then close your eyes and create a feeling of wonder and relaxation.

Now let a vision of your remo "pop" into your mind, whether it be a strong sustained visual impression, or the mere flash or fleeting glimpse of an image. This should be done now before reading further.

SELF-IMAGE

This vision will be the symbolic embodiment of how your remo feels about itself at this time, regardless of what strange or wonderful apparition appears to you; whether it be a little boy or girl, an infant, an egg with arms and legs, an animal, Christ, God, an insect, Superman, the devil, an angel, a monster, a mobster, an inanimate object, the opposite sex, etc.

How negative the image is depends on the degree to which status has been dominant over synergy when the remo was being raised as a child. However, avoiding, ignoring or criticizing the remo, because of the way it feels about the self, is not going to change the way the remo feels or believes. It is only with a complete acceptance of your remo, "as is," that is going to eventually permit you to make a positive change and resolve any negative or unpleasant imagery.

If your remo appears as some animal, like "Hobbs," or some terrible monster, it does no good to reject this image. You will only be rejecting your remo, which already feels rejected. This rejection is what stopped the remo from becoming emotional mature to begin with. You have to accept the worst in your self before you can change it. So if you do not like your remo's self-image and want to change your way the remo feels, you first have to accept this objectionable vision.

Actor and writer Peter Ustinov talks about his early years in his book "Dear Me,"(121)

"I was a motor-car to the dismay of my parents. Psychiatry was in its infancy then...There was no one yet qualified to exorcise an internal combustion engine from a small boy...I switched on in the morning and only stopped being a car at night when I reversed into bed, and cut the ignition."

One day his mother suffering with a terrible toothache and all the noise from young Peter's automobile caused her to reprimand Peter severely. His wise old grandfather is reported to have remarked,

"Never shout at him! I know it is irritating, even without a toothache, dear child. But don't think of it as the sound of an automobile, but rather, as the sound of his imagination developing and then you will see, it will become bearable."

Whether an Oldsmobile, Edsel or whatever, your remo will become bearable. You should have no doubts that your remo will grow and change for the better later on. There are specific reasons for your remo's responses that you can gradually modify. But if you try to reject this image, or be critical of your remo's feelings, you will accomplish nothing, but drive your remo away from you.

IMAGERY

Imagination has a reality in feelings which can be very real to the remo. Images that come into your mind, fantasies or illusions which flitter by are the expression of feelings of the remo. The remo's needs are immediate. Vicarious feelings and images can answer these needs. They reflect real needs in the world of the remo.

You now want to use this ability of your remo to create imagery. Direct questions which your remo may now respond with the use of the image created by simply nodding the head "yes" or "no."

When alone, you should try to spend some time at this level of interaction with your remo, communicating about past and current events. When you've successfully completed some job, you can celebrate with a secret hand shake with your remo in your visual mind by locking thumbs, locking fingers, bumping elbows, etc. When listening to your favorite music, for example, while driving, you should have this image of your remo dance to the music in your mind's eye. While you watch your remo move to the music, and put on a show for you, you might make little minute movements along with your remo. Now when you go out on an actual dance floor you'll want your remo to show you how to move in your mind's eye. You want your remo to move first using your imagination to get in the right rhythmic mood before starting your first moves to a dance.

Whenever you can, try to have a good time and enjoy your remo, by using the behaviors of the "approach" response. For example in your mind's eye you can smile and wink at your remo, as you develop loving feelings between your rao and your remo.

CHAPTER 25

LOVING
AND HATING

LOVING

When social status hierarchies dominate strongly, the reaction to love is often either indifference or contempt. Arduous efforts often go unrewarded, as results seem to bear little relation to the efforts made. But if you can shape an environment of synergy, so that you can feel emotionally secure, then how much you love is a function of the love you feel for yourself. The more you can love yourself, the more that loving feelings can become effortless, and the more you can feel love for your spouse, children and others.

The success of a personal relationship requires first an awareness of your own feelings, and second an awareness of another's feelings. If this includes loving feelings for yourself during these social events, then you have improved the quality of the exchange, as this tends to raise the esteem of yourself and those around you.

The selflessness of loving others requires the selfishness of loving yourself first. Understand that this does not ask you to fall in love with an image of yourself, as you look in the mirror, like Narcissus, for this would be like treating yourself as an "object." Rather you want to appreciate yourself by developing warm and loving feelings between your rao and your remo, then you can develop a natural affection for those around you.

You can develop this higher quality of pleasure within yourself by generating feelings of care, affection and love between the rao and remo. As humans, we learn and develop the ability to love. We do not have the instinct to do things automatically. So we learn.

Love is a relaxing stimulant. It integrates relaxation with excitation to provide a feeling of comfortable stimulation. In love, pleasure is inextricably bound up with care. Care means you are giving full attention and meaningful importance to the interest you consider significant. Thus, loving the self involves the enjoyment and pleasure you can derive from the meaningful care and attention you can give yourself.

Now along with your remo's image created in the last chapter, you can also produce an image of your rao, for example as you appear in the mirror. In this way, the two images can appear together. Now to start out on the road of learning to love yourself you can imagine your rao and your remo giving each other an affectionate hug. Practice the integrative "care" response from the care period to give full expression to loving feelings.

When you learn to love and enjoy your remo, you have found one of the best remedies for what ails you both physically and psychologically. A supportive acceptance, or even better, a caring, affectionate relationship, between your rao and your remo creates a synergetic relationship that can be a source of inner peace and strength. In addition, the fun and good feelings will help you gradually build up your esteem and confidence. You can acquire this self-curative well-being by applying the acceptance of synergy, enjoying a love of life, a love of people and nature, and a responsible affectionate caring for yourself.

THE REALITIES OF HATING

One who can love very much can also hate very much. Love and hate stem from the same root, which is a strong tendency to care.

Often, those you care most about can also be those who have hurt you the most. So these feelings can create problems and conflicts. And those who are riddled with anger and hate from their past need a method to purge these hostilities. So instead of stifling your anger, or the harmful expression of your wrath, there is another choice available to you to handle your remo's hostilities. A catharsis of the pent-up anger can be brought about with the use of "aggressive" fantasies.

What we are interested in is some expression of the hostility in a more mature manner. When expressing "aggressive" fantasies, you want an emotional release of the remo's hostile feelings. Since these feelings may have been augmented by the internal reality of the imagination, we want to use this same inner channel to decrease or eliminate the hostility. By using your inner reality, you can relive or even increase the intensity of past hostilities, onto which you will then apply your "aggressive" fantasies. Paradoxically, this can eventually reduce the animosity and lose this emotional baggage that can drag you down.

You need first to review your past history of those devastating moments that distress your remo, then arrange them into a hierarchy so that you start at the top with the most distressful remembrance.

ELDER CAITIFF

Angry feelings from the past will often be about someone close to you, such as your parents, spouse or friends. If, for example, ELDER CAITIFF hurt you badly by some unforgivable deed, then you want to relive the experience in your mind and try to resolve it. Then you may punish ELDER CAITIFF in any manner you want within your inner imaginary realm. First create an image of yourself along with ELDER CAITIFF in your mind's eye. Now you can take your revenge with an envisaged rapacity. You are allowed to use and do anything you want toward him within your mind. You can go as far as you desire. You can use any verbal or physical abuse, or any bizarre method you want. And it is best to give your remo a free rein to create the punishment in the "aggressive" fantasy.

The important thing is the purging catharsis which you achieve by the intense expression of your feelings of revenge. This exorcism of hate may last a couple of minutes or a couple of hours, but it should continue until you no longer desire to indulge in the mental retaliation. Then you will reach a state in which your thirst for vengeance is quenched.

When your anger and revenge are replaced by a complete indifference, and when you no longer feel anger nor enjoy the abusive vengeance, "then" you have relieved yourself of a damaging emotional burden. And you will have personally experienced the reality of the remo's inner world.

If you had allowed the negative feelings to ferment suppressed underneath a social facade of forced civility, then when you personally encountered ELDER CAITIFF in the flesh, the possible degradation of the social situation could result in an awkwardness and tension. Instead with your "aggressive" fantasy you will have achieved a much better control of yourself and the social situation.

This type of hate, one has for another, has to be controlled in a status system to maintain order. Besides the law, conformity is also able to take on the function of controlling people and making them cooperate.

CHAPTER 26

CONFORMITY VRS. MULTIFORMITY

CONFORMITY

Conformity may take the form of customs, traditions, fashions, popular ways, or dictates of that which is proper, correct and appropriate. Even advertisements of products on TV, radio, newspapers and magazines often take on the role of tellings us how we should be. They all function to weaken some of the harmful effects of a status hierarchy by creating some semblance of unity.

Conformity keeps you from being dismissed as unacceptable while being given a chance to make an impression of your social skills, maturity, performance abilities, etc. Conformity does not guarantee your acceptance, but it permits you a chance at competing for acceptance. You may conform in many ways and still not feel you belong, because you may still have to prove yourself.

Conformity itself can create problems. Conformance, your performance ability to conform, can lead to uncertainty and a lack of ease with yourself. As you adopt the behaviors, opinions and characteristics of the people you want to be accepted by to gain approval, then the facade of this conformance is given credit for the acceptance received. This leaves a guarded uncertainty on the impression you are making that can prevent you from being comfortable with yourself.

Conformity itself is not bad. Conformity is only bad when it makes use of the punishment of disapproval. But conformity depends on punishment to operate effectively. Conformity punishes others with disapproval of those who are different, and rejecting those who do not want to play by the rules, even though no harmful behavior has occurred.

What makes conformity especially reprehensible is the snooping, meddling and gossip often used to enforce codes of behavior. Social hierarchies make many people feel worthless, or if not worthless their lives tends to be empty. To take their mind off their own meaningless affairs they snoop around into the affairs of other people. Those who do not want to conform, and act the way others think they should, are punished. But to punish improper behaviors indiscriminately punishes both the good and the bad. Not only are the harmful ostracized, but also those who want to live a creative, spontaneous life.

The punishment of harmless behavior is what makes conformity particularly unwholesome. Although conformity offers some balance to the harmful aggression of a status hierarchy, it is no solution. Instead we need to weaken the source that disrupts cooperation which is the social status hierarchy.

MULTIFORMITY

In a status culture the restrictions that conformity places on people tend to create a boring existence. So to spice up the humdrum of the daily routine many rely on juicy tidbits of gossip that peck at others esteem.

However, the best way to spice up your life is to allow and encourage a multitude of actions and behaviors to exist. When you adopt synergy you are choosing to believe that there should be no such thing as doing something improper or inappropriate, unless you are hurting someone else, because the ideal is not conformity, but its opposite multiformity.

The essence of multiformity is the belief that there are many correct ways of doing things and many forms of excellence. "Superiority" is a comparative of the state of conformity, whereas a state of diversity has a less comparative basis. It would permit a multitude of different qualities contributing to a form of excellence. Now the diverse inequality of talents and abilities can be a desirable asset, instead of being used to set one apart, either below or above others.

There are many creative ways to live life that can provide a boundless source of pleasure and interest. Since multiformity allows greater diversity, than other people become more of a positive source of pleasure and rewarding experiences. The eccentric person can be a welcome novelty and provide a desirable contribution that adds interest to living instead of being someone to evade.

CIVILIZATIONS

Besides using laws and conformity to control the people, all of the great civilizations of the past had the same limitations in common. They did not incorporate the minorities and the low status people effectively; instead they provided privileges for special groups.

During the rise of these civilizations, the special groups could control the harmful effects of status hierarchies because of the many prospects available during the rise of a culture. When there is expansion, opportunities bloom with abundance to provide the hope that can create a desire for people to pull together in a cooperative spirit.

But the limits a status political system places on the development of new technology, with its beliefs in the status quo to protect the powers that be, eventually fills the capacity for the advancement of a society. As potential growth is realized, then the aggressive energies of a status society turn more and more from constructive to destructive objectives. This eventually starts the descent that leads to a disintegration of a status society.

There were no options available to the leaders of past declining civilizations but to try to force more cooperation from people with more punishing tactics. These civilizations got to the point where they offered little hope to the people and had to depend more and more on punishment to maintain control. This is happening in our society as prisons can't seem to be built fast enough. Without much hope, people will tend to retaliate to the violent nature of punishment in a similar manner.

So, during bad economic times, social hierarchies produce the worst possible conditions for a society, and the society's status system gradually destroys the cooperative spirit in its people. When the promises of growth are realized, the inequalities and injustices of a status hierarchy can no longer be tolerated, and a society will slowly be destroyed with either internal dissensions and violence, or externally with wars to relieve the internal strife.

The way you improve the economy of a nation is the same way you improve relationships. You develop and encourage cooperation. Just as relations between the rao and the remo, between family members and between neighbors improve to the degree they adopt synergy, so the economy of a nation will improve to the degree it adopts synergy. So the most important goal you can set for yourself should be directed towards developing synergy.

CHAPTER 27

GOAL-DIRECTED PERIOD

2 - 1/ 2 TO 3 YEARS

CHILD STAGE

The prior "care" response was an integration period that provided the energy for the "engine" of motivation. That is, it allowed the emotional circuits to be united for the emotional arousal to do something. The "goal-directed" period is also an integration area, but it provides the steering apparatus to guide this motivational "engine." The "goal-directed" circuit gives guidance to the remo's motivational engine, so the remo can direct its energies towards more significant and practical goals.

In other words, during the "care" period, the remo tended to be overly concerned about everything, but in the "goal-directed" period the "care" response has been restricted to more important and practical goals. This allows a higher level of organization, as the remo guides the self towards more pertinent goals.

Up to this level of development, the remo's determination has been dependent on directions from others. That is, one can do a good job with conscientious effort as long as there is someone to tell one what to do. But now the rebel develops who wants to do things one's own way, to follow the beat of one's own drum, and one who would prefer to be self-employed, or some equivalent freedom in work, over being employed and having to follow orders.

During the "goal-directed" period, the motor system is dominate. The "care" circuit developed an emotional mobility in the last period that allowed a spontaneity in regard to what one may feel. Now a motor mobility is developed that provides muscular expression to one's feelings so that feelings can be acted out with more skillful behaviors.

The circuitry involved in the "goal-directed" period has been found to be a very pleasurable reward area in the brain.(86 & 87) And with the "goal-directed" behaviors of this period, there are a hundred and one things to be doing, things to be said, expressions to be expressed, feelings to be felt. And the anticipations of goals act like gasoline on the motor cortex to drive and excite the remo. On the other hand, when there is nothing to do, then arousal can be overstimulating, creating anxiety, boredom, etc.

When people first take up a skill, sport or occupation, they often may get a "bug" for it. Many people become enthused over golf, because they have 7 or 8 things to do at the same time during a golf swing when learning the game. They may be "hooked" for years, because nothing can get the remo so impassioned as trying to do several things at the same time, as is needed in mastering a golf swing. Thus, many people may enjoy the many challenges of a goal more during the early learning stages, than after they have become quite proficient at it.

The problem solving ability of the remo that started developing in the last period, now increases with a compulsive intensity. The practical creativeness of this "goal-directed" period is much more likely to make contributions of a problem solving nature, both during waking hours and at night during dreams. When your remo can effectively work out your problems in dreams, then your remo has well developed "goal-directed" and "care" circuits.

The "goal-directed" circuit provides the components for the development of a shrewd "Sherlock Homes" quality that searches diligently to get to the bottom of a problem. But this also can create other problems as suspicions involved with jealousies now can be relentlessly pursued for affirmation. However, when directed towards the field of science and research, then invention and innovation can result.

A strongly developed "goal-directed" circuit will encourage a strong love of variety, and a desire to experiment with all the different ways and methods of doing something to find the best way. This experimental attitude where everything reasonable has to be tried at least once, along with anticipation and imagination, allows the remo to be very innovative, inventive and original.

The "goal-directed" circuit produces a very industrious active life. But more important than the activity is the planning and organizing of activities ahead of time and ironing out the problems that might occur.

The pleasure in the anticipation of a goal provides the motivation that keeps one oriented towards achieving the goal, and provides a searching awareness for the necessary tasks needed for that goal. The greater the anticipation in doing what one wants to do, the greater the potential pleasure.

The joy in anticipation, the pleasure involved in the problem solving process, and the elation in finding a solution are some of the pleasures of this area. The more things one can plan and carry out that benefit the self, then the more pleasure can be experienced, especially when one's actions not only help the self, but others.

Since this is the most productive and innovative period of all, then those fortunate to be able to do things they want to do have the greatest potential for happiness. Thus the farmer or self employed businessman who works 14 hours a day does not do that just for the money expected, but more for the pleasure found in the many "goal-directed" activities involved. The desire for money can only get one started. It cannot maintain the activity. It takes pleasure to do that.

However, one can be so completely engrossed in the attainment of personal goals, that one seems to be disinterested in others. This persistency in driving towards a goal regardless of the obstacles involved may give the impression of being inconsiderate of people. But this belies the loving nature that can reside underneath these appearances, as there can be a deep need for others that provides the motivation for a very caring relationship with others.

The elation in solving problems can also cause trouble with sleep and keep one awake all hours of the night. On retiring at night, problem solving episodes can create conflicts between the rao and the remo, when the rao wants to sleep but the remo wants to find the solution to a problem. If one's life has some synergetic order or one has a remo who has matured beyond this stage of growth, then the remo can function in a problem solving way in dreams without disrupting the rao's sleep. But if not insomnia can disrupt the biological rhythms, making the next day dreadful.

BEHAVIORS

To develop or strengthen the "goal-directed" circuit requires you to communicate with your remo at the higher levels, the higher, the better. Investigation and experimentation are the essence of this period. For example, if you're cooking, you want to cook a dish in a new way. But instead of going to a cookbook, talk it over with your remo about the different ingredients you might add or substitute. Be daring! Let your remo come up with something unusual. You should study cookbooks to see new ways of combining ingredients from various dishes.

If you like to play some sport, suspend your desire for excellence for a while to experiment with new ways of performing a movement. Go to the library and refer to several books on a sport to give you ideas to apply during practice sessions. If you really want to develop the "goal-directed" circuit, the library is very necessary to sharpen your investigative skills.

You should also experiment with various emotional behaviors and skills to develop your acting ability. Try to imitate behaviors you see in others, on TV, at the movies, etc. You should even try to do impressions of famous people to activate this "goal-directed" circuit. But most of all you want to experiment and express yourself in new and exciting ways. You want to improvise and express your own variation of the emotional behaviors of the various growth periods.

The "goal-directed" period represents a time of double jeopardy for the 2-1/2 year old child, as the remo's jealousy of the parents and other members of the family can stop the growth of the remo, as well as the rejection felt from disapproval.

THE PARADOXICAL AGE

The information in this section was obtained from Gesell and Ilg.(40) Spankings and punishment are reaching a peak around 2-1/2 and 3 years of age, because it is the most exasperating age of all to adults. He tries his parents with contrary extremes.

"Yes and no, come and go, run and stop, give and take, push and pull, assault and retreat" are some of his behaviors that can represent the range of his desires.

He may demand to be fed, then turn around and refuse to eat. He may change from being very active to being passively peaceful; or be screaming loudly one moment and mutter in a soft whisper the next. His enthusiastic helpfulness and sociability may suddenly shift to a desire to withdraw into isolation.

He is caught between alternatives that at 18 months were not so desirable or pressing. And the avoidance and shyness of 24 months now includes their opposite behaviors of approach and aggressiveness. He needs to try both ways to find out which is best for him.

Children at this age want to be with other people, but their easy excitability makes it difficult for them to handle people. They usually play best with one other child, especially one who is older that he can respect and accept.

When children of this age come together in nursery school it creates a conglomeration of the extremes of sociality. The play is mainly self-centered with each independently following her own devices, but the rudiments of cooperation are beginning to form in parallel activity. And the desire of each to imitate the other is forming a kind of mutual collaboration that is creating a social bond. She may eagerly show playmates her favorite toys, but she can't bring herself to let go of them and share them with the others.

She doesn't have the overflowing warmth of the two year old, as her affections have taken on more of a detached superficiality. Affection often is expressed in rigid form such as a kissing ritual. Something keenly desired may be ignored with indifference once it is possessed. And her mother may be dismissed from the nursery with a thoughtless "good bye.

Her growing independence is shown in her behavior on walks as she either runs ahead or lags behind. When she knows what she wants, she can make emphatic demands, and go after it with determined dispatch. She may ask her mother to leave the room when she feeds herself for part of a meal or when she goes to the bathroom. She may throw a temper tantrum over dressing conflicts, and she may not permit her mother to touch her when she insist on dressing herself.

The natural communication between the rao and remo begins at 2-1/2, as an interest in an imaginary playmate comes spontaneously from within the child. This internal relationship will usually reflect and satisfy some inner need, "whether it is for companionship, someone to beat, someone to look up to, someone to do things for or some one to boss." Sometimes his identity may shift at 2-1/2 to become an animal.

When alone his activity is accompanied by constant talking. Speech, the motor expression of his experiences, is now put into practice within the security of his own private room or at bedtime when he may talk to his teddy bear.

When being put to bed he likes to have things in there proper place. His tenaciousness is making him resistant to change and he may fly into a temper tantrum when his routine is disrupted.

All is not well with the world of the 2-1/2 year old. He does not laugh quite so freely. He takes himself too seriously, because he is caught in the rigidities of ritualism, perseverance and negativism. His domineering manner may be hard for others to accept. He verbally asserts domination over other members of the family. "He may command one to sit here, another to do something else, and still another to go away."

His imperial demands show a new excitable energy source that provides a determination that can be helpful in putting things away, carrying out simple task around the house, and going on errands. This energy comes from within himself so he cannot be forced, he can only be activated in the right direction.

His new vigor and easy arousal is causing difficulties in relaxing readily to go to sleep. When scheduled to take a nap, he usually consumes over an hour in different self-activities. He may get in and out of the bed several times, before finally going to sleep.

The 2-1/2 year old may express jealousy of younger siblings. His intense energy causes high tension, stuttering, and sudden fatigue. He is proud of his ability to do things. And his energy allows him to do things he could never do before.

GOAL-DIRECTED CIRCUIT

The medial forebrain bundle (MFB) seems to undergo development now, as the main intergrating aspect of the "goal-directed" circuit.(See Fig. 8) The MFB has been found to be the most pleasurable reward area in the brain. Rats will stimulate this area with 8,000 lever presses per hour for 24 hours or more until they drop from exhaustion.(87)

The highly motivating reward area of the MFB is concerned with "goal-directed" behavior. This "goal-directed" circuit is concerned with goals that are an expression of the oral and genital functions essential for self-preservation and the preservation of the species.(66)

This is the circuit that initiates the sexual development of puberty. Since the remo develops from 10 to 15 years, then this development should begin around 12-1/2 years of age. The variations of the beginning of puberty would be an indication if a person's rate of growth is normal, or if he/she is a late bloomer. In the rao's hemisphere this circuit would be developed between 17-1/2 and 18. It is said that men reach there sexual peak at 18 years of age. There are also sexual peaks at 23, 28, 33 and 38 years of age that occur at dimishing levels of intensity.

Fibers from the reticular formation, mediated by the lateral region of the hypothalamus, are carried in the MFB to provide a tremendous energy and action system that can make the individual restless and full of desire to be doing something.

The descending reticular formation arouses motor pathways in the lower brain stem to influence motor activity and muscle tonus. As long as the individual is

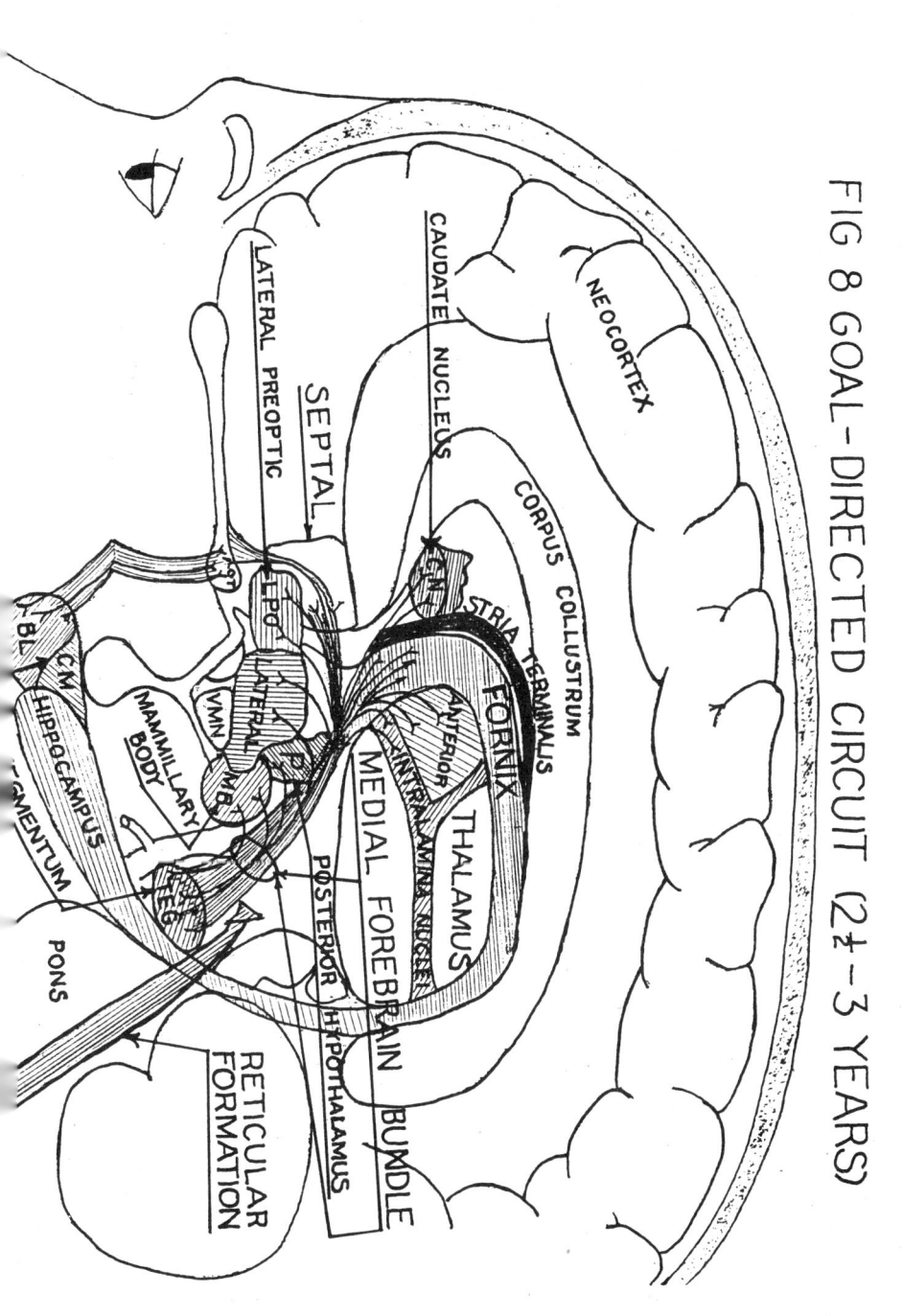

FIG 8 GOAL-DIRECTED CIRCUIT (2½–3 YEARS)

actively pursuing a goal, then the control exerted by the innervation of the reticular formation in the midbrain region can effectively reduce excitation to a tolerable level, so that the individual is more able to handle anxiety. Also the mental energy, involved in the anticipation of a goals, uses up the arousal created by the reticular formation in a pleasurable way to keep the individual functioning effectively.

While the energizing ascending reticular formation provides arousal and alertness, it also acts as a motivational apparatus to provide the drive impetus also needed for muscular activity. So in many ways the MFB is to the limbic system what the motor pathways of the internal capsule are to the neocortex.(66)

This widespread and diffuse interaction of the MFB provides a greater period of integration than the prior period, as the autonomic and motor components of the lower brain stem mediated by the hypothalamus is brought into a unison of activity with the "care" region by the MFB to channel arousal into specific directions.

CHAPTER 28

ACCEPTANCE

The overriding drive of the remo is a desire for acceptance. On a psychological level there can be a threat to your existence that is felt by the remo as non-acceptance or rejection. The remo's psychological need for acceptance is comparable to the biological need for food and water. Although physical blows are not a concern, verbal and nonverbal blows go on between people which can be just as damaging.

If you have ever once experienced the devastating alienation of being an outsider, then you may understand how this can be comparable to being denied a place in life. A very primitive social environment like status creates these conditions where others are used to punish, via criticism, disapproval and rejection.

Although the remo's need to be accepted is required for emotional survival, the rao may not be aware of the degree of this psychological need. This discrepancy happens because of a lack of awareness of the remo. And the rao does not have the need for the same degree of acceptance. Thus, autonomy and independence from others can be claimed without any awareness of the discrepancies between one's words and the remo who will usually be very dependent on the acceptance from others.

These discrepancies within the self can result in conflicts. As long as an occasion is of no significance, these disparities may be rationalized away. However, when a real threat to one's acceptance from important others occurs, the burning need for acceptance will be felt as self-criticism, bad feelings, discomfort, anger, depression, headaches, etc.

Acceptance is often associated with success. If you're successful, you're in! If you're not, you're out! By hooking success and acceptance together as a motivation system, we are using a sledgehammer where we should be using a feather.

The process of learning requires making mistakes. In fact, the best way to learn is from your mistakes. But the status system insidiously creates an undercurrent of insecurity and inhibition that encourages failure. Then mistakes can make the learning process an emotionally dangerous undertaking, because the fear of being a "flop" encourages avoidance, rather than the approach behavior needed for learning.

Even worst, when this success/acceptance connection is adopted by your remo, then it is applied to your relationship between your rao and your remo. This undermines your very foundation of life and living. Once your esteem or worth is determined by this success/acceptance link, then your mutual supportive relationship with your remo can be easily shaken or crumble.

Thus, there develops the need to be successful at a job or profession, socially in a group or at a party, socially in a one-on-one relationship with a friend, business partner, family member and relatives, socially in an intimate relationship with a lover or spouse and even a need to be successful in some sport or hobby. What happens is you can't win. You can be successful in one or more areas but if you're unsuccessful in other areas, your remo can still be unhappy.

But the pleasures of success can never equal your remo's punishment for not being successful. As the need to avoid the punishment of sadness or pain is much greater than the need to achieve happiness.

Once your remo gets caught up in this status belief of connecting success and acceptance, then it becomes a Pavlovian response. So unless you're superhuman, your chances of being happy in life are considerably diminished.

You can only be happy and enjoy life to the degree you develop synergy, both internally and externally. If you would rather be into pain, displeasure and unhappiness, then maintain your status belief system with values concerned with discipline, obedience and control.

The first essential step into synergy is an acceptance of yourself as you are with all your faults. But this supportive relationship needs to be consistent. You need to realize your remo can feel love for yourself, but not really be accepting of yourself, as when your remo loves the self for some success and hates the self for some failure in this success/acceptance response. This kind of limited acceptance, called "conditional acceptance," does not create the right conditions for a basis of care and support.

"Conditional acceptance" is an attitude where you are acceptable, that is you are not disapproved of, if you do what is right, if you do what is expected, and if you are successful in what you attempt to do. This negative status approach to life erodes confidence, as you hope to get through the day without making mistakes.

CRITICALNESS

In the eyes of your remo, when you are critical of others, you are not accepting them. Your rao may not be aware of this. But a critical attitude towards others is like a trap you are laying for yourself that will ultimately be as harmful to yourself as others; when you are critical of yourself, you are not being accepting of yourself either. Thus, how critical you are of others will be how you are of yourself. As being unaccepting of others is how unaccepting you are of yourself.

First, you have set a measure of behavior for others which you do not want to fall below. Since you are not a perfect performance machine, but a human, you can be assured that you will either slip below this performance level during low energy periods when your spirits are down, or be apprehensive that you might do so. Even when you are just being critical of others in your thoughts, you can inhibit your own freedom and actions. This can produce discord within the self, making you more critical of the self.

Second, you are often the most critical of those things you dislike within the self, such as inhibitions, shortcomings, or inadequacies. Rejecting these imperfections as not being an acceptable part of the self, may be despised out of all proportion when encounter in others.

People who cannot accept their own shortcomings may come to despise those with whom they should have more of a feeling of identity. Instead of sympathy and kinship, there is repulsion. As a result, disharmony often disrupts their relationships. So when you dislike another, who has not hurt you and you don't know why, you should take that as a signal that you may not be very accepting of yourself.

Regardless of how many shortcomings you may have, it's important that you, through your rao, still accept your remo. If you do disagree you can still accept your remo while holding some reservation for future change. You will find most conflicts can be resolved much faster by making your remo a loving supportive friend.

OMNIPOTENCE

A lack of acceptance creates a need by the remo to make up for this psychological deficit by exaggerating personal worth. Feelings of greatness will be expressed to the degree that there has been a lack of acceptance felt either now or in the past. When your remo does not feel acceptance, it can feel rejected and inferior. Feelings of superiority are almost always imbedded in feelings of inferiority. The degree of the feelings of superiority will be the degree that your remo has been beaten down in life.

Some religions may inadvertently encourage this internal feeling of superiority when they persuade the vulnerable individual to look inside their self to find God, to find a unity of the body with the spirit, or to "search within yourself to find your savior," "carry God in your heart," "be one with God," or "God is a part of you." This can persuade the remo who feels hidden and unknown to the rao to take on the role of God. This sets up the remo who has felt rejected in the past to have omnipotent, godlike feelings.

As the remo takes on a god-like persona, then a prayer to God becomes a kind of talking to yourself, using wishful self-suggestion in a sort of self-hypnotic state. The initial euphoria that this brings to the individual whose esteem has been smitten in the past can be a heaven sent salvation. But later on there will be some dues to pay, because of all the internal conflicts this creates.

This sets up the internal status conditions of inequality where the rao needs to be perfect to live up to these new high, god-like standards. The discrepancy between the remo's image of the self and what is really the self creates tremendous conflicts. Since the rao can never live up to this great image, an enormous dissatisfaction with the self can build up a hate that neither the rao nor the remo can understand. The hate may be directed towards others, through self-righteous expressions of rage, or it may be directed inwardly to demoralize the self with overwhelming guilt. The hate and destruction can be so great as to even create a belief that the person has been invaded and possessed by the devil. Because of this phenomenon, any authoritative religion that started without a devil would soon have to develop one.

Other grand feelings may be discovered when the remo feels like the frog waiting for some magical kiss that will transform one into all that one was meant to be. Or the remo may feel like Superman, carried in the guise of the rao, Clark Kent. The fact that these sentiments were personified in popular media is a good indication of the emotional climate, and the needs operating within the people of our culture.

If you discover omnipotent feelings operating within yourself, you will want to know how to deal with this problem. An example of how "not" to treat your remo would be to punish your remo disapprovingly for being a "bad boy!" With the critical "go to your room!" approach. This can only makes matters worse.

One of the bad results of getting upset would be to drive your genie back into the bottle. This could result in your cutting off the communication you desire, and interfere with your ability to get at these problems and deal with them. There is usually a good reason for most behavior. First, you need to understand what purpose omnipotence serves. Why does it operate?

You need acceptance in some form to survive emotionally. If you do not receive it from others in the outer reality, then you have a substitute for this vital need in your inner reality. If your worthiness is not confirmed by acceptance from others, then from what source is the motivation to survive going to come?

You need acceptance to create a belief in yourself. This is essential. When this great need for acceptance is not satisfied, then you have an alternative available that acts as a substitute in the form of your remo's inner omnipotence. So when alienation from others occurs, the remo is able to compensate with some attitude of personal greatness. Omnipotence then builds an internal "ego" that serves as a defense or a substitute when the greatest of all the remo's psychological needs is lacking.

If you take away your remo's omnipotence, you take away the spirit, the fight and the struggle to exist. You wind up with an incapacitating hatred, apathy or depression that can lead to violence towards others or suicide.

The degree or strength of the omnipotence will reflect the degree that your remo does not feel acceptance from others now, or in the past. If you attempt to eliminate your remo's omnipotence, you would only be "jumping out of the frying pan into the fire" by removing a protective symptom, while making the underlying cause worse than ever. As a result you would be trading off one problem for a worse one.

The best way to handle this problem is with acceptance, and to allow the remo to indulge in flights of powerful fancy. You should maintain the attitude that you may not agree with it, but will go along with it. When you can develop feelings of synergy around and within you, you can increase feeling of acceptance and affection for the self. The supportive acceptance and a sense of belonging that synergy develops provides emotional security that would represent a more realistic substitute for these feelings of superiority.

Never take omnipotent feelings too seriously. You will be much better off if you can even enjoy them and deal with them in a playful way. As you develop an atmosphere of acceptance and synergy, the omnipotence will eventually go away.

ALCOHOLISM

The prevalent attitude of conditional acceptance, is an important factor in many other behavioral problems besides omnipotence. Take alcoholic addiction as an example. An alcoholic is a person who may have first drunk to look for acceptance in friendly fellowship, but gradually used alcohol as a source of escape to get away from the displeasure and pain that goes on so subtly in our status environment.

The remo, whose nervous systems can operate in the bottom layers of the grey matter of the neocortex much more effectively, is able to carry on and function after top layers of the neocortex have been subdued by alcohol. As a result, after drinking a lot of alcohol, the rao tends to be less dominant, leaving the remo, the child within, more influential in determining actions. This allows some personality aspects of the remo to emerge that are normally suppressed under sober conditions. However, many of the abilities found in the top layers of remo's neocortex have also been impaired by alcohol, so one does not see a true and complete picture of the remo.

Becoming drunk can serve many purposes. There is temporary numbness that lowers one's inhibitions and conscientious level of "care." It blunts awareness and dulls a person's senses, to provide an escape from the unpleasantness of status conditions; the saying, "happiness is ignorance" has a ring of truth here. The status system also restricts the free expression of our inner child, the remo. Being drunk excuses behaviors that normally aren't tolerated, and creates conditions where we feel as if we are more personally acceptable.

When the alcoholic finally realizes that the addiction makes one less human and life is worse, then there is a readiness to give up alcohol. But usually there is nothing better to come back to than what was there before. One effective way to stay sober is a unique organization called Alcoholics Anonymous (AA).

The AA was organized by former alcoholics who recognized that what an alcoholic needs is acceptance. They created a group that offered support, acceptance and solidarity among its members.

A feeling of acceptance can be felt with a confession of past wrongs. Confession by itself however, does not give relief. Confession becomes an effective purging agent when the person can feel some acceptance from those who have been exposed to the confession.

When a new member of the AA is taken in, he is encouraged to confess about his weaknesses, to spill his guts of past vileness, to appear at his very worst in front of all. This shows him there are people in this world who will accept him, after exposing all of his terrible turpitudes, as he is. This begins to relieve his doubts about himself, and rebuilds a trust and confidence in his acceptance as a human and his worth in life.

When a group's main moral criterion is acceptance that says the best way to be for yourself is to be for each other, then you have found a synergetic atmosphere. But you also want to create a synergetic atmosphere internally, between your rao and your remo. In the next communication level you can exchange feelings using the visual aspect of the imagination.

CHAPTER 29

EMANATIONS

For your fifth communication step you want to create a large close-up of the remo's face, on which feelings can be expressed visually in your mind's eye. The emotions shown in a large close-up can tell you things about your remo that were not feasible before. Instead of passively responding, intricate feelings and attitudes can be conveyed via complex facial expressions. Now your remo can become more actively involved in the creative expression of needs, desires and emotions.

By conveying feelings with the visual effects of imagery, the remo can express more complex ideas and subtleties, such as the rao and remo giving each other a hug. Or the rao and remo can give each other high fives and butt bumps to celebrate some correct response or success. Now the remo can relate needs and desires with a new facility that was not considered available before.

Fantasies may have been experienced before and shrugged off as being illusions, figments of the imagination, or stimulus from the memory banks of the brain. Such whimsy may have been either ignored or regarded as having little importance by the rao.

Now the expressions of the remo can be accomplished in your mind's eye with a shrug of the shoulders, a furrowed brow, an affectionate pat or hug, a turned-down mouth, a turned-up nose, a smile, folded arms across the chest, etc. These types of expression and much more can all take place almost instantaneously in the theater of the mind, using the remo's creative imagination as the vehicle of expression.

SOUNDS

Next, in order to progress, you will need to experiment with a new dimension of expression. The remo is not only capable of creating visual images, but also the sounds of auditory thought or words within your mind.

Using the image of the remo's self, you want to direct questions towards your remo as before; but now instead of shaking the head yes or no in a visual response, you want your remo to respond with the sound (in your mind's "ear") of a verbal "yes," "no" or "I don't know," using the natural auditory sounds of words that occur within your mind. These auditory sound processes can occur with the visual image your remo has created. Again try to use arousing questions that are provocative and stimulating to your remo, questions about some exciting activity.

Don't try to anticipate the answers. The rao is usually the leader. So the remo will often merely concur in agreement, regardless of how the remo really feels. You need to let your remo's words "pop" into your head quickly. If your rao's intruding efforts or anticipation still occur, then a daydreamy feeling or a sense of wonder should be created so your remo can respond without interference. If you have trouble achieving this level, then you can resort to an alternative method below in the next section.

IMAGERY ENDEAVORS

Since families who believe in the values of a status system almost always use physical and psychological punishment to raise children, the remo may have been emotionally impaired by not maturing, and may feel too ashamed to reveal the inner self. Also, an emotionally immature remo, that feels inadequate, may not have the energy, or the motivation to communicate.

The remo may also enjoy the control of remaining hidden from your awareness. This way the remo's psychological misdeeds can be blamed on the rao, as the remo remains free of direct responsibility. This must be overcome. The more your remo hides, the more you need to communicate. It is essential that if you want to develop your remo, you have to take charge and break through this communication barrier.

If your remo is reluctant to come forward, then the conscious rao can create a mental image of the self. The most effective is a facial close-up, as you look in the mirror or of someone you admire. Superimposed on this conjured up facial close-up will almost always be the remo's feelings, attitudes, beliefs, etc. A facial expression will tend to be automatically expressed like a reflex, because the remo is very impulsive and spontaneous. So when you want to ask your remo about something or somebody, you can use this method to communicate.

Most status seekers will probably have to use this last method, because the cut-throat world of a status system requires that feelings should not interfere with success. Interacting with the remo does not come easily to runners in the rat race.

The remo wields a lot of strong motivating power, and as long as the child within you can remain secret and concealed it can encourage a sense of irresponsibility. However, for growth to occur the remo needs more expressive freedom; and by being more accessible to the rao, problems can be tackled and developed together with the esprit de corps of a team.

Communicating with your remo and synergy are two sides of the same coin. It's very difficult to communicate with your remo without an atmosphere of synergy. And it's very difficult to develop synergy as a social system without communicating with your remo on higher levels. When you are in close touch with your own feelings, you will be in close touch with the feelings of others. This is the essence of synergy.

CHAPTER 30

SYNERGY

BENEDICT'S SYNERGY

Ruth Benedict discovered and wrote of a common characteristic or quality she referred to as "synergy," that ran throughout the different primitive cultures, she studied.(74)

In societies with "low" synergy every act that was to the advantage of the individual was a victory over another. There were strong beliefs in the ability of power to defeat and humiliate others. In these very competitive societies each would take what he could get. This rivalry often took the form of heaping up goods in competition; and sometimes even letting them rot, rather than share them with others.

Tribes with low synergy were revengeful, acquisitive, jealous and greedy. They were people who felt very insecure, as anxiety was found to run through out their society. Real power was believed to reside in those who could inflict the most harm; while those who did good by helping others had no power at all. They developed powerful gods whom they feared. They trembled in the presence of these gods who used punishment and vengeance.

On the other hand, members of tribes with high synergy greatly prized their personal skills, because any ability that was for the good of the individual was at the same time good for the group, where members supported each other in a kind of social solidarity. Private possessions were treasured, because they could be shared with others. Since everyone is provided for, there was no fear of poverty. And anxiety was missing to a degree that seemed incredible to Benedict and her colleagues. These were societies of good will, where murder and suicide were virtually unknown. They developed kind gods with benign spirits whom they had no fear of and that brought benefits and protected them.

ORIENTATION TOWARDS PLEASURE

Those tribes with high synergy often had festive joyous ceremonies where everyone would take an active part in the singing and dancing. Even in their worship there was no conflict between the pleasures we associate with a general good time and those we associate with a solemn mass.

In like manner, the main principle of synergy is an orientation towards pleasure, and that people are naturally "good." On the other hand, status says that people are naturally "bad" and must be made to be "good." The truth of this last statement rests in the ability of status hierarchies to bring out the worst in people. The status competition for acceptance insidiously cultivates the "badness" found in people.

People are "good" under synergy. First they naturally wants to approach pleasure and avoid displeasure, i.e. avoid hurting others. And second, people will control their offensive aggressiveness not because they are unselfish and puts social obligations above personal wishes, but because synergy arranges personal desires and social duties so the two are identical. This happens because the mutual support and acceptance of synergy develops a sense of belonging. And the need for selfishness and harmful aggression gradually disappear.

Synergetic relationships operate on the pleasure principle. Of all the behaviors and defenses that are possible, pleasure is the most significant for emotional, mental and physical well-being. Therefore, an orientation towards pleasure is your main behavioral defense. As an example, to chuckle at your own mistake can make learning a new task much more pleasant. All your emotional growth periods and behaviors involved with social coping skills has a basis in pleasure, especially during the developmental phase.

An orientation towards pleasure promotes a spirit of cooperation, both between people and between the rao and the remo. And pleasure permits a greater flexibility, with greater alternatives of adaptable behavior than displeasure.

Pleasure and cooperation go hand in hand. It generates versatile thinking that includes the remo's problems solving ability. This increases the remo's participation in life. When facing a challenge, you can operate on a higher level of emotional and mental ability when you can more effectively include your remo as a partner.

On the other hand, status operates on lower intellectual levels. People oriented towards status values can't be bothered by the time consuming effort it takes to reason, compromise and workout a solution, instead they react with a mindless reflex of simple aggression to a problem.

Instead of using the mind, they can efficiently respond with some thoughtless power move to force a solution. Thus, if a child or employee is doing something wrong, instead of using reason to figure out ways to distract the child or solve the problem, they can simply use the threat of punishment to force a quick solution. This is because status operates on a belief in discipline that uses punishment, or its threat, to force cooperation.

In the same sense, pleasure has a different purpose under status. Authoritarians look on pleasure as a vice, a sin to be avoided. They maintain and increase their power by keeping people miserable and dependent; the more dominate the master, the more subdued the slave. To have people happily support each other, cultivates a strength and independence that those in authority can find threatening.

But even within a status culture, pleasure is often used in a negative way to ridicule or laugh at another, as seen daily on TV's sitcoms. The enjoyment derived from "put downs" is a corruption of pleasure that temporarily elevates the status of one as it demotes its victim.

Punishment and pain are the strongholds of the status system. An orientation towards pleasure is the forte of synergy's motivational system. As synergy generates more pleasure in your life you will naturally be more accepting of harmless behaviors and life-styles. All living things are accepted, respected and protected. This is especially true with people. Your acceptance by others is taken for granted as a part of life, whether you perform at your best or at your worst, just as long as no harm is inflicted on another.

Status and synergy usually operate side by side in various strength to determine the type of relationships people have with each other. In our society you can find many pockets of synergetic attitudes operating among small groups of people who reject ideals of status. They have to exist to a certain extent, because people would not cooperate enough to prosper. You will never find status hierarchies or synergy functioning alone, but there will be various mixtures of the two operating with one having more influence over the other. For example, there should always be status hierarchies operating that puts the hurtful people and criminals at the lowest levels.

You needed to discriminate the synergistic behaviors that can increase harmony and productiveness, and the status responses, that can tear down cooperativeness. Then you should try to strengthen synergy and weaken status values from the inside out, and never in the reverse order. Synergy should be developed in the relationship within yourself first, i.e., between your rao and your remo, then within your family, then with your friends, then within your community, and so on. In this way you are improving the quality of your internal and external environment by choosing the values of synergy over those of status.

All efforts in the past have been directed in the opposite way, and will be doomed to failure, because a government cannot force equality onto its people. Synergy will not work in this reverse order, because although it is possible to create a benevolent government, it will not work if the people have strong social status hierarchies operating among themselves.

A big stumbling block to synergy operating among people, is the lack of emotional maturity in the population. For example, during the juvenile stage of emotional development cooperation unfolds. The calming effect of the behavior of this period provides social energy and courage needed for cooperation and concurrence to operate more effectively among people.

CHAPTER 31

STABILIZING PERIOD
3 - 4 YEARS

THE JUVENILE STAGE

STABILIZING RESPONSE

The emotional problems of the "child" remo (the 2 to 3 year old remo) boil down to caring too much. To worry, anger, fret and be upset are often the way of a person with a "child" remo.

The "stabilizing" response provides the ultimate method of controlling these displeasures. It is so effective at reducing displeasure that once your remo has developed a strong "stabilizing" response, then emotional pathologies such as a psychosis, neurosis and personality disorders seem to be no longer a threat.

However, the "stabilizing" response is only effective at controlling displeasures such as fear during the early stages. Once a full blown response overwhelms you, you can lose control. So the remo at the juvenile stage is susceptible to phobias, if the sensory nervous system (N.S.) is dominate, or antisocial behaviors when the motor N.S. predominates or being a dropout when the autonomic N.S. is the strongest. If all three nervous systems are balanced a person could be a claustrophobic, sociopathic bum when overwhelmed with status social rejection that leads to a breakdown of emotional behavioral defenses.

The ability to care from the "child" stage has to be modified with an ability to discriminate as to when, how much, or what to care about. The problem is, if a remo worries about everything, then the quality of care loses some of its significance. For caring to have more meaning then the remo has to be able to not care, to be able to have a choice. Caring takes on more importance, as it is a choice made from options.

The last period developed a control of anxiety while engaging in "goal-directed" activity, so that anxiety was allayed as long as one was busy doing something. But anxiety is still a problem when muscles and behaviors are restricted. When one reacts with fear or anxiety at the "child" stage without being allowed to fight or flee, then the remo is not able to effectively handle displeasure. However, the development of the "stabilizing" response provides the skill to control anxiety in the early stages.

The "child" remo believes that the way to do something is to try hard, and that the way to solve a problem is to go over and over the conditions of a situation. So the "child" remo often becomes a slave master or a boss over the rao, because it comes to believe it is the effort that counts the most.

This is not to say that persistence, concern and trying hard are wrong. These are often the right responses to solve certain problems, but they can be the opposite of what would be best.

But the great motivation and care involved at the "child" stage can work against the self, as the excessive stimulation of high excitation can hamper performance ability. Over reactions, or strong states of arousal, can interfere with performance skills.

Not caring is an important attitude of the "stabilizing" response that functions as a means to reduce or control displeasure. Other phrases that represent equivalent attitudes of not caring that may carry more meaning are indifference, detachment, objectivity, nonchalance, impartiality, business-like, matter-of-fact attitude, etc. They all represent an unemotional attitude that is neither pleasurable nor displeasurable, but resides near the center between them.

MEMORY

Although memory started developing during the "goal-directed" period as an important aspect of problem solving activity, it is reaching a peak of development in the "stabilizing" period.

The memory process of the "stabilizing" response is able to control emotional states that create distractions that disrupt the recall process. Emotional distractions result from the easy excitability of the "expectancy" and "avoidance" circuits.

The "stabilizing" circuit can subdue your excited reaction to something new or novel in the environment. This permits you to sustain attention over longer periods, so that information can be evaluated and rehearsed.

The "stabilizing" circuit nips excessive arousal in the bud to permit the absorption of ideas and materials that need to be learned. This allows you to listen, read and study for longer periods of time without interference, because the immediate need to gratify desires and impulses can be delayed by the inhibitory controls of the "stabilizing" (hippocampus) circuit.(42)

The rao's recall of memories is the attitude that activates the "stabilizing" response, while an awareness of the remo's corresponding feeling state should be noted for recall later. So the memory recall process is primarily the same as the "stabilizing" response. It operates the "stabilizing" circuit to maintain an optimal state of arousal. The recall process makes your past experiences available, so you can apply them appropriately to the present situation.

The "stabilizing" response controls displeasure, because you learn not to care for situations, people, objects, etc., that cause displeasure. That is, through this memory response, the remo learns to attach less significance to things that cause displeasure. This in turn, reduces the amount of emotional arousal involved. Now, things that result in bad feelings can be looked at objectively by the remo to ascertain their value and determine whether these things are worth the price of caring.

The "care" responses provide very desirable emotional states. It is your primary source of excitement, stimulation, and motivation for growth and intelligence, as long as it is pleasurably oriented. But displeasure can offset the scale of balance and make caring more undesirable than desirable. Namely, to most people, it takes a great amount of pleasure to willingly accept the punishment of a small amount of emotional displeasure.

ASCETICISM

The Eastern belief in asceticism seems to be related to the development of the "stabilizing" circuit on the surface. But in reality, it is not. The self-denial of asceticism reduces the things you desire down to a minimal level. But this reduces the things you "care" about in a pleasurable way. The problem is, it throws out the good with the bad; it throws out pleasure with displeasure.

This is the type of not caring of the "infant-child" remo that has not learned the integrative "care" responses. This tends to be a general, passive, unresponsiveness that represents a gradation of the "vegetative" response.

Its slower rhythm can effectively terminate or suppress physical and emotional desires. This "vegetative" response of not caring represents a self-discipline that is a generalized not caring of all but the essentials that maintain life. This represents a regression in adaptivity to a lower level of development.

This is not to take away from the essential necessity of this defensive behavior as part of a repertoire of behaviors. But any behavioral circuit can become a detriment to well-being when it is relied on exclusively, as it encourages an autonomic fixation that puts one in a "rut," and reduces adaptability.

The "stabilizing" response has vitality and energy, compared to the placid "vegetative" response. It projects an inner alertness over an outer calm which allows an adaptable response of concern to always be at the "ready" to help realize your desires.

The "stabilizing" response, using the memory recall process, distinquishes those objects that bring pleasure from those that create displeasure. It values things that bring pleasurable rewards. Conversely, the "stabilizing" response devalues sources of displeasure by reducing arousal, so that you can care less.

The remo at this stage learns not to let things bother it. Instead of going over and over a hopeless problem, it learns not to care, and uses its energies more constructively. Instead of being jealous, the remo simply cares less about the person involved. This helps the remo to be objective, detached and to suspend emotional involvement to bring about more self-control.

The "stabilizing" response is most helpful in regards to bad memories of the past. Instead of becoming depressed or angry when recalling past displeasurable events, the remo learns not to care about what has happened in the past. Instead of letting past mistakes gnaw away, creating feelings of inadequacy and pulling the remo down, a "cool" indifference about these past events encourages a positive attitude and self-confidence to build.

ALCOHOLIC EFFECT

Alcohol can temporarily deaden the "stabilizing" circuit to impair memory and to hamper your ability to control aggression. So alcohol can make you very susceptible to violence.

Although alcohol appears to create the "stabilizing" feeling of not caring, what it does in reality is knock out the sensory system of the "care" circuit so that it no longer functions effectively. Since alcohol represses the sensory system, then the next day you have a double rebound effect from sensory deprivation.

The sensory rebound is experienced as a hangover with symptoms of an overreactive sensory nervous system, namely fatigue, headache, anxiety, nervousness, depression, increase in dreaming, sensitivity to light, sound, etc. So the effect of lowering your sensitivity one day is a double dose of sensitivity the next.

The individual often mistakenly seeks relief from this tension with more alcoholic consumption. This creates more sensory deprivation. This can start a cycle of abuse which is often viewed as a compulsive addiction. But any compulsion is simply a motivational impulse by the remo. The remo can see no other solution to the displeasure created by the sensory deprivation, then by "drinking." Thus it is often motivated not so much for pleasure as to avoid displeasure.

PERFORMANCE

The remo learns at the "stabilizing" stage that trying too hard and caring too much impairs his ability to acquire skills and to perform well. He discovers intuitively that being less emotionally aroused permits better performance and control.

The more detached approach along with the superior use of the memory pathway tracts in the "stabilizing" response creates the conditions for one to achieve a higher level of development in skills of speaking, listening, facial expressions, etc.

Participating in the sport of tennis or golf is an excellent aid in developing the "stabilizing" response. Under a pressure shot where successful results are important, the remo at the "child" stage tended to care too much about the results. Thus, a state of over-arousal could inhibit the smooth functioning of the muscles to cause one to possibly "choke" and miss a shot. A person with a "child" remo can be a pro until crunch time, when there is a lot riding on a shot.

But with the development of the "stabilizing" circuit the remo is able to inhibit its arousal so that muscles and emotional arousal work in harmony to provide the optimal amount of muscular tension and excitement. When the rao and remo work together for the best performance, then the rao can try hard to make a shot while the remo simultaneously reduces the care about the consequences.

This is a gambling, risk-taking quality, where the relaxed carefree feelings of the remo, permits aggressive action by the rao. Thus, the rao can play a more dominant role when under pressure to achieve the utmost skill and control.

BACK PROBLEMS

Posture involves the large gross trunk muscles of the remo. So the problem with bad posture is usually not a problem of will, but a problem of an internal feeling state of the remo. When the remo's growth has been stopped at the "child" stage, a person's sensory arousal system often creates tension, so that he tends to be slouchy and droopy in his posture. He slumps and becomes careless in his posture to reduce the tension within the body, to try to be less uptight.

However the tension of arousal is reduced with the "stabilizing" response, allowing one to throw one's shoulders back, and hold one's head high and be relaxed. It permits one to expand one's chest and breath capacity, while maintaining the chest and shoulders in an uplifted position, yet still be comfortable and relaxed.

Many back problems are caused by a lack of development of the "stabilizing" response which results in bad sloppy posture. Those with bad back problems and who tend to have poor posture, will find that if they practice the proper erect position while sitting or standing, yet still maintain a state of relaxation by using the "stabilizing" response, this will be a remedy to their back problems.

COURAGE

Premeditation, the memory process of knowing before hand how you are going to respond, can give you confidence and courage. And the habitual attitude of using your memory banks to recall past similar experiences can help you handle emotionally stressful social situations.

The "stabilizing" response can maintain a reservoir of energy to "project" an inner strength of self-confidence. On the other hand, the prior "caring" responses produced states of emotional excitement and agitation that deplete energy sources to cause fatigue, and erode self-confidence.

Easy excitability tends to expend energy. The more you care, the more vulnerable you are to be anxious, timid and inhibited, so that you are less able to think in terms of others. This cuts down your ability to interact with others in a mutual social reciprocity.

The more uptight you get, the more unacceptable you are. The more unacceptable you are, the more you care for this same evaluation of your worthiness from others. This sets up a cycle within a status social system that can lead to avoidance behaviors and an introversion of feelings. And when the concern is about things, it can create a penny-pinching, stinginess, that some might think is selfish.

OBJECTIVITY

The "child" remo, who wished to approach the "good" or pleasure, and avoid the "bad" or displeasure, created a judgmentalness that lacked objectivity, and viewed events as either black or white. Now, at the "stabilizing" stage, a third response in the grey area between good and bad judgments is available, as the indifference of the "stabilizing" response allows a greater objectivity, thereby reducing the remo's prejudices.

Inhibiting arousal at the early stages can create a desirable indifference. There are times when a detached objective approach is an effective way to handle certain situations; especially those concerned with fairness, justice or professional relationships. Involved in this is an ability to delay impulsiveness. This allows you to postpone judgements until more facts are present to provide more impartiality and fairness to decisions.

The "stabilizing" circuit is able to reduce overpowering emotional threats to a level that permits reason and memory to operate. This leads to judgments with greater understanding and sensibility.

This is an extremely important ability for your remo to have. It permits a greater trust in the natural impulses of the remo to reduce the problems that black and white appraisals tends to create. For example, instead of love-hate reactions, indifference can modify these extremes. And differences and conflicts between people can be discussed in a sensible manner without leading to overreactions, heated arguments and bad feelings.

PROJECTION

Since there are less problems and concerns with the self, once the "stabilizing" response is developed, you are able to move outside of yourself to deal more with the real world. As feelings come under more control, it gives you the confidence to "project" your feelings out towards others. This "projection" ability is a prerequisite to developing the social skills, and is experienced as a kind of controlled energy, referred to as extroversion.

Those with a dominant autonomic and motor nervous systems will tend to be more extroverted than others, even with a "child" remo, because of their plethora of expressive emotional energy. "Projection" is a kind of mental, emotional giving of the self that takes energy. Generosity is primarily a function of energy. Those who have an excess of energy can afford to be more generous than those who don't. Generosity develops now, because the inhibition of arousal keeps energies from being depleted, so it may be "projected" out with control.

Pleasure is also an important factor. Pleasure "projects" to permit one to be expansive and giving. And extroversion requires pleasure as an impetus for development. That is, to safely and confidently "project" your feelings, you need to be into pleasure. When "projection" is accompanied by displeasure, it can make a person antisocial. And when accompanied by chronic displeasure, "projection" can create a sociopath or a paranoid.

Thus, sociability depends both on pleasure and a "projection" of feelings. When you are oriented towards pleasure you are usually comfortable with your self, and feel good in the presents of others. And the pleasure of self-complacency can be "projected" out towards others, allowing approach behavior to motivate the development of social skills.

The memory activating process allows you to recall past behaviors for the greatest spontaneity within the relevance of the social conditions. This process requires emotions to be on a mobile mental level, to develop a carefree attitude that produces the charm needed for social skills.

Spontaneity is possible only if pleasure is dominant in a social situation. If displeasure predominates, then the "stabilizing" response requires you to be more premeditative in your behaviors instead of spontaneous.

In order to handle displeasure, spontaneity is not so desirable; the "stabilizing" response is most effective in the early stages of arousal. Once a full blown displeasurable response occurs, then the "stabilizing" response is no longer so effective in quelling the overwhelming displeasure. However, overwhelming fear and anxiety can be controlled at the next adult-child stage of development.

CHAPTER 32

DEVELOPMENT OF THE STABILIZING RESPONSE

The "stabilizing" response is activated by premeditated thought that innervates the memory process. It can provide the ability to discriminate and to anticipate displeasurable conditions so that it can employ readiness along with controlled indifference. The "stabilizing" response works best by inhibiting arousal in the early stages, which involves a premeditation function of the "expectancy circuit. The "stabilizing" response maintains a sense of readiness to sustain a state of equilibrium.

To maintain the flexibility of a state of equilibrium, then anticipation and premeditation are essential. That is, you can't just walk into a troubling situation and expect to control excessive excitation after it has already been initiated.

During the initial phase of developing the not caring attitude of the "stabilizing" response, you need to be aware of the remo's corresponding feeling state. Generally a new attitude as such does not have much of an affect on the remo. So the remo learns a new behavior by learning the emotional feeling involved with the behavioral attitude.

This is not to say the remo does not have attitudes, but they are more the domain of the rao, just as the rao is capable of feelings but not nearly to the extent the remo is.

To ask a "child" remo to not "care" is pointless. What probably will happen is a displeasurable response of some kind, as the "child" remo will probably equate not caring to mean the same as being irresponsible and completely impersonal to other people, which it is not. Rather, it is a response that keeps one centered in a state of equilibrium between pleasure and displeasure. However, an orientation towards pleasure can still be maintained and is preferred.

The feeling that occurs with the rao's attitude of the "stabilizing" response consists of an alertness, associated with a lack of emotional arousal during this memory recall process. The corresponding feeling state of the remo could perhaps be described as a mobile fluid state.

This fluid, emotional, searching movement by the remo that facilitates the memory recall process is similar to the problem solving process. During the "goal-directed" period, a rudimentary aspect of the "stabilizing" circuit was activated when problem solving was attempted. The next time you try to solve some absorbing problem, try to be aware of the sensations that occur within your mind and yourself via sensory feedback.

The inner emotional freedom of the not caring "stabilizing" response involves an inner and outer awareness. There is a cool, calm, nonchalant outer appearance as the intense look of the eyes subdues to permit a greater freedom of movement.

The carefree emotional state one feels when staring off into space by the rao, while the remo uses the memory banks of recall, would perhaps be a good description of the not caring "stabilizing" response, except that the eyes are focused and actively used. There is a versatile energetic state internally that provides more control. And the readiness of the "stabilizing" response operates on a higher energy level, while appearing to be "externally" relaxed.

An outer appearance of indifference permits an internal condition of arousal to exist for a relaxed state of readiness. Or conversely, a lively external performance acts to belie an internal state of relaxed indifference. In other words, a new physical and emotional control develops internally that does not allow the environment to control or dominate you with approach/avoidance conditions as it did in the prior periods of development.

The not caring "stabilizing" response should operate to control harmful displeasure. And usually the signal for the performance of this response is the anticipation of some displeasure or during the early stages of displeasure.

When you find yourself in an unpleasant situation, uptight, or starting to get anxious or depressed, then you want to activate your memory recall circuit. For example, you might want to recall some pertinent passage from this book, or recall similar situations or experiences from your past to elicit the not caring "stabilizing" response.

Remembering situations from your past that created bad feelings is an excellent way to practice the not caring "stabilizing" response. You can rehearse indifference in regard to these bad memories in your mind until they no longer make you uncomfortable.

This is especially true with bad memories concerning people. You should let no one gain such an advantage over you that they create a lingering hate or hurt. Instead of giving that person status over you by lowering yourself, and suffering from anger or sadness, you can practice an indifference towards the person with the imagery of the mind until the memory no longer bothers you.

Now you have reached a new level of maturity. Instead of overcoming your hate by destroying your enemy via the imagery process referred to earlier, you can overcome the displeasurable harm by a more healthy inner resource of indifference, if that is your choice.

Another method to elicit the "stabilizing" response that can work, uses the facial muscles in the eyebrows of the forehead. Referring to a right handed person, when you are in a stressful situation and find you are getting nervous, your rao can raise the outside corner of your right eyebrow, while the inside corner near the bridge of the nose should be forced down. This can create the alert indifference of the "stabilizing" response.

Using your mental ability to activate the memory recall process along with this method will strengthen the "stabilizing" response even more. You should also try to use the memory process to recall that you want to be oriented towards pleasure while employing this method. Be sure to keep your sense of humor. This will allow you to avoid the displeasurable circuitry pathways in the brain even more.

After your rao has become proficient with this method, you want your remo to learn this behavior by practicing with the left eyebrow. When your remo can response automatically using this method, you will have a powerful behavior to add to your defense arsenal.

When you experience more excitatory energy then you can handle, it can create a nervous feeling with facial tics, impatience, bouncing leg, tension, driving too fast, getting irritated with other drivers, etc. Now, when this method is used to induce the "stabilizing" response, you can eliminate these displeasures or reduce the negative energy to the level appropriate for the situation.

MOOD ELEVATOR

The "stabilizing" response has the ability to arouse you when you are sleepy, morning, noon or night. Thus, when you are tired or fatigued, and you have to be "up" for a business meeting or social event, employ the "stabilizing" circuit to elevate your mood and prevent drowsiness. You can be awake and aroused to the degree that you want when you make use of the "stabilizing" response.

After driving on the road for an extended time, when there is no safe place to pull over and sleep, you endanger your life and others when you start getting so sleepy you can hardly hold your eyes open. However, the "stabilizing" response has an exquisite ability to raise your level of arousal, so you can continue on your way fully alert!

LISTENING SKILLS

The "stabilizing" response adds a sense of emotional maturity to your life. When bored the person with a "child" remo can feel an inattentive restlessness or discontent that is hard to conceal. This impatience and internal tension could cause a friend, co-worker, employer, neighbor, spouse or family member to feel slighted or even insulted, because their company doesn't appear to appreciated. But with the "stabilizing" response, you can calm that internal tension and irritability while at the same time raise your arousal and attention level to become an excellent "listener." This higher level of self-control was something a person with a "child" remo was often incapable of accomplishing.

COOPERATIVE PLAY

The information in this section was obtained from Gesell and Ilg.(40) The 3 year old has himself well in hand with emotional and physical self-control. "He is no longer as paradoxical and unpredictable as he was at 2-1/2 years."

This is an imitative and social age. He is making important distinctions between physical obstacles and personal ones. He is becoming mildly affectionate, and the expression of emotions, such as sympathy, is becoming more apparent. With a strong tendency to establish social contacts, he likes to visit a friend's house during the day.

Instead of the contrariness of the past, this is a time when he tries to please and conform, and he is most pleased when he pleases others.

The 3 year old's independent play is less reckless and rash, than it was in the last period. Self-dependence and sociability are more balanced to help him to fit in more comfortably with others around him.

Although he is capable of self-initiative, he tends to be influenced more by social suggestion. He is more susceptible to praise, so suggestions are more effective then direct orders. In fact he may do things he does not like to do if he is given a good reason. He gladly helps his mother put his toys away and will go to the toilet on a slight suggestion.

"The conflicting extremes of a half a year ago give way to a high degree of self-control." His greater self-control has its basis in motor responses, and his motor expressions are more evenly balanced and fluid.

The smooth and cooperative play of a group of 3 year olds is more spontaneous yet more calm and self-reliant compared to the stormy 2-1/2 year old group. Several children are likely to participate together in some type of activity with much laughter and verbal humor accompanying play. Since the gross motor drive is under the child's control, there is a greater freedom with fewer environmental restrictions.

He enjoys helping others when he can. His growing self-reliance allows him to help in small household task and to help in getting his room in order. The 3 year old is proud of his own increasing abilities, and is more capable of solving his own problems now.

The adjustment problems of the 3 year old are infrequent. His time consuming demands are lessening as a more cooperative adaptivity is developing. There is not the need of rituals for self-protection, because his personal relations are more flexible. His advances in his ability to handle personal-social relationships is one of the most difficult and complicated task that the growing child will have to encounter.

Because the 3 year old is less turned in on himself emotionally, he is more sure of himself and superficially shows some savoir faire. His motor action system is in a state of equilibrium so that everything is working together effectively. He is becoming a man of the world displaying a certain flair when he makes his entrance into the nursery. And he may occasionally shout and sing with exuberant confidence. Three year olds may insult each other and use swear words to indicate that they are not afraid to be a little bad.

He has developed the ability to judge and is ready to choose between two rival alternatives. Instead of the doubt of before he now can enjoy making a choice within the realm of his experience. When walking into the nursery he may survey the situation for a moment and then with deliberateness choose a child or an activity that he is interested in.

The three year old is developing an ability to limit his interest to a smaller area, and he is able to focus his attention and interest longer. The daily routines do not have to be rushed as before. He can make comfortable transitions and adaptations, because he can wait his turn. You can bargain with him now, because he can delay doing the things he wants to do, and hold himself in anticipation.

If he cannot fall asleep during nap time, then he is content to play at "napping." If he inquires and finds out that the required time to sleep is not up, then he will usually return to his "play napping" without protest.

Memories of his past babyhood are relived at this age as he likes to recall his past experiences and achievements. His memory process is actively felt as he is bursting with interesting stories about his home experiences even before he enters the nursery. With a new confidence in his utterance, he has an eager desire to talk; and if encouraged some could talk indefinitely.

If he has confidence in the security of the routine, then he can shed his dependence on his mother with an indifferent good bye on entering the nursery. But when the parents leave him to go "out" then he may cry until he vomits, or until the parents return. The mother is the more favored parent now. The 3 year old clings less at bed time and usually falls asleep more quickly than at 2-1/2 years. He is beginning to report dreams.

His imaginative life reaches a peak at 3-1/2 years in the form of an imaginary playmate. He relates this imaginary companion intimately with his own activities and home life, so that he may have a place at the table, go for a ride in the car, and sleep in or under the child's bed. "The child is often very demanding about the rights of his imaginary companion and very solicitous in teaching him many things." Although he does not bring the companion into the nursery school, he may bring him as far as the nursery door. This imaginary companion may recur up to 8 or 9 years of age with some children.

STABILIZING CIRCUIT

The "stabilizing" circuit refers to the hippocampus and its pathways. The fornix connects the hippocampus with the septal region and the hypothalamus. There are two primary divisions within this "stabilizing" circuit each with different functions. (See Fig. 9) The dorsal hippocampus sends fibers to and from the mammillary body by way of the postcommissural division of the fornix, while the precommissural fornix contains fibers from the ventral hippocampus that project to the septal.(104 & 82)

The ventral hippocampal fibers that connect the septal area inhibits the sensory (arousal) nervous system while the fibers from the dorsal hippocampus that connect the mammillary body restrain the motor/muscle (arousal) nervous system.

The hippocampus participates directly in the memory consolidation process. The hippocampus, working in conjunction with the entorhinal area, operates as an

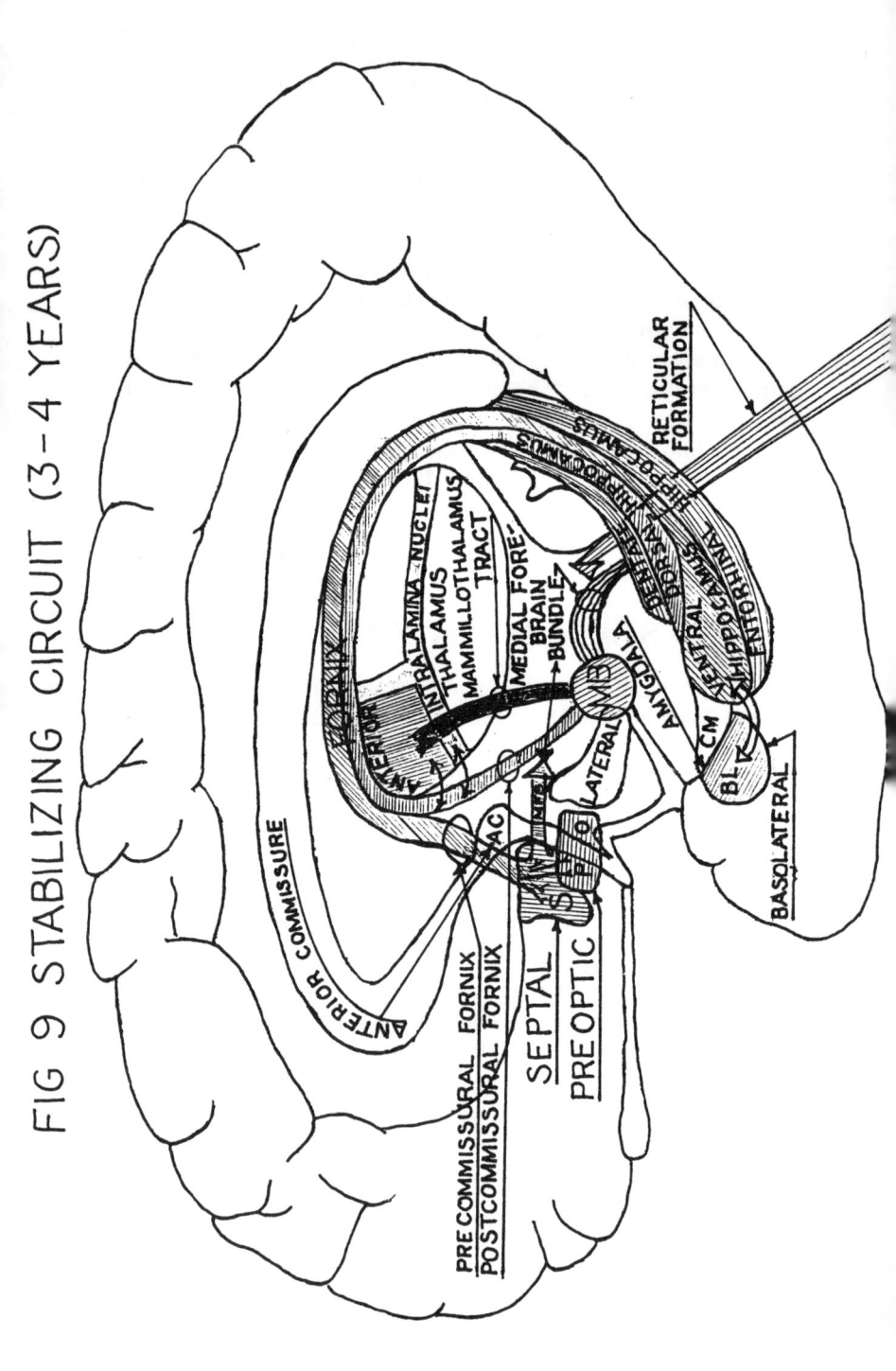

FIG 9 STABILIZING CIRCUIT (3-4 YEARS)

intermediator to retrieve memories impressed on the cells by absorptive ability of the sensory nervous system. On the other hand, the retrieval of a memory from storage depends on the "projection" ability of the motor aspect of the hippocampus.

In other words, to effectively lay down a memory into a storage area depends on the emotional implications and "meaning" that can make a strong impression on sensory cells of the sensory (arousal) system while the retrieval of a memory in storage depends on the motor (arousal) system, so that the sensory impressions are "projected" from the entorhinal hippocampal areas.

Imagination aids memory by creating a reverberating feedback where impressions and "projections" oscillate rapidly back and forth, as the input and output aspects are completed in a circuit and then gradually consolidated by this echo process.

The hippocampus has long lasting inhibitory effects that reduce cell excitability. And one of the most important behaviors that the hippocampus develops during the "stabilizing" period is the ability to inhibit arousal in the early stages. The hippocampus has diffuse 2-way connections with the amygdala and it is able to control the excitation of the basolateral division which has important connections with the pituitary adrenal stress mechanism.(106) The hippocampus especially has an inhibitory influence on ACTH secretion of this rapid alarm system.(29, 54 & 51)

The hippocampus is innervated by the reticular formation in the early stages of attention which in turn restrains arousal from the reticular formation in a mutually inhibitory relationship.(106)

Basket cells in the hippocampus have feedback pathways that reduces excitation, so that the more the pyramidal cells fire, the more it activates the feedback inhibition that stops cellular firing. This gives the basket cell neurons the final decision as to whether the impulse will be conducted down the axon.(2)

This not only keeps down the level of excitation, but effectively participates in cell integration that can modify patterns of neuronal responses by shaping impulses into specific forms of neural performance.(26)

So the hippocampus seems to have the common function of analyzing sensory input for relevant information in terms of experience and the current situation. It can inhibit unwanted responses and exploratory behavior and allow appropriate responses and exploratory behavior, and appropriate responses to novel stimuli.(106)

During evolution the neocortex was derived or was developed from the hippocampus, and the hippocampus acts like the neocortex of the limbric subcortical system. In contrast to the inflexibility of the basolateral amygdala rhythms, the hippocampal rhythms have an exquisite placticity.(106)

The frequencies of its rhythms vary from the 3-7 c/s theta waves to the fast waves of 40 c/s by providing different degrees of synchronization and random firing in its cells. As such the hippocampus represents the highest level of control for the innervation and suppression of excitatory impulses below the neocortical level. The frequency of the hippocampus rhythm seems to be a function of the degree of motivation.(91) When arousal is needed for motivational behavior, the slow theta rhythm of the hippocampus inactivates the hippocampus to permit maximum attention and EEG arousal of the neocortex. Fast waves of 30-40 c/s in the hippocampus inhibit the reticular formation to reduce arousal in the neocortex.(106)

The "stabilizing" response of the hippocampus tends to maintain a kind of emotional equilibrium. When the neocortex shows low EEG arousal with alpha waves, the hippocampus can elevate one's mood to prevent drowsiness and maintain a state of equilibrium. In the opposite sense, when the neocortex is overly aroused, then the hippocampus also maintains a balanced equilibrium.

In other words, the hippocampus is capable of keeping one near the center on a horizontal plane to maintain a balance between the para-sympathetic and the sympathetic nervous systems, and on a vertical plane between pleasure and displeasure in the sensory (arousal) system. Thus, the hippocampus allows one to maintain a state of equilibrium.

The hippocampus is able to inhibit excessive energy that causes displeasure from the basolateral amygdala. The hippocampus can either inhibit the energy impulses or redirect the energy. So this energy can be used in the motor (arousal) system for action, or in the sensory (arousal) system for pleasure or learning, according to one's motivational choice.

When the fornix was severed it produced excessive emotional reactions in animals.(96) Chronic ferocity was produced in a monkey with bilateral hippocampus lesions.(88) Excitatory hyperactivity was so strong in rats with dorsal hippocampal lesions that they could not stay on a "safe" platform to keep from being shocked.(117)

When the inhibitory cells of the hippocampus, neocortex and motor pathways are destroyed with hydrophobia or rabies, there results extreme fear where a slight sensory stimulus can bring on convulsions of fear, demonstrated by spasms of the larynx and pharynx. Convulsions become so intense that breathing is paralyzed and death results.

Bilateral lesions of the hippocampus causes a memory loss of verbal and non-verbal material even if the patients let their attention wander for one second.(106)

In Korsakoff's psychosis, there is a degeneration of the hippocampus, fornix and mammillary bodies resulting in gross memory defects and an inability to learn or retain new facts and skills.(123 & 58) In this psychotic reaction, there are acute fear, hallucinations, disorientation, suggestibility and tremor. This is found in chronic alcoholism, especially in an attack of DT's (delirium tremens).(118)

Patients who suffer from this acquired less information and forgot it faster; new associations were quickly lost and there was no relearning. They could not handle any learning task that involved more than two items. There seemed to be two basic disabilities, a fragmentary impression of events without any connection with the experience it was associated with; and a fixation on a limited set of behavioral responses.(75)

CHAPTER 33

MORALS

With the development of the "stabilizing" response a person is better able to deal with others socially. This greater self-control can start to place one in a role of leadership to influence others. So after establishing a synergistic relationship between your rao and your remo, and within your family, you want to have some influence on encounters with others in your daily social environment. To do this you should have one simple moral system, one that discriminates and disapproves of harmful behaviors.

Harmful behavior is any act that hurts another either emotionally or physically. An example is the act of being critical of another because of weakness, ineptness, stupidity, tactlessness, crudeness, inconsiderateness or a lack of energy.

A behavior such as inconsiderateness results because of status, where a sensitivity to others can be punishing. People develop a lack of awareness or harden their emotional sensitivity as a means of self protection. Once the displeasures of status can be reduced or eliminated under synergy, then a sensitivity to others can find rewards in pleasure to produce a greater awareness of others.

Punishment, such as criticism and disapproval, should be used to control harmful conduct. But when punishment is used to establish control of behaviors that are harmless, it loses its effectiveness to control really bad behaviors.

The inner nature of the remo has a real sense of fairness so that punishment for harming another is likely to be taken as being deserved. But when you belittle another in regard to some blunder, you have inflicted pain for an act that hurts no one. This is a behavior that can really hurt someone. It is much more harmful than inept behavior. To belittle another is the behavior that really needs punishment.

The tearing down of others with criticism is the thing that is despicable under synergy. This reverses the priorities of a social hierarchy where the inadequacies of others can be used for personal advancement. When you ignore or stand by and let a person minimize another, you have fertilized the seed that will eventually grow into the ugly status weeds around you.

It is up to you to rank harmful activity, e.g., gossip, criticism, etc., as being unwholesome. Being inconsiderate, inept or inappropriate hurts no one, but when these behaviors are criticized, they are creating harm to another where no harm existed previously. However, if your feelings have been hurt by someone being inconsiderate, then you need to tell that person so directly.

If a person puts another down with some form of disapproval, such as criticism or gossip, then that behavior need to be confronted directly with criticism, shaming or complaint. It should be unacceptable to let harmful behaviors pass, as we presently do with the status system.

In other words, you should accept all behavior except harmful behavior. You should be critical of criticism, except when the criticism is of harmful behavior. This implies that it is your responsibility to use your mental ability to discriminate and make inferences that are for the good of others from those that have the purpose of harming others.

An example of what often occurs in a social hierarchy is that people stand meekly by allowing someone to belittle or even slander another. Those who use criticism are playing a dominance game, so that their momentary influence of superiority is used to advise and persuade others to adopt their opinion. Thus a pressure is applied to influence the beliefs of others to agree with the speaker within this hierarchy.

However, you can fight these status behaviors and start to be protective of others by discouraging this type of behavior as soon as it starts. You actually make yourself a much stronger person when you disapprove of such harmful practices. In addition, you are undermining the status system and creating a more supportive environment.

For example, if a person you are conversing with criticizes or minimizes someone not present, it behooves you to call the speaker down, and take him to task for undermining another. You can say for example, "He hasn't hurt anybody with that behavior, but you are actually hurting him. Besides I don't agree with what you say at all, I have found him to be very sincere, positive, etc." Or as Thumper said in "Bambi", "if you can't say sumthin' nice, then don't say nuthin' at all."

If the person is not corrected, then he doesn't realize, and doesn't learn, what it is he is doing that is detrimental to himself and others. It also erodes the trust between people. If you talk about others behind their backs, you could also talk about those who are present behind their back. On the other hand, when you are standing up for another not present, then there will be a trust that you will stand up for those present also.

However, if the criticism is related to some harmful behavior, then this is a different matter. Here criticism is used for the purpose it was intended. Disapproval to correct a harmful behavior is called for if synergy is to work as a social system.

In addition, it is important that a person understand how feelings came to be hurt, because you have to deal with harm in terms of very real human experiences, and not use the common status ploy about some potential threat of harm to try to control another's behavior.

You also have to direct the remo's thoughts away from being critical of the self. As soon as the remo is critical of the self or others, it is a signal that you are into the harm of a status hierarchy. Curtail this criticalness within yourself. These minor deeds of status may seem insignificant, but this is where your control is most potent, because it can soon grow to cause most relationship problems.

ACCEPTING THE SELF

Will Roger said, "I've never met a man I didn't like." This quote is often repeated because it is such an unusual occurrence. Rather for one human to dislike another, when no harm has occurred, should be the unusual occurrence. It is unnatural, because the degree that you dislike others, may be a measure of the dislike you have for the self.

One way to accept yourself is to make a concerted effort to like someone you dislike who has never harmed you. When you can succeed at that challenge, you are more likely to find a comfort with yourself. Status can not give you this self acceptance. It can only provide a conditional acceptance that lasts only as long as you can perform adequately to prove yourself.

Those oriented towards synergy believe all life forms and all behaviors are acceptable. This implies a trust in people as being "good;" a belief in pleasure as being essential and beneficial; and an indulgence of others to allow them to be at their worst and yet still be accepted as they are.

A group of people who organize their relationships around synergetic principles will accept each other's inner feelings and weaknesses. Those in a synergetic group might have a need to meet together as a group to iron out any misunderstanding or social problems that arise. The Japanese keep personal problems in the workplace down to a minimum with similar types of support meetings.

Being critical of hurtful behavior must be tempered with some concern for the uncertainty and mistakes to which humans are susceptible. So a stipulation needs to be added that the purpose of criticism under synergy is to enhance the supportive reciprocity between people. In other words, for disapproval to be effective, there must follow some attitudes of forgiveness, which in turn would bring about a feeling of acceptance and cooperation.

Disapproval should be expressed at the time of a harmful occurrence, and then forgiven and forgotten. This will facilitate cooperation and permit a supportive relationship to start anew. If unable to express disapproval at the time, then do not carry it inside, because to harbor resentments will not do any good and can make matters worse.

Putting on a brave front after a "put down" to show that you can take it is one of the bad "macho" values of a status system. The feelings suppressed with such a show of control can fester and await an opportunity for retribution. You should not stand for personal abuse. Instead of taking disparagement you should immediately express any feelings of displeasure, and then let it pass in an air of conciliation.

RESENTMENT VRS. FORGIVENESS

Under the status value system when you show forgiveness without paying back, you are demonstrating a lack of courage. The benevolence of forgiveness is a status sign of weakness. The concept of being a "man," or to be tough like a "man," as in macho, is a major signpost of a social status hierarchy in operation. Revenge shows a virility that is nurtured in a macho attitude of "I'll get you back for that!" Or "You'll be sorry you messed with me."

Revenge maintains a passive defense in resentment. To carry resentment and a desire for revenge are bad defenses, because there is a constant replay of negative emotions which may eventually harm the psyche. A price is paid when you relive a situation involving bad feelings. Although it may arouse you, you will be residing in the displeasurable pathways and circuits of the brain, which can disrupt your psychological and physical well-being.

Having a forgiving attitude is taking a step towards a pleasurable orientation. Actually, forgiveness is a prerequisite for pleasure. You cannot expect to be oriented towards pleasure, and also carry the spitefulness of vengeance.

The rewards of forgiveness are not divine, they are pleasure. If you can't develop an attitude of forgiveness, then you will have trouble developing the attitude of having a orientation towards pleasure.

AT YOUR WORST

If you harbor resentment, then to suppress those feelings requires a lot of energy, especially when you need to appear at your best. When dealing with status oriented people, there is a need to keep your best foot forward to make a good impression. But when you try to impress others, the primary concern is not with others as much as trying to advance yourself. Energy is used to gain status, to maintain the status quo, or to guard against a loss of esteem.

In contrast, a synergetic group allows you to be at your worst. If you try to hide your weakness in shame or disgust, then you are still into status. It is only through the exposure of all your imperfections, showing your inadequacies, faults and fears, followed by the supportive acceptance from others, that you will be able to accept yourself.

It is not important that one is better than another; rather, it is assumed that an inequality exists. The idea of one being better than another loses much of its importance when each is accepted.

However, to develop any skill so you can be at your best comes about, paradoxically, when you are allowed to be at your worst and are allowed to make mistakes. When you are free to be at your worst, you will be free to be at your best.

A common social status paradox happens when you find the greatest acceptance occurs while performing at your best when muscles are at their peak of efficient control with an abundance of energy. Ironically, this is the time when you can feel relatively free of care and when you need acceptance least of all. But during low energy periods when you have little confidence, when you are at your worst, or when you have the worries and burdens of care and concern, is the time you have the greatest need for acceptance. Unfortunately this is when it is least likely to be forthcoming.

This is such a common occurrence, you need to be aware of the internal synergetic feelings that can deal with the blues. When you are feeling down, this is the time when the rao and remo need to count on each other. When you feel depressed, you need to create loving feelings between the rao and remo. And the last communication step can facilitate this mutual bond.

CHAPTER 34

COLLOQUY

You want your remo to move beyond verbally replying to questions with a "yes" or "no." You now want ideas to be communicated using the verbal ability of your remo to express complete sentences within the privacy of your mind. That is to say, your remo should be able to create a voice in your mind's ear to exchange thoughts and ideas, or to carry on a conversation with you.

"The little voice in your ear" that you may have experienced, or heard about, is actually your remo conveying a message to you. By making use of this ability of your remo, you should be able to exchange words of comfort or conflict, and mentally talk things over. When combined with the previous steps, you can even have complex visual and audio exchanges with your remo within your mind.

You want the sounds of your verbal communications to take place privately within your mind. Do not speak out loud; use your mind and speak silently without making a sound. Preferably, converse using your remo's mental image to express facial and bodily gestures, while using your mental ability to create verbal sounds of words.

Now along with synergy you can create the most healthy internal emotional environment possible, by having your remo become your "imaginary" mate. And there is no needs for anyone to know about it, if you don't want to tell them.

Gradually introducing you to your remo a step at a time can reduce or eliminate the shock of the final communication step with your remo. When you can achieve this last step, the full range of communication tools and skills will be available to either put an end to all your social and emotional problems or allow you to have control of these problems.

For example, tension headaches occur because the remo creates tension in the shoulders and neck muscles. This tension is caused by the remo's reaction to the stress created by status conditions. Now if your remo agrees that synergy is the way to live your life, and that such self-punishment needs to be eliminated then have your remo transfer that tension to the diaphragm as you practice taking deep breaths using the "vegetative" response; or some other fitting defensive growth behavior that allows you to shift the negative energy into more pleasurable pathways.

This last communication step may occur naturally around three years of age, when your remo appears in the form of a child's imaginary playmate. Many children are able to reach this sixth level of communication with their remo naturally, often referred to as the imaginary companion.

With an imaginary companion the child has a natural way to grow, while having fun at the same time, in a mutual cooperative effort of play. The remo takes the form of an imaginary friend to provide a means to solve problems, resolve conflicts and reach some kind of compromise by talking out opposing desires in exchanges of give and take. Using verbal imagery is a natural way to enjoy yourself, to get along with yourself and learn to play and care about yourself.(72) When you practice communication with your remo, your "mate," you will be amazed at how much wiser and intelligent you will eventually become.

However, the status system makes us such socially primitive people, so ignorant about ourselves, that those concerned about conformity, often suppress this activity with subtle non-verbal disapproval, or even ridicule. So children eventually give up this cooperative bond and suppress their imaginary companions. The result is that we are often encouraged to be alienated from ourselves from an early age. Even today, parents still have an uneasy attitude towards a child's imaginary companion, especially among fathers.(13)

VERBAL   ABILITY

You will want to develop and increase the ability of your remo to use words. For instance, if something is bothering your remo, instead of creating tensions or tying your stomach up in knots, you want your remo's distress expressed verbally by opening new channels of expression within your mind. Instead of expressing disagreement by creating tension in the neck or with a headache, you want your remo to learn to use this more cooperative way of communicating and dealing with problems.

Language development is equal on both sides of the brain until about five years of age. In most adults the remo's hemisphere has a vocabulary of a fourteen-year-old and the grammatical ability of a five-year-old.(130) The reason the remo's speech does not continue to develop is because of status conditions which discourage people from tapping into this great resource which is the remo's half of the brain.

Words can be pleasurable for the remo to play around with, as they are simply labels or symbols for more complex ideas. As the interactions between your rao and your remo within your mind increase, you may find the remo is verbally very creative. By increasing your remo's ability to use words, you truly can become more of a natural conversationalist.

When you increase the verbal ability of your remo, it can increase your literary creativity, increase your ability to absorb new words, increase your ability to find words, make you more articulate, and make you more fluent by reducing hesitations.(19)

The effects of our culture and school system have tended to neglect the remo's abilities by developing the rao's brain through reading, writing and arithmetic, so that the remo's great motivational half of the brain is left out in the cold. As a result, our culture has most of the population operating on half a brain, with pleas to our school children "You have to try harder!" Or "You're just not making an effort."

When an educational situation was created to enhance the functions of the remo's right hemisphere, there was found an increase in the student's self-esteem. They were interested in a greater number of content areas and investigated to a greater depth the arts, sciences and humanities.(98)

Finally, communicating with your remo will cause your remo to not only be more involved with life, but enjoy life more. When the general sociability of your remo is allowed to develop fully, it provides not only that get-up-and-go spirit, but increases common-sense. Your remo has a social "street sense" that can handle the many complexities of a social situation simultaneously. This permits you to react to new situations in innovative ways. We need to realize that the remo is an equal partner with the rao, equipped with a brain that can match the mental capacity of the rao.

As you communicate at higher levels, you will begin to stick up for your remo's hurt feelings. You need to protect your remo as you would a child. So if your remo's feelings have been hurt you need to inform the offender with assertive feedback.

CHAPTER 35

FEEDBACK

ASSERTIVENESS

Synergy must use assertive feedback to inform another that feelings have been hurt. Many who lack sensitivity need this feedback to know they've hurt someone, and then given a chance to contribute in a cooperative spirit.

When you feel offended, and hide your remo's hurt feelings by putting on a brave front, you promote the harmful actions of status. This lack of communication between people can lead to misunderstanding, resentment, alienation or revengeful feelings. On the other hand, expressing feelings of mental distress when hurt is the best way to discourage harmful behavior.

Many belittle pained reactions after they inflict hurt on others, believing that you "ought" to be able to take it, as if it was a responsibility not to weaken. There even exists an attitude that if you can't hide these feelings, you should feel ashamed; you should feel bad if you can't carry through and cover up with courage.

But this type of bravery is the very thing that makes weak and ineffective individuals. It has its basis in the rejection of personal feelings which can eventually lead to self punishment or a remo who is angry at the rao. Thus, assertive feedback is necessary if a social solidarity is to develop, because it informs another of injured personal feelings.

TURNING THE OTHER CHEEK

A faith in authority can substitute for a loss of faith in the self, as personal insecurity strengthens authority. One of the best ways to entrench a status system into a culture is to encourage a passive nonresistance to harmful behavior. When harm becomes permissible by letting it pass without correction or reproach, then you insidiously shape a social status hierarchical system.

The idea of "turning the other cheek" is the perfect way to have people become alienated from their self. This artificial way of reacting to harm can humiliate the remo, and cause the remo to resent the rao. This not only creates a deep division between the rao and remo, but invites the harmful aggression of a status system. Such standards of behavior can propagate the dominance of status over synergy.

It has been shown in our society that the great majority of people have proven to be apathetic or even accepting to the violations of their rights. A number of experiments were carried out in a study by Moriarty titled "A Nation of Willing Victims"(78), which concluded that the passive acceptance of the violation of personal rights is partially responsible for the current climate of crime and fear we live in, and that rights not defended can soon wither away.

Representatives of authority, by giving advice not to resist harmful aggression, discourage the solidarity between people. This encourages the attitude that getting into a hassle to defend another is not worth the involvement.

On the other hand, people can develop more courage once they have an emotionally reassuring environment. A supportive environment is encouraged and harmful behaviors are discouraged by defending those that have been harmed or wronged.

NEGATIVE FEEDBACK

Negative feedback is a function of conformity. Basically, it disapproves of your behavior. Such feedback presupposes there is a perfect way of performing a behavior, and your performance was inadequate. Negative feedback is undesirable. It uses the punishment of disapproval to control harmless behaviors to indicate how a person is somehow different. Or it presupposes that you are doing something wrong that needs to be corrected, adjusted and changed.

The encouragement of negative feedback that didn't discriminate between harmful and harmless behaviors was the main trouble with encounter groups. Expressions of anger, hostility and a dislike for another were often indiscriminately promoted as a purging release. While such expressions do provide this immediate effect, they actually encourage these misbehaviors to increase in strength, as people lose their inhibitions to control harmful behaviors.

Harmless weaknesses were criticized as often as they were given support and acceptance. The problems this promotes is shown by the fact that members of encounter groups were discouraged from associating with each other except during the encounter hours, because of the backbiting and critical judgment that often occurred to create factions within a group.

Negative feedback's use of punishment intimidates and elicits suppressive and avoidance behaviors that can demoralize. And this punishing criticism and disapproval is a major cause of depression.

CHAPTER 36

OVERCOMING DEPRESSION

People are vulnerable to all kinds of losses. There are physical losses of loved ones or friends. In this instance when you're sad and you feel like crying you should not hesitate to go ahead and cry, especially if you're a male. This is the most healthy thing you can do both emotionally and physically.

Or another option, when your remo first starts feeling depressed from a physical loss, you can activate the "stabilizing" response to avoid the depths of displeasure. However, if you've waited too late and your spirits are so low, that you feel depressed, and you have to face people, then this is a time you especially want to call up loving feelings for yourself between the rao and remo.

When you are down, it is practically useless to initiate the excitement of the sympathetic division of the autonomic nervous system, except via the "care" circuit. The rao and the remo are capable of creating loving feelings for the self even through depressed. The sweet sorrow of the blues can activate enough excitement of the sympathetic division so that you can carry through and interact effectively with people.

On the other hand, if your depressed and you don't know why, or if you're suffering because of a loss in self-esteem from the put downs and rejections that are so common in a status culture, then take a radically different approach to rid yourself of this displeasure.

If your depression is not the result of some obvious physical loss, then your depression stems from your remo punishing the self. When the remo gets angry, and the anger isn't expressed outwardly, then it can be turned inwardly and experienced as depression. This anger is almost always a result of a belief in social status values, and is therefore, futile.

However, even though the remo may concur about the evilness of the status system and wants to adopt synergy, the remo tends to react automatically from habit to status assaults on self-esteem. So you will have to teach the remo to react in a new way.

Depression is a state of anger turn inward to punish the self. Thus, if you make a stupid blunder, the remo may lash out at the self with self punishment. But if you believe in synergy punishment should be restricted to harmful behaviors. Also performance ability should not be a measure of your esteem.

So now you need to find out if your remo agrees with these ideas, by asking the remo. And you want to talk this out, so there is a complete understanding. Remember, just because the rao understands something doesn't mean the remo does!

Next, you need to relive those situations that caused you to be depressed, and have your remo respond with the "stabilizing" response of indifference. Within your mind the remo's first instant reaction to these devastating events should be the "stabilizing" response of a matter of fact indifference. When you activate the "stabilizing" circuit you short circuit the negative energy of displeasure and redirect it to a positive source. You are pulling your self up, by your own boot straps, out of displeasure into a state of calm indifference. The more you can practice this, the sooner you will defeat this scourge.

You may also want to imagine some future depressing scenario at work, with the spouse or friends, etc.. to practice this response. If you practice this daily, after a month or so this response will "lock-in" as an automatic behavior of your remo to provide you with a major victory over a troubling emotional problem.

If you've been put down, rejected, snubbed, insulted, etc., you need to realize these are the vile conditions of a status system. First off you should never stand and take such punishment from another. You need to let them know in no uncertain terms, that they do not have the freedom to treat or speak to you that way, if at all possible. And once your remo has developed the "stabilizing" response along with the "integrative" response of the adult-child stage, you will be able to unleash a verbal assault to unjust treatment towards the offending party while maintaining complete self-control.

Next, if you were unable to stand up for your self, but believe in the values of synergy, then you should realize your esteem and worth is not dependent on others in a status system. The feeling of equality synergy engenders should gradually build feelings of self-confidence within you. You do not want to give anybody the right to evaluate you and determine your worth.

So if your remo agrees, you want to rehearse reacting to these status situations with the "stabilizing" response of indifference, instead of self-punishment. You should practice reacting to instances from your past over and over until's it an automatic response. And you should conjure up possible future situations to also practice this new response.

If you have problems with depression you should plan ahead and visualize circumstances that can cause future problems. Thus, you might imagine responding to being fired from your job, getting a divorce, being rejected by a friend, etc. Remember your essence is not determined by the job you hold, being able to maintain a marriage, or someone else's opinion of your self, if you hold synergy's values.

However, if the remo still believes in status values because of an allegiance to a dominating father, an authoritative religion, a cult, etc., then you have a real sales job of persuasion on your hand. Since it is the remo's belief in status values that is the source of your depression, you need to sit your remo down like you would a child, and have a long serious talk. And you should review those chapters about status and synergy.

If this doesn't work you may have to resort to giving your remo a good tongue thrashing. Your remo is using punishment for harmless behavior, and you should not put up with such status actions. So unless you've hurt someone, admonish your remo silently with the verbal sound in your mind with a stern lecture, that you are not going to put up with such irresponsible behavior. And then reread those chapters on status to show the remo how harmful and terrible these status values are to your well being.

If you want to be rid of depression, your rao has to take command and guide your remo towards synergy. During this period of training your rao has to raised your remo like you would a child. But this all depends on the communication breakthrough.

If you don't have the courage to interact with your remo as an imaginary mate, then your chances of overcoming depression are considerably diminished. This lack of courage is strictly a result of social status hierarchies. For example, as a young child, the status value system can impair the emotional growth of the "stabilizing" response when a child can learn to control fear and anger. And as an adult, this same status system can also threaten your security by endangering you acceptance and your place in society as a human.

On the other hand, status and "macho" attitudes often produces insecure cowards who can be scared to death to communicate at higher levels with their remo. Thus a lack of courage and being cut off from your remo are intricately bound up in a belief in status values.

If the remo is reluctant to communicate, you should take charge and command your remo to cooperate. Your rao is your leader that guide your remo. If you make a demand that your remo communicate, your remo will follow.

Once you're communicating with your remo, you need to present strong arguments for synergy and against status values, and watch your remo's reactions in a facial close-up. But if the remo still wants to keep the stern iron will authoritarian values of your father or some religion, then you want to grab your remo firmly by the shoulders in your mind's eye, and tell your remo in your mind's ear, in no uncertain terms, you are not going to put up with such mean spirited status behavior. That it has to shape up and get rid of those status values of using punishment against the self.

For one thing depression destroys the pride you feel for yourself. And pride in the self is an important quality you need for synergy to function smoothly.

CHAPTER 37

QUALITIES

PRIDE

Positive feedback can make you feel proud of yourself. Pride is an important quality you need to embrace. To feel a positive pride about yourself is a very powerful motivating force. Pride can become an impelling force to encourage your pleasures of goal-directed activities, and a desire to share your achievements with others. When you share with others, openly, the pride you feel about your accomplishments, you will feel good about yourself, and you will feel good about others. This will in turn encourage the cooperativeness that is the essence of synergy.

Conversely, pride in a status society is corrupted. Because the remo wants to be accepted by everyone within a group, the remo wants to rise as high as possible within the social hierarchy operating. Your remo may feel this can be accomplished by expressing the pride you feel about some accomplishment. But this can lead to feelings of superiority, that you are somehow better than others, which can also minimize others.

The problem is, a status society creates feelings of alienation among people even within an organized group, so that most people's remos tend to feel some degree of inferiority or insufficiency. So pride can eliminate these unwanted feelings, and be used to compare the self and judge others to create superior feelings. But the more there is an underlying feeling of inferiority within your remo, the more arrogance that is felt. Because of the lack of acceptance that operates among people pride easily becomes a negative, undesirable quality under status conditions.

On the other hand, synergy eliminates these problems so pride becomes a positive, desirable quality. Under synergy pride takes on a sharing quality. For one thing, pride is contagious. If a person feels a high positive regard for the self and freely says so, then it spills over, causing others to feel equally good and proud.

The remo's ability to generalize feelings is the source for this contagious sharing. When feeling proud of the self, the remo will tend to generalize these feelings with others who are around. This way each achievement becomes a source of pleasure that can be shared with all.

Under synergy the esteem felt in pride can be a substitute for the remo's need for status, that's why orthodox authoritarians think pride is a sinful quality. The culture that can handle the energies of its people in a beneficial way, instead of a destructive way, can best be achieved by encouraging the expression of pride.

People should be encouraged to sing their own praises with the attitude that what is good for one is good for all. This provides a tremendous motivating force to develop skills and talents to the utmost. When accomplishments are not only benefiting the individual but are benefiting others, this substantially increases the motivation to achieve goals.

When pride is felt, expressed and shared, it develops the confidence of everyone. Pride generates an increase in esteem that rubs off on others, making everybody feels important. This high morale can boost the confidence of all to create both a personal strength and independence, and paradoxically a solidarity or unity with others. So this can create a situation where there is no one leader; each can be a leader in his or her own right.

LEADERSHIP

The ideal of leadership is the very essence of a status society. Since a status culture not only hinders the ability of its people to organize, but hinders their ability to cooperate by interfering with personal relationships, then there is a tremendous need for leadership. Good leadership is able to elicit cooperation without having to resort to forceful methods. But in a status system this calls for extraordinary qualities.

A leader needs the charisma of an actor, the tact of a statesman, the wit of an intellectual and the cool judgement of a wise man. A leader needs a toughness in relationships so that those who do not measure up can be discarded. A leader needs to be in close contact with people, yet detached from people.

A leader usually experiences a lack of warmth and closeness with subordinates; a respectful deference is the main solace for this distance. Since a leader is usually not in close touch with subordinates, then relationships with members can discourage exchanges on a free and equal level. What often happens to a leader is that after a brilliant start, all the problems inherent in status hierarchies begin to create trouble.

The most important problem is a disruption of the lines of communication. First there is a breakdown in the free and easy flow of ideas. This communication gap can cause a change in expectations of subordinates. These expectations may not represent the reality of a situation, as a leader gradually loses touch with those under him. This gradually erodes a cooperative spirit, as the leader asserts his power to get things done. Thus, the influence and power a leader wields can become corrupted so that force wins out over reason and finesse. After a time under a status system a leader can go from a director, to a disciplinarian, to a strict boss or master, to an authoritarian, to a dictator.

In addition, a leader often takes on most of the involvement that requires decisions and responsibilities. Typically, subordinates need a lot of drive and ambition to encroach on these areas.

Unless there is some incentive where the leader is willing to share some of his power and responsibility, subordinates too often give way and do only what they are told. Usually their actions have been determined as they carry out orders. Thus, subordinates are made sufficiently dependent to make them mentally inert or inactive, so that they may be more easily led.

ORGANIZER

The need for leadership becomes minimal in a synergetic atmosphere. Japanese businesses have shown, that their workers are able to organize their jobs and think for themselves. In such a cooperative atmosphere people can get things done in a much more effective manner as communication flows more smoothly. Also, responsibility and involvement are not bound up in one leader but are spread out to others.(60 & 9)

Of course no one can deny that there is often a need for an individual member to organize, coordinate or put things together effectively, so as to minimize wasted or duplicated efforts. But these are qualities many are capable of, unless they have been crippled by the value system of a status culture.

Such organizers should not have any special privileges nor should they be expected to perform roles that would separate them from a close working relationship with the people involved.

Since cooperation is an essential part of a synergistic atmosphere and because help, support and input is coming in from all sides, then the responsibility of an organizer doesn't require superhuman qualities. Also, as many individuals as possible should have the responsibility of an organizer with the understanding that this overview provides. The behavior that facilitates your ability to organize is the "integrative" response which develops during the adult-child stage of growth in the next chapter.

CHAPTER 38

INTEGRATIVE PERIOD
4 - 5 YEARS

ADULT-CHILD STAGE

THE INTEGRATIVE RESPONSE

Although the astrological signs, a system where people can make judgements to accept or reject you using your date of birth, are absolute hogwash, the "earth" sign temperament describes compliant qualities similar in nature to the behaviors found in the circuits of the infant-child stage of development. The "water" sign temperament depicts attributes of the "child" stage. The "air" sign temperament portrays qualities of the "juvenile" stage, while the "fire" sign temperament represents qualities of the "adult-child" stage.

The "adult-child" remo is lively and spontaneous, because all the excitatory energy sources and their controls are brought together to provide great vitality and great self-control. You are now capable of cooking on all 12 burners at the same time. And you are able to emphasize those behaviors most adaptive to the situation at the moment. The "integration" circuit gives you all the equipment you need to develop good social skills, and to be a good actor. This can give you self-confidence and a sense of self mastery.

Spontaneity and vitality comes into full bloom now, because a greater trust is generated in your remo's natural impulses. The ability of the "integration" circuit to allow you to express yourself with complete self-control lessens the discrepancy between inner and outer realities. As emotional desires are being fulfilled in the outer reality, there is less need for the emotionally charged atmosphere of the inner reality to express the remo's needs. This produces a greater trust in your remo's impulses and judgements, resulting in a greater freedom.

The "goal-directed" circuit and its activities is the key behavior to innervate the "integrative" circuit. The "goal-directed" circuit was concerned with goals related to objects and skills needed to deal with the environment. In contrast, during the "integration" period your goal-directed activities are related to social activities with people.

The development of the "integration" circuit requires the stimulation and socialization that only other people can give. This "integration" period is a time when you needs to be among adults and to be treated and accepted as an equal adult. It provides a multitude of behaviors to better meet the diverse needs of a social situation with a greater versatility.

The "goal-directed" period tended to produce an individual with a "one track mind" where all responses were centered on a concern for the purpose at hand. The "integration" circuit opens up new avenues while pursuing a goal. This versatility improves your problem solving ability as it allows you to be open to see alternatives.

The "integration" circuit can activate all three nervous system, the sensory, motor and autonomic, simultaneously. First, the autonomic system provides the "vegetative and approach" responses to help you relax and maintain a sense of self-contentment. Second, the sensory system can provide both an alert, exciting, sensual awareness of the environment with the "expectancy" response, along with some kind of "care" response. And third, the motor system, where muscular performance skills in speaking and facial expressions, is utilized at an optimal level of arousal via the "goal-directing and stabilizing" responses. (See Fig. 10)

All of these emotional growth responses or behaviors can occur simultaneously and can be felt and expressed in a relaxed comfortable way or in an energetic way, depending on your energy level at the moment. The "integration" circuit permits a facile ability to shift back and forth between responses and energy levels as your needs and capacities directs you.

The "integration" response is performed with a fluid emotional mobility, sort of like the movement involved with the "figure eight." This allows a constant movement in all directions away from and back towards a feeling baseline of equilibrium.

Thus, you can move from one response to another with the facile ease of a butterfly. This is because the "integration" response allows you to express all the many responses mentioned above as one response. But one moment the "vegetative" response can be more dominate over the others. In the next moment, the social situation may call for the "expectancy" response to have more emphasis. Then if you become overly excited let the "stabilizing" response have the most influence, etc.

Of course, there are endless variations and different combinations of behaviors that can be infinitely expressed in their shades of feeling, depending on the social conditions. An internal dramatization of social situations in thoughts, meditations or daydreams becomes an excellent abode to practice these different feeling responses and behaviors.

The "integration" circuit provides a versatile behavioral arsenal to deal with social problem. Practice and experiment with as many of the emotional growth responses as possible. Learn to switch back and forth between behaviors with a fluid agility.

For example, using the problem solving aspect of the "goal-directed" circuit, think of as many responses as you can for the conditions of the social situation. Using your memory bank to recall the various behaviors initiates the "stabilizing" response. You may also want the "approach" response to prevail over the other circuits to support and encourage other people. If you feel your energy getting low, let your "vegetative" response have the most influence to recharge your batteries. Or if you would rather pep yourself up, then the "expectancy and stabilizing" responses can be combined to reign supreme.

Next, you may want to create feelings of love for the self or others with the "care" response. Get a "buzz on" with feelings of warmth in your chest area and face with the slower alpha brain waves.

The main point is that as you practice and experiment with these behaviors, all your circuits and all your behaviors can come alive. And all these behaviors can be expressed as one response, that can flow to emphasize one particular behavior as being more appropriate than the others for the social situation at the moment. And to add to your enjoyment, realize that there are few things the remo enjoys more than doing several things at the same time.

SOCIALIZING RESPONSE

If you've been alone all day working, studying, reading, etc., and you're thrown in suddenly with a number of different people, you can be taken aback when you're not prepared. So any time you go out socializing or partying, you need to be in a mood that will allow you to enjoy yourself.

First of all a love of the self between your rao and remo is your most effective socializing response, but if this presents a problem, then you want to integrate the "stabilizing" response with the "expectancy" response and the "vegetative" response as one behavior. Combining these three social behaviors together as one response, using the "integrative" circuit, will be referred to as the "socializing" response.

A prerequisite for these behaviors is an orientation towards pleasure. Your goal is to integrate all three responses so they occur as one behavior. When the "socializing" response has been incorporated it can give your remo great adaptive skills to deal with people or any kind in social situation.

While learning, there will be a lot of premeditation involved with the "socializing" response, but after it is established as an automatic reaction of your remo, this is primarily a spontaneous, impulsive response. As you gain a trust in yourself, the spontaneity of your remo provides a kind of fun emotional playground as you explore various social adventures with synergetic people.

These behaviors can help you have control over your life so you can enjoy life and enjoy others, as you create an atmosphere of support and acceptance. However, if you are looking for this to make you a "super" personality so that you can be better than others, then you are into a deleterious game that will defeat your purpose.

Once you've achieved the abilities of the "integrative" response you can easily rise to the top of social status hierarchy you operate in. But once you start being socially competitive with others then you are into a status belief system. There may be moments of euphoria during those transitory periods of dominance and status when you initially realize your new level of power. But with this attitude you start to put other people down, thereby accumulating enemies who will start to sabotage your chances of having the pleasure that these responses depend on. Even if successful, dominance habituates quickly. Eventually it becomes an insatiable desire for power that spreads misery.

CONCENTRATION PROBLEMS

Some people have bad study habits. They hate to study or read non-fiction books, because they clamp their jaws, grit their teeth, suspend their breathing or take minute swallow breaths. So after 10 or 15 minutes, there body has a build up of carbon dioxide to make them tried and fatigued with a need to take a nap. They're tired because they're not using their innate abilities of breathing naturally while relaxing the mouth region, involved with the "vegetative" response.

One problem is the misconception that exist among many people, that to learn you need to be non-emotional or you need to study with a lack of feelings in order to be objective and impartial. Nothing could be further from the truth. To learn and retain what you learn you need to be emotional and excited. And the degree you can be emotional about a subject will be the degree that you can potentially become more proficient and adept on a subject.

Learning is a problem solving exercise that should completely engross your remo. But an indifference attitude effectively excludes your remo's involvement. If you approach a subject you want to study with indifference then the indifference can move from boredom, uneasiness, discomfort, dislike, to dread, abhorrence and hate.

And when you read, your remo likes to change words into symbols. A picture is worth a thousand words to your remo. So the more you can use your "imagery" circuit to express ideas you are reading about using visualization, the more you're going to enjoy and retain what you're reading.

You need to try to find a hook to get you excited about a subject. And then you need to approach studying using your emotional coping skills. Ironically, the "socializing" response is the ideal behavior to employ when you want to absorb a new subject, even though you are alone. By integrating the "expectancy, vegetative and stabilizing" responses in the "socializing" response, you'll find the energy and alertness needed to study for hours without fatigue. However, you may want to practice this in your mind before studying or reading. Or if not, have a two or three minute timer to remind you to practice the "socializing" response while studying until this habit is established.

THE ABILITY TO SLEEP

Once a full blown displeasurable reaction sets in, the ability of the "stabilizing" response to regain self-control is impaired. However, the "integration" circuit can provide control by integrating the "vegetative and stabilizing" responses for an extremely effective control of overwhelming displeasure. In addition, your ability at integrating these two responses determines your skill at going to sleep quickly and easily.

People whose autonomic nervous system is dominant over the sensory and motor systems usually have little trouble sleeping. But a dominant sensory nervous system can cause a lot of sleeping difficulties.

Some may be sleepy, yet may not be able to go to sleep because the sensory excitation of the "imagery, expectancy and care" circuits are able to effectively disrupt the rhythmical activity needed for sleep.

It is the rao's hemisphere that is concerned with consciousness or the lack of consciousness in sleep. While the remo instead of sleeping just switches from an outer to an inner reality.

The problem with sleep production is that when you are conscious of the sequence of events, this consciousness defeats your purpose. And the harder the rao tries to sleep the less likely sleep will come.

To facilitate this loss of consciousness, or to interfere with the remo as little as possible, the rao has to become immersed in something else. The rao needs to become lost in some thought that is not too stimulating. Or become riveted and engrossed in a dreamy stare at some object. People have had car accidents by falling asleep while driving on the freeway. They become lost in reverie while their eyes are glued in a fixed stare, immersed on the road ahead.

The primary sleep center is the "synchronal" circuit involved in the "vegetative" response. The secondary source is the "stabilizing" circuit. Low stimulation of the hippocampus ("stabilizing" circuit) depresses the arousal system to facilitate sleep by eliciting the behaviors that precede sleep such as yawning, stretching, etc. (56) You initiate the "stabilizing" circuit for sleep by forcing down the outside corners of both eyebrows.

The integration of the "vegetative" and "stabilizing" responses is referred to as the "sleep" response. With the development of the "sleep" response, you will increase your skill and ability to go to sleep easily whenever or whereever you want.

First, establish deep relaxed rhythmical breathing by sniffing the air. The "vegetative" deep breath is felt when air is taken in through the nose only, so that it rushes past the deep, back part of the throat. If you begin respiration by flaring your nostrils it will facilitate your breathing. Take a slow deep and expansive breath, so it is performed in a relaxed rhythmical manner. The breathing rhythm is just as important as the air.

If you have a lot of tension in your body, transfer the energy of the tension so it's concentrated in a downward pressure on the outer corners of your eyebrows, and on your diaphragm located in the bread basket of your stomach region, allowing you to draw air in and push air out in deep forceful rhythmic breaths.

Next, relax and immobilize all your muscles. Your muscles should not only be relaxed, but try for a suggestive feeling state where you are not able to move a muscle without a strong exertion of effort. This produces a heavy feeling in the muscles that makes them relaxed but immobile. Also, there should be a thickening of the tongue and lips that makes them feel heavy, moist and immobile.

Third, you want to experience a chilled, cold tingling or buzz sensation within your body. However, the buzz you experience with feelings of "warmth" should not be associated with going to sleep, but more with loving feelings, because warm feelings may cause the release of histamines which can interfere with sleep. If you can you even want to feel a chill. The cooler you are, the easier it is to sleep. The warmer you are the harder it is to sleep.

Beta brain waves fire randomly at 20-25 cycles per second (cps). You experience beta wave when you feel excited or when you are highly active. As you relax you lower the frequency to 8-12 cps when alpha waves are dominant, or lower still to 4-6 cps when theta waves are operating which can make you feel drowsy and sleepy. As the frequency goes from high to low the cellular firing goes from a helter-skelter disorder to a harmonic unity.

When the cells fire together in a "synchronal" manner that means the para-sympathetic division is dominating. The synchronized firing of cells together in unisonance may be experienced as a "buzzing" feeling for alpha rhythms and a "rumbling" feeling for the slower theta rhythms. These slower rhythms produce a heavy lethargic state that make one feel drowsy and sleepy.

Now you want to use the "integrative" circuit's agility to flow back and forth between the ideas or steps above, represented symbolically as the fluid "figure eight" moment within your mind, while integrating the "vegetative" and "stabilizing" responses in the "sleep" response.

Since sleep is the proper domain of the remo, then you have to practice these skills until they can be adopted by the remo. The remo can take over when these behaviors become automatic habits. Outlined below is one method you can use to develop an ability to go to sleep easily and quickly.

For your remo to learn the "sleep" response, you need to use an imaginative, symbolic form the remo can handle. Here is an example, but you can make up your own symbols.

A METHOD TO FACILITATE SLEEP

YOU'RE FLOATING IN A CLOUD OF CAULIFLOWER AND MASHED POTATOES. THE CLOUD IS VIBRATING CAUSING YOU TO HAVE A CHILLED, COLD TINGLING "BUZZ" OR "RUMBLING" FEELING, AS YOU STRETCH. THE OUTSIDE CORNERS OF BOTH EYEBROWS ARE PRESSED DOWNWARD TO MAKE YOU YAWN. YOUR EYES LOSE THEIR SPARKLE, AS THEY BECOME FIXED IN A DULL STARE.

NEXT, YOUR LIPS PROTRUDE, THICKEN AND YOUR JAW SLACKENS AND DROPS SO THE CORNERS OF THE MOUTH COME CLOSER TOGETHER TO KISS THE MOST DESIRABLE PERSON YOU KNOW WHO IS COMING TO GIVE YOU MOUTH TO MOUTH RESUSCITATION. YOU CREATE A GENTLE SUCTION ON YOUR TONGUE THAT CAUSES YOU TO TAKE DEEP RELAXED BREATHS WHICH YOU HOLD IN A FEW SECONDS, THEN SLOWLY LET OUT.

YOUR LIPS AND TONGUE BECOME ENGORGED WITH SALIVATING WATER AS YOU ROLL OVER TO CREATE A LIGHT RAIN. AND THE CLOUD OF MASHED POTATOES GENTLY WRAPS AROUND YOU TO MAKE YOUR LIMBS IMMOBILE AND RELAXED.

THEN YOUR REMO TURNS INTO A "BUZZING" BEE AND FLIES FIGURE EIGHTS AROUND EACH OF THESE IMAGES.

Here the "sleep" response has approximately 10 or 11 responses you need to learn. You want to combine as many of these steps together as you can, so that eventually all of these behaviors will occur simultaneously as one response using the "integrative" response. You need to practice the images of the "sleep" response, with their corresponding behaviors, while sitting up, not in the bed you sleep in, until your remo absorbs them completely.

You can get away with initiating these behaviors for a few minutes upon going to bed. But after that you don't want to be thinking of any of these ideas. If your rao continues to try to apply any of these thoughts to induce sleep, you will take the job of sleeping away from your remo and suffer with insomnia. Going to sleep is strictly the responsibility of your remo.

You should practice the "sleep" response as much as you can every day until these behaviors are soundly established or integrated. Those with an emotionally mature remo, or those with a dominant autonomic nervous system may have little trouble developing this ability. But for those whose sensory nervous system is very dominant, this ability could take much longer to become established.

You should practice during the middle of the day when you have some privacy to take a little 5 or 10 minute catnap. And after this ability has been integrated by your remo, you should be able to shift into this response even when among people to take little micro-naps. These can revitalize you so much, you will find you will need one or two fewer hours of sleep each night!

Even if it takes you several months to learn this response as an automatic behavior, it is well worth the effort. This is a powerful behavior to have at your disposal. Once you're good at initiating this "sleep" response within a moments notice, you will be able to maintain a sense of self-control for practically any emotionally stressful situation.

OVERCOMING FEAR

The remo at the juvenile stage of growth could be overwhelmed by fear or anger if it was not caught and controlled at the early stages. But now you have the tools to control angry temper tantrums and high panic states of fear that are overwhelming. You can do this with the "soothing" response.

Fear and anger creates a lot of negative energy. You need to know before hand how to cope with all this excess negative energy. You need to understand what happens when you are overwhelmed with anger or fear. If you can fight or run to save yourself from harm, then there is no need to be concerned about being overwhelmed. But since we no longer live out in the wild, we need to learn how to handle all this excessive energy.

There are four avenues of control. On a physical level this excessive negative energy can be both transferred and reduced. Negative tension can be transferred to the diaphragm to initiate deep breaths, to the lips as they pucker and protrude, to the nose as it flares out and to the outside corners of the eyebrow as they are pressed downward.

On the other hand, the amount of negative energy is reduced by acting out the behaviors of the "vegetative" response, such as a slacken jaw, deep rhythmic breaths, enlarged tongue, puckered lips, etc. These behaviors function like a Pavlovian response that can automatically reduce arousal.

At the mental level, this excessive negative energy can also be transferred and reduced. The "sleep" response which consist of the "stabilizing and vegetative" responses can both effectively reduce the energy level. The "vegetative" response does it by sychronizing cellular firing and the "stabilizing" circuit does it by inhibiting arousal in the neocortex. And to transfer negative energy at the mental level you employ the "expectancy" response. When you activate the "expectancy" response, the attentive awareness and readiness can divert a tremendous amount of energy away from the displeasurable pathway into the "expectancy" circuit.

When you combine the "expectancy" response with the "sleep" response, this will be referred to as the "soothing" response. So when you integrate the "expectancy and sleep" responses you both divert and lower the amount of negative energy and tension by deploying the "orienting" reflex of the "expectancy" response that you've seen in a cat, while depressing the outside corners of both eyebrows down using the "stabilizing" response. And you also want to redirect tension to the diaphragm so you take deep rhythmical breaths.

After you have integrated all the behaviors of the "sleep" response along with the "expectancy" response and they become an automatic response of your remo in the "soothing" response, you will always be able to quickly regain your composure no matter how overwhelming the crisis. You will always have the ability to pull in the reins and take a momentary break to calm yourself!

For example, if you're in a high anxiety state, and activate the "soothing" response, you can return to a state of normalcy in a remarkably short time! But be sure to redirect the negative tension from fear to the areas previously mentioned. It is important to restore deep rhythmical breathing by transferring the negative energy to your diaphragm muscles to inhale and exhale deeply and to a downward pressure on the outside corners of both eyebrows while also transferring energy to the "expectancy" response. Even if you are overwhelmed with fear, you can quickly pull out of a panic state to regain self control, when you employ the "soothing" response.

This is true for a fear of heights, fear of flying, claustrophobia or a fear of small places, like elevators, fear of crowds, bugs, animals, open places or anything. However, make sure you have mastered the "soothing" response first. Then imagine yourself in the fearful situation while practicing the "soothing" response before you actually put yourself in emotional jeopardy.

OVERCOMING ANGER

To control anger you have to determine which kind it is. Some anger is justified and some is not. Unjustified anger results from a belief in the status value system. The source is the remo, which needs to believe it is superior to protect the self from its fear of inferiority. To boost the self the remo will make unreasonable claims, or want special privileges. Then the remo can easily become angry when it isn't granted some right, exception or freedom.

Also, those who think they are superior, have to control others, again out of fear of their deep inferiority. Thus, when a spouse, a worker, a driver, a clerk, a child or a rule breaker doesn't obey them and doesn't do what they think is "right," the foundation for their esteem can be shaken. So their remo needs to deny and protect their self by projecting out this threatening negative energy as anger.

To control this anger, the outlook is bleak if a person doesn't want to adopt synergy. But if your rao, believes in synergy and your remo will go along, then your anger can be controlled and eventually eliminated.

Those who have a fiery temper haven't developed or aren't utilizing the emotional behaviors of the "juvenile and adult-child"stages. When a person has a dominant motor nervous system, and one's emotional growth has been stopped at the "child" stage, then the remo's temper tantrums that occurred early in life, and during the terrible twos, will tend to continue, unless the rao makes enormous efforts of will to suppress the remo's anger.

First to control your anger, practice accepting and tolerating all kinds of people and behaviors. Next, integrate the "expectancy, vegetative and stabilizing" responses, so they can be expressed as the "soothing" response. You want to practice this response as often as you can to develop the emotional skills of your remo. The stronger you can make your remo with these behaviors, the healthier you will be both emotionally and physically.

Then you change the remo's automatic responses that trigger angry reactions. Recall past irate episodes and employ the "soothing" response, as your remo's initial quick reaction. The more you practice this exercise, the faster you can eliminate anger as something you have to guard against. Spring past situations on your remo, so it can eventually react instinctively with the "soothing" response. Envision possible future troubles that might create a short fuse, and practice the "soothing" response, so the remo can develop more adaptable reactions.

If you are driving in a car, and someone is driving slowly or cuts you off, your first reaction should be the "soothing" response, instead of the futile attempt to control the behaviors of another driver and "lose" it. You may have to rehearse these types of situations using your imagery circuit with the "soothing" response a few times before you are actually on the road.

If someone cuts in line at a queue, you can use the "soothing" response, to correct them with a calm indifference, humor and/or the power of self-control, instead of getting hot under the collar and creating a scene with possible tragic consequences.

If some family member, spouse or relative sets you off, you'll have to decide if you want to control them or control yourself. If you want self-control you will have to rehearse your response to different familial situations in your mind. You want your remo to employ the "soothing" response, as often as possible so your remo can grow and become stronger. As your remo matures you'll be able to handle difficult situation like these with ease.

CONTROLLING HIGH BLOOD PRESSURE

When there is no apparent physical cause such as arteriosclerosis, most scientists believe less than 10% of the cases of hypertension are caused by disease, while emotions seem to be the problem for the rest.

High blood pressure seems to be a result of a rao keeping a tight lid on a "child" remo. So "child" remos often maintain an outer calm that belies the repression of inner turmoil. But a price is paid with this type of controlled repression that can result in damage to the body. For example, to maintain this lid of control, intimate conflicts with an important other dare not be communicated directly. So those with high blood pressure resolve important conflicts with explosions, if they are resolved at all. But your blood pressure can be gradually lowered as you develop the emotional behaviors of the "juvenile and adult-child" stages, and use the "soothing" response to rehearse and resolve stressful situations before hand, using the method referred to in the last section.

MAINTAINING YOUR DIET

If you have problems staying on a diet, the "soothing" response can give you the self-control you desire. The "care" response can produce great desires for food, while the "goal-directed" behaviors can produce great drives to obtain food, regardless of the obstacles. When these emotional states predominate, they create a restless discontent.

To calm this internal uneasiness, there develops a belief by the remo that the pleasure found in eating food is the way to ease these internal tensions. While eating, the sympathetic division kicks in to provide exciting simulation. Then with satiety, the para-sympathetic division provides a kind of relaxed sleepiness to allow an escape momentarily from these internal discomforts of life.

The problem is that food is used inappropriately to quell an internal discontent. But now you will find by employing the "soothing or socializing" response that you can lull that high strung state of irritability into the calm state of equilibrium. When you're out with others employ the "socializing" response, but if your alone use the "soothing" response. Or try them both in different situation to see which is the best for you.

To lose weight you have to able to communicate with your remo at higher levels. You'll have to ask your remo if it really wants to lose weight. You will need your remo's cooperation and even enthusiasm for this project. You want to tell and direct your remo to take care of your body and that you want this to be a high priority. So you'll want to depend on wholesome foods for pleasure, like fruits and raw or cooked vegetables.

The problem is the remo reacts automatically. The remo doesn't think ahead about the consequences concerning daily activities like eating. Although your remo may want to lose weight, when caught up in your daily routine your remo's automatic habits kick in. If you're a little off guard you may find yourself snacking at certain key times of the day.

So the way to maintain a diet is to change your remo's established habits and develop new ones with the emotional controlling behavior of the "soothing or socializing" response. You have to prepare for these periods of weakness ahead of time. You need to think of all the situations that tempt you, and practice the tranquil indifference of the "sleep" response or the "socializing or soothing" responses.

If you tend to snack during TV commercials, then you have to be prepared before hand to counteract your remo automatic actions. You need to picture yourself in this situation and even see yourself reacting to the sight of other people eating during a commercial, then you want to calm your desires by practicing the "soothing" response with a relax nonchalance.

If you're addicted to food this is not going to happen overnight. You need to organize your life around a sensible diet. You have to plan ahead, even for a week if you can. Plan out what time of day and what kind of food you want to eat. Make this a fun project using your "goal-directed" behaviors. Go to the library and investigate vegetarian cookbooks and diet books for ideas on creating a plan.

The big problem with dieting is when you lose fat you also lose muscle. So you need to use your "goal-directed" circuit to plan some daily exercise routine so it can become a habit with your remo. It's better to exercise with others, because it's more fun and it gives you a greater sense of obligation.

You need to find other pleasures in life that can take the place of food. Using your "goal-directed" circuitry of behaviors look into various stimulating hobbies, sports, or social activities you might like. With the development of the "integrative" response you should be enjoying your relationships with others much more. So you may want to become more involved with different social groups.

You might even want to form your own synergetic group of like minded people who can participate in social activities, like snack free parties or get togethers, going to the theater without eating popcorn and candy, vegetarian dining, rock and roll, ballroom or square dancing, etc.

But the next time you get an urge to eat junk food is an excellent time to excite your memory banks by exercising your "stabilizing" response. Instead of eating sweets, start practicing your "soothing" response. You will simply be amazed at how effective it is at maintaining a state of balance equilibrium and self-control. Your daily accomplishments will give you a sense of pride and pleasure from the self-mastery you achieve.

Try it, you'll like it!

CONTROLLING OTHER ADDICTIONS, DRUGS, TOBACCO AND ALCOHOL

Cigarettes are smoked and drugs are consumed for the same reason that food is used, and that is to quell an internal nervousness or irritability. People lose confidence in their ability to deal with all the daily difficulties in a status society. So they depend on whatever can get them through the day. The biggest problem in getting over any addiction whether food, tobacco, alcohol, etc. is not having a supportive group of people around you and a supportive remo within you. Your remo needs to feel a sense of belonging to freely interact with others. You need to strengthen you remo's abilities and behavioral skills, but first you need a nurturing atmosphere. So you primary approach is to target the status value system for attack. You want to adopt synergy values between your rao and your remo, and you want to cultivate friends who are oriented towards pleasure and synergy.

Next, you want to develop your remo's emotional coping skills so you can have more self-control. The method used above to control the food you eat is the same technique you use to control any addiction. Just substitute your drug of choice for the food that is avoided to achieve weight control.

You may be able to defeat your personal addiction without a supportive group, but then you will need to depend mostly on your intimate relationship with your remo. In this case, your success will depend on the efforts of your rao and the desires of your remo.

ATTENTION DEFICIT DISORDER

A hyperactive child has a remo who has been stopped in development either in the child stage with the "goal-directed" circuit dominating or the infant-child stage with the "action" circuit dominating. So to overcome this problem the child has to learn the growth behaviors of the juvenile and adult-child stages. If you have a hyperactive child, and you want to teach the child how to develop these abilities, you first have to create a desire in the child to want to change.

Find the answer to questions like; is the child happy? Or not? Make a list of things the child wants to change, things the child likes and dislikes. Does the child want things to stay the way they are or the way they've been? What are the child's dreams and aspirations? You need this information to motivate the child to develop and practice the emotional coping skills to achieve self-control.

Next explain the differences between the rao and the remo using figure 1 from chapter 1. Spell out how it is the job of the conscious rao to lead, guide and direct the remo. This role has been reversed in hyperactive children. The excess energy of the remo causes the child's rao to be overwhelmed and lose control of the self. The only way possible for the rao to regain the upper hand is for the child's rao to visually and verbally communicate with the remo, for example as an imaginary playmate. To get started play a favorite piece of music and have the child's remo dance to the music in the mind's eye.

The behavior of choice is the "soothing" response. You need to review the section in this chapter on "Overcoming Fear." Assuming you have mastered the "soothing" response, you need to convey the ideas and behaviors to the child, and practice the behaviors together. You need to explain how to control all the excess energy. Ask the child if he would like to use his mind to reduce the energy whenever he wants; and to use his mind to redirect the energy to use it in a positive constructive way.

You should spend as much time together as you can rehearsing the behaviors while imagining different difficult situations that the child has to deal with, at school, in a restaurant, visiting friends, at family gatherings, etc. When you are out with a group of people, the hyperactive child is very vulnerable to feelings of inferiority. So if no one pays attention to the child, he can experience a feeling of rejection or that he doesn't belong. But instead of being overwhelmed with fear, this excessive negative energy is channeled into the motor nervous system and expressed with anger.

And most important, you absolutely cannot use punishment to teach any behavior. You should approach it in a playful way. And approach the learning situation as a cooperative effort, that the two of you are a team working together. Try to have fun and realize you may only be able to convey bits and pieces of the information at a time until the child's rao can regain control.

SEXUAL PROBLEMS

Great or anxious anticipation of the sex act can cause pre-ejaculation or impotence in men and a lack of lubricating readiness or frigidity in women. Now you have a cure for that problem! Using the "soothing" response to calm down the fearful anticipation of sex can make you an effective sex partner.

The negative anticipation that caused so many emotional problems at an earlier stage of growth can now be used in an opposite way to rechannel energy to a positive source and control excitation. Anticipation used in conjunction with the "expectancy, stabilizing and vegetative" responses in the "soothing" response can create an about face to subdue and calm, instead of creating excessive excitement. Thus anticipation can work for you to reduce excitement and maintain a state of equilibrium.

First if you're uptight and can't relax, use the "soothing" response along with a light pleasurable banter to get in a relaxed mood. Now the anticipation of an exciting sexual adventure, can reduce arousal to keep you in a state of relaxed readiness. And when men use the "sleep" response during sex, they can greatly extend the sex act. As they approach an orgasmic state they can initiate the "sleep" response to cool down and prolong their pleasure and their partner's pleasure!

On the other hand, some have just the opposite problem. If you have no problem relaxing, have a low sex drive and would rather get excited about sex, then you need to use the emotional behaviors involved with the sensory system. The primary circuit for sexual activity is the "goal-directed" circuit involved with motor(muscle) movement for both men and women. The secondary source comes from the excitement of the "expectancy" circuit as it is integrated with the "goal-directed" circuit. Then employ both the visual and auditory aspects of the imagery circuit(see Appendix A) with erotic fantasy. Next move into the pleasure pathways of the brain by evoking feelings of love with the "care" circuit. And last the mood elevating aspect of the "stabilizing" response can also be used to increase excitement.

EPILEPSY

Some who suffer from epilepsy will find if they activate the "sleep or soothing" response when they first feel a warning signal, they can prevent an attack. However, much more emphasis should be given to the "stabilizing" response, as this "stabilizing" circuit is the main source of control. However, when out among people the "soothing" response should be used for the most control. But if you're in a quite subdued atmosphere, the "sleep" response may be more effective.

Epileptic seizures appear to originate from the basolateral amygdala,(27) which can create a fight or flight reaction. When this reaction is not possible, it spreads the excess negative energy to stimulate the entire neocortex in waves of excitation that can bring on convulsions. So the ability of the "stabilizing" circuit to inhibit arousal of the basolateral amygdala in the early stages should prove to be a control of epilepsy!

SOCIABILITY

The information in this section was obtained from A.L. Gesell and F.L. Ilg.(40) "The 4 year old is very versatile. What can he not do? He can be quiet, noisy, calm, assertive, cozy, imperious, suggestible, independent, social, athletic, artistic, literal, fanciful, cooperative, indifferent, inquisitive, forthright, prolix, humorous, dogmatic, silly, competitive."

His blithe and lively activity pattern and contrariness is typical of 2-3 years. But this is not a regression; the mental behavioral achievements at the age of 3 serves to stabilize, and he is now functioning at a higher, more adaptive level in all the motor, language and personal-social areas of his behavior.

"If at times she seems some what voluble, dogmatic, boastful and bossy, it is because she is a blithe amateur swinging into fresh fields of self expression."

She prefers a very creative dramatic type of play where her ability to shift rapidly allows her to play her "roles" with a facile ease. Through social dramatic play, she is striving to identify herself with her culture and to assimilate it into her world of behaviors.

She likes to dress up and act like an adult, often with excellent behavioral imitation and acting ability. This is a most effective way of maturing, and shows she is more interested in being socialized into the culture, rather than having a resistance to it.

"The 4 year old is a truly social being. He not only wants to join a play group every morning, but he wants to be with playmates every afternoon."(40)

He is most happy when with one adult. And his endless questioning is not so much a pursuit of knowledge as a social device to practice speech and listening behaviors. He likes to make faces to identify with adults and improve his skills using facial expressions. These are used as mean to understand and incorporate the complexities of his culture.

While three had a conforming mind, four has a fluent lively mind. His high drive combined with a fluid mental organization provides the key to understand the four year old. His mental effervescence and fluid flights of fancy make it possible for him to dramatize any experience, besides making him a good fabricator of alibis.

Her mental agility provides a diffuse ability to use words with an abandoned ease. She is excessive in her speech. She may exhaust every verbal possibility while running a topic into the ground. She is a great talker who is believable, because her burgeoning language often camouflages her lack of knowledge. A kind of dramatic poet, she enjoys learning new and different words, especially for their humorous affect. Verbal and physical exaggerations amuse her, as her showing-off on the trapezes is performed with flying commentary.

Another key to understanding the four year old is his high energy drive associated with his extremely mobile mental organization. While three was agreeable and compliant, four on the other hand is assertive and expansive. He surges ahead with both muscles and mind. "He tells tall tales; he brags; he tattles; he threatens; he alibis; he calls names." He is proud of his creations and achievements and praises himself by a boastfulness that reaches its highest level. He resists confinement around the home and is trying out his new found powers. "It is the four year old who runs away from home."

Relatively self-sufficient, she enjoys her times alone, which can be a very creative period. With more self-control, she can do two things at one time and no longer has to stop midway in what she is doing when she begins to talk.

He may be jealous of his mother and father together. He expresses strong affection at bedtime and falls asleep rather quickly. He can take a preparatory nap to stay up late in the evening in contrast to the two - three year old who will become so excited that he will be unable to sleep. He wakes up in a happy mood, greets his parents with conversation instead of the romping abandon of a year ago. And his imaginary companion takes part in his dramatic social play that is closer to the realms of likelihood.

INTEGRATIVE CIRCUIT

The habenula nucleus and its many tracts form the "integrative" circuit. The habenula brings together the past eleven periods of circuit development. (See Fig. 10)

One of the habenula's tracts, referred to as the stria medullaris, connects the same nuclei as the medial fore-brain bundle (MFB) of the "goal-directed" circuit, including the interconnections between many of the hypothalamic nuclei, although the MFB by-passes the habenula.(106)

The stria medullaris is the major input system of the habenula complex. Since the MFB connects the same nuclei as the stria medullaris, then it would follow that "goal-directed activity is the key behavior to innervate the habenula.

Some of the other habenula tracts hook up the "synchronal" area, the midline and dorsomedial thalamus to the prefrontal lobe, the hippocampal area, the amygdala complex, the mammillary bodies, the anterior thalamus, the interpeduncular nucleus with the cingulate, and the limbric midbrain areas.(42 & 82)

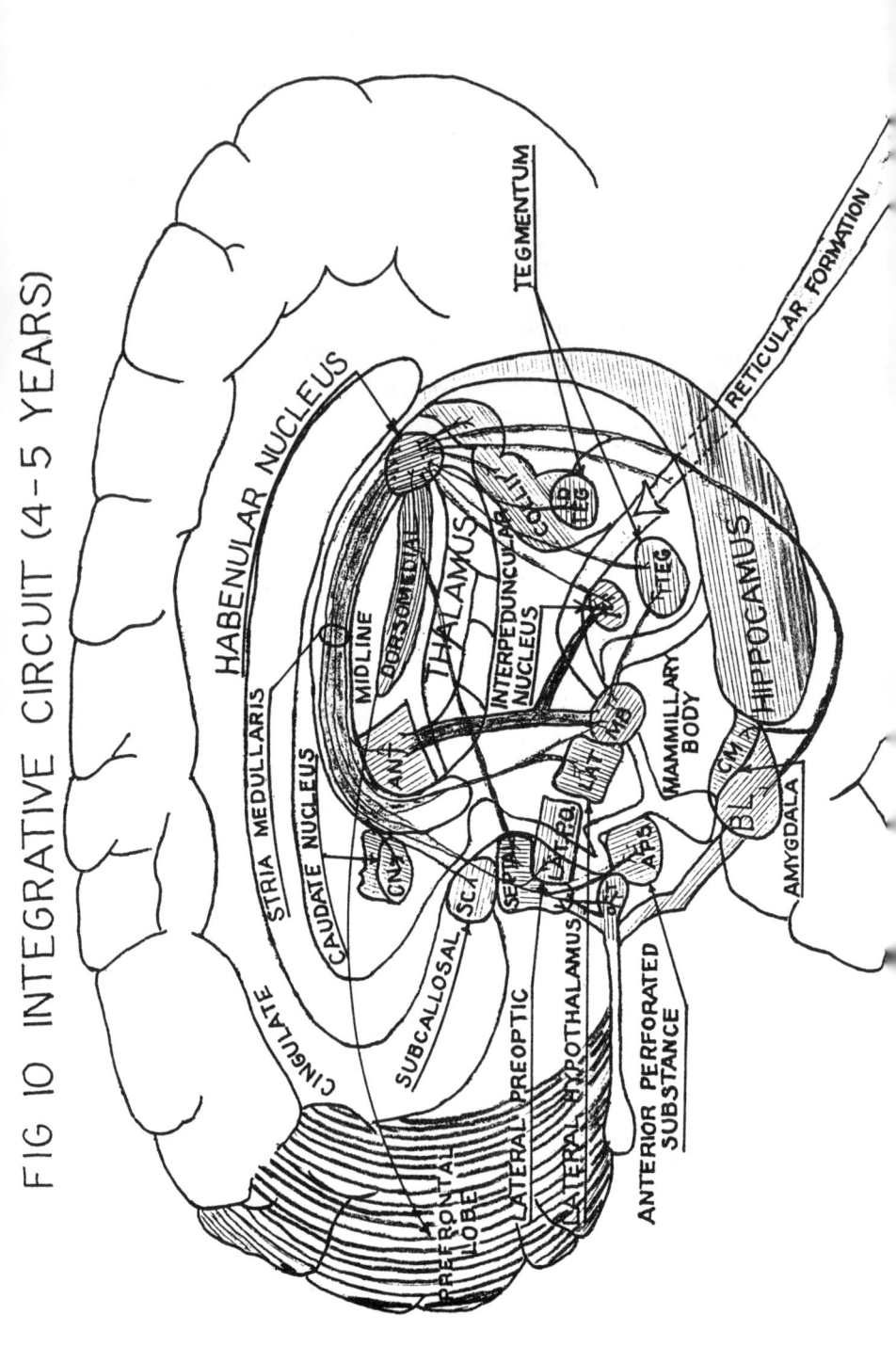

FIG 10 INTEGRATIVE CIRCUIT (4-5 YEARS)

CHAPTER 39

RELATIONSHIPS

The "integrative" response gives you all the emotional tools to develop good social skills. So you will find your relationships with others will be more enjoyable and fun. And it will be filled with pleasure when you can set up your acting stage with a synergetic backdrop. Your drama of life should have a synergetic scripts with plays of comedy. On the other hand, if you want to dominate and control, then play your status script with its pathos and tragedies in the theater of cruelty.

A belief in the values of a status system produces almost all of the unhappiness found in relationships. This is true for the relationships between relatives, workers, friend, lovers, etc. Thus, the degree that a marriage is unhappy and troubled is the degree that the relationship is oriented towards status rather than synergy. When the relationship of the parent toward the child is oriented toward control, obedience and discipline using punishment, then the unhappiness, misery and abuse are often evident, although many other problems are created that are not so obvious.

Status puts people on unequal levels, so that they can feel inferior, isolated, or alienated even when they are physically together. The lack of a term that identifies synergy is an important reason for status being so dominant. A term like synergy allows you to grab hold of the concepts of this social system, so you can more effectively discern whether status of synergy is operating in relationships.

The Japanese male may be the "lord and master" of his household, but he still would rather spend time at work rather than with his family, because he doesn't understand the difference between the synergy operating at the workplace and the status operating within the family unit.

This is no utopian concept, but rather something you are involved with everyday, as you constantly move back and forth between status and synergy without any awareness or control of what's really going on.

COMPLIMENTS

Your relationships with people become very important in a synergistic setting because they are not only a source of support and acceptance, but also pleasure. To look for the good points in the person you are relating with is a synergistic value. Even nonverbal compliments will develop a positive regard for yourself and those around you.

This is not only a conscious effort but also a feeling of pleasure and contentment with yourself and others. You don't have to verbally express or pay compliments in words unless you enjoy doing that, but rather, it is the pleasurable approach and positive way you look at people and yourself that is important. The rao is usually not aware of the ability of the remo to intuitively pickup nonverbal compliments and criticisms from others.

People tend to be naturally good. They will even talk to plants and wish them well to encourage good growth. Yet it is extremely difficult for them to convey such good feelings to others because of the status values that put them at odds with each other, and places them on unequal levels.

Under synergy the more you support and encourage those around you, the more you create an environment that can improve your quality of life. When you look for the good points in your self and others, you are combating a status hierarchy in a very effective way. In contrast, when you look for bad points in the self and others, you are promoting the status system.

EXPLOITATION

In a status system relationships with people are not that important. Contentions or conflicts can arise even over trivial matters; being right and in the know can elevate status, while trying to save face for being mistaken can lower feelings of status. Winning an argument or proving a point can often be more important than a relationship. There even develops a desire to not only make others agree, but to make them think the same way. Thus, the need to control others can generalize into a desire to control the mind and thoughts of another.

The need for respect and repute is usually acquired via a rise up the status ladder. Thus, there develops a need to be "in" with those near the top of the acceptance chain. Greener pastures can create a restlessness or dissatisfaction with a relationship. So as a status seeker envisions prospects of an improved position within the social hierarchy operating, then a relationship with those on lower levels can create conflicts of desire.

For example, if an opportunity presents itself to be part of the "in crowd," then relations with a friend may be considered a liability or a time consuming impediment to this advancement in social ranking. There may be a choice to be made as to what's more important, a friend or a gain in social position. For the status seeker the friend usually comes in last.

COMPETITION

The competitive struggle under status pits man against man, so that they have to strive for positions that put them on unequal terms with each other. What helps one is at the expense of another. This competition for status is a competition for acceptance, usually perceived as being respected and admired. There often is a competition to court the friendship and curry favor of those felt to be the most important in the social hierarchy operating within a group, whether in a business, in the community, etc.

Social games people play on each other are devised for advancement in a social hierarchy. Games are played in order to win over another perceived to be of good social standing. This can be analogous to winning a victorious prize. Gamesmanship is used to "hustle" and captivate another in order to gain a friend, like a trophy.

With other competitive games for social status, compliments are used as "come ons" to make another feel obligations, or to get the upper hand. Here, relationships can take a back seat, and are exploited for whatever advantages can be gained. These games are based on the concept that superior qualities and abilities can be used as personal advantages over others.

The number one argument used to justify a belief in the harmful practice of the status system is the dire need for competition. Status believers say, "We need competition to motivate people to be productive and to strive to improve themselves!" There is no argument the status system does have a strong need for competition. However, this is because it has such few sources of motivation. And the hostilities a status environment creates need competitiveness as a channel for the release of aggression.

People are driven into this rivalry with each other by the status system; we must get the best of others, or better yet, destroy them.

We are driven into rivalry not because we are evil or because we are selfish but because the status system operates that way.

In Kohn's book, "No Contest: The Case Against Competition," on debunking the myth about competition building character, more than 400 studies were analyzed. Kohn concluded, "Regardless of our definition of character, research suggests that competition is more likely to be detrimental than constructive. Indeed, competition is to self esteem, as sugar is to teeth." (57)

There is not much faith in the power of pleasure as a motivating force under the status system. When competition dominates over pleasure as the main source of motivation, what often results will be a disappointing and low quality product.

Competition in the workplace has been shown to be hogwash by W. Edwards Deming's method of Quality Control, used in Japanese businesses. Here the cooperation of his system by far outstrips the strife found in the competitive status oriented workplace of the U.S.

Another low quality product that competitive motivation produces can be found in most public educational systems. High schools have such strong social hierarchies operating that it has often been said that the only students who are happy are the "captain of the football team and the head cheerleader." The lack of self-esteem that status hierarchies generates, creates not only personal hurt but also interferes with learning.

However, under synergy, motivation is not a problem. Once you have the security that a feeling of belonging and a supportive acceptance provides, the pleasures found in goal-directed activities create an over abundance of incentives and motivation.

DOING YOUR OWN THING

A status society needs many inhibitory controls to limit people from doing what they want. The suppressive control from authority and conformity is needed, because of the animosity a status environment creates between people. Many have a desire to make others suffer, while many more are indifferent to that possibility.

In addition, people are discouraged from doing what they want because of a status society's need for conformity. To pursue the personal pleasure of doing what you want is often considered selfish. But selfishness is primarily a function of the social status system.

Under synergy people are not so alienated from each other. With a greater sense of belonging and trust in their acceptance they do not have to worry about other people emotionally hurting them or bringing them down. Then selfishness would lose much of its significance, because what is good for the individual is good for the group, and anything the individual desires and does would be for the good for others. This creates a concern and thoughtfulness for others. And a thoughtfulness for others often provides a great amount of freedom for people to do what they want to do.

CHAPTER 40

POSSESSIONS
AND OBJECTS

POSSESSIONS

Both synergy and the social status system create a care and responsibility for the self. But under the status system most people have no desire to see beyond the self. They operate on a lower energy and mental levels that pulls back from sharing the self, territory or material possessions.

The status system creates a simple dichotomy where things are viewed as being either yours or mine. And a competitive belief prevails that whatever is out there is up for grabs with the simple notion that whoever gets there first, with the most influential and aggressive demands, or claims of strength, e.g. money, personality, class, power, privilege, etc., gets to acquire these goods for their personal benefit. This can create an artificial condition of scarcity, because of the waste that is created by the hoarding of materials. This is especially seen in the third world countries.

However, a group of people who believe in the ideas of synergy can operate on a broader integrative level and with higher mental and physical energy levels. Although the desire for personal gain still operates under synergy, the individual can now function on a more expansive level. Now what one does for the self, is also done for others. And what others do for their selves, they also do for the individual.

Instead of the objects in the environment being limited and made scarce by wasteful accumulation, they are made more available by sharing with others. It isn't a matter of giving up anything. The gains are not only material but psychological. This is because sharing can create mutual feelings of trust and cooperativeness. The atmosphere of belonging and support that synergy creates can alleviate both the insecurity and the possessiveness of a selfish nature.

To people who believe in status values this idea of sharing is so far removed from their realm of possibilities that the concept could just as well be from Mars.

GUARDING SKILLS

In a status society worthiness and acceptance is often determined by the skills you "possess." So what you do for a living can determine not only your acceptance but your personal esteem and worthiness as a human.

Skills become secretly guarded for the good of the individual, at the expense of others, instead of benefiting others. Skills and trades are kept within a family or are taught to a privileged few. Lawyers write the laws in unintelligible language, so only they can know what the law is about. And knowledge is power, so important information is kept secret under status. Secrecy then justifies rights and privileges that develops a legitimate relationship with authority.

OWNING PEOPLE

Possessiveness, also has a detrimental effect on the relationships between people. In a status system people become objects that have to be dealt with and handled properly. When people are objects of desire, they become a good catch, or they are like a prize to covet and own. Once possessed the picture changes as they are treated like possessions, as an object. Especially when this ownership can be made legal, as with a marriage license or birth certificate.

A mastery of the object, namely, a control of another, is very important. This attitude can result in indifference, contempt and degradation. Practically anything may be done without much thought. Even harmful abuse may be inflicted and justified without much concern to keep the object of concern under control.

OBJECTS

When you are confident and happy, others will accept and include you, but when you have personal problems or doubts, you can feel isolated and alone in a social status system. To find some comfort and solace, people often turn to pets to assuage the remo's need for emotional acceptance. And many others may turn to material objects for involvement and emotional pleasure. But the problem with this is, their personal worth and esteem may eventually become bound up and equated with material acquisition.

Possessions often form an important security tie with the world. An emotional involvement and time is invested in inanimate objects that cannot give anything back in return that is emotionally substantial. The pleasure things give at first can easily change into the uncertainty and fear that someone may steal or damage their prize possessions. Or things can become so important that it's hard to let go of anything, as they are transform into a hoarding "pack rat" accumulator. Thus, possessions may substitute for a lack of real emotional involvement with people, but these material riches can ironically create even more insecurity.

The stronger the belief in status values, the more that possessiveness develops into hoarding, stinginess or greed. Suspicion and fear that others would like to take their things away, can alienate people further. And the chasm is widened, as desire, jealousy and envy create resentment of material success. So the very object that could be shared to give the self and others pleasure and enjoyment now gives one person an inner emptiness, and gives others an uneasy desire and resentment.

The object that could be a source of happiness can be instead a source of conflict and misery. Some would as soon die as give up their belongings. Suicides have been committed after the destitution of financial loss. Some losses can create health or heart problems, or crippling emotional traumas, comparable to losing a limb.

These conditions come about because people have worked all their lives, placing all their faith in material possessions for their salvation and acceptance in the world. When acceptance is equated with success, and success is measured by material wealth, a Pyrrhic victory can be achieved that leaves an emptiness inside, and an alienation from others, which is probably acceptable to them as long as they can feel they are better than other.

CHAPTER 41

IN CONCLUSION
YOU NEED TO
ACCENTUATE THE
POSITIVE AND
ELIMINATE THE NEGATIVE

As you move to the extremes of a status hierarchical system, you will find fascism/Nazism, McCathyism, perversions, gangs, skin heads, KKK, etc. All of these grim realities are caused by one thing and one thing only, and that is a status hierarchical system. What Pandora found when curiosity made her open a box that let out all the human miseries and ills into the world was an authoritarian force that besieged humankind with a social status hierarchical system.

Rid yourself of as many authoritarian status values as you can, such as trying to control another; using punishment to bring about obedience and discipline; being intolerant or being critical because of another's race, religion, sexual orientation, laziness, mental illness, obesity, coarseness, ill manners, cowardliness, or other differences, such as being strange, weird, odd, creepy, crazy, freaky, outlandish, etc.

Status values undermine the support and acceptance people need for each other. They produce a sense of alienation that can result in a climate of fear and isolation. When there is no sense of belonging, a feeling of emptiness is created. These status attitudes can make life cheap. And they lower the quality of life to such an extent, making people feel so helpless or worthless, that many believe life isn't worth living, and strike out at others or back at the self.

Status may or may not be eliminated from personal relationships but to the degree that it can will be the degree that a more healthy environment is created on physical, mental and emotional levels. And this is the degree that cooperative, harmonious relationships can be established between people.

Just as there is a clash between status and synergy in the external world that permits you a choice on how you want to relate with others, the same battle goes on internally to allow a choice as to how to feel about yourself. Synergy requires both a supportive acceptance of the self, and a belief in pleasure, instead of punishment, as a motivating system. You want to try to adopt this cooperative system to enhance the quality of your life.

The biggest obstacle to controlling the harmful and violent behaviors in our society has been the inability to discriminate between status and synergy, which operate jointly and in competition with each other. As long as there is a lack of knowledge to tell when status or synergy is in operation, then status will dominate and win out over synergy, but only because of the ability of displeasure and pain to dominate pleasure.

However, once people learn to discern the cues and signals in behaviors that distinguish status and synergy, then status can no longer maintain its dominance, because then you can "fight fire with fire." You can fight displeasure with displeasure, attack pain with pain, become critical of criticism, and disapprove of disapproval. When you reserve and restrict these punishing tactics to real harmful behaviors, instead of harmless behaviors, you strengthen the effectiveness of punishment to control emotional and physical damage.

Once you start to discriminate between the two social systems, then status cannot dominate, because synergy will naturally unite people to support and protect each other. Then status aggression by a few can never break that type of strength and solidarity.

Status thrives on a state of confusion that it creates among people. A lack of conviction exist in most people, because they don't understand what's operating socially, externally or internally. Thus, in a debate between two authoritarian experts on opposite sides of an issue, the opinion of the people listening can vacillate back and forth like the heads of tennis fans watching a tennis match. They can be convinced of one point of view one minute and swayed to the opposite point of view the next. Never mind that one or both of the official experts may have the personal integrity of a snake. Those who hold power in a status system depend upon this state of confusion and lack of conviction, so they can sway or bamboozle people to support their agenda.

On the other hand, once there is an understanding of the two social systems that are constantly in competition with each other, then a confidence in personal convictions can develop that can put an end to a state of confusion that many find themselves in.

The belief in giving support and acceptance to all people is the essence of synergy, while the status system, which believes in the individual pulling himself up by his own boot straps, produces a society where each man is out for himself. Even with primitive man status demonstrated it was not the most effective system, as Ruth Benedict and others have shown.(74 & 114)

This is because the human brain makes status obsolete in terms of evolution. Animals need this principle of power makes right, because they do not have the mental development that would give them the choice of another option. We have taken the animal's system of primitive organization, and tried to develop it, and make it more sophisticated with laws, conformity and authoritarian concepts.

Now the historical situation has changed. A small number of men in a number of different countries can potentially destroy the world. The odds of status producing a sociopathic leader is unpleasantly greater than you could ever imagine; we've already had Stalin, Hitler, Chairman Mao Zedong, Pol Pot, Saddam Hussein, etc. in this century. In addition, as long as nations are oriented towards status, they are going to fight, because that is the natural inclination of a system where each thinks they are superior to the other.

A nation is status oriented to the degree that it is patriotic. Patriotism implies "WE" are superior, and other cultures are inferior. And when other nations have the same patriotic fervor, then you have an unstable condition, especially when communications and understanding are minimal.

The relationships between nations is similar to the relationships between two communities, two people or between the rao and remo. The greater the equality and communication, the more that harmony and cooperation will exist. So when other nations exhibit patriotic fervor, the superior feelings created among the people can mislead them to think people in other cultures are insignificant, even animal-like beings or objects that can easily be defeated. In addition, using patriotism is an easy way for an egotistical, macho, psychopathic leader, crazy for more and more power and territory, to rally people into a state of passion to back his demands.

Furthermore, this patriotic nationalism, augmented by the social sickness that status hierarchies create, makes the possibility of men destroying themselves a plausible consideration. And in the relationships between nations there is almost no controlling mechanism to ensure peace among them, except for the weak and ineffective United Nations Organization.

Only if we can get along with each other and work together, by being supportive and accepting of other people, will the conditions be created that will permit our survival. Adopting synergy and discouraging status is the only way this can come about. Continuing to employ status principles will be to our own demise. Thus, it is time we move out of the emotional dark ages and move into an era of emotional responsibility.

CHAPTER 42

CEREBRATION

CREATIVENESS

The creativeness and problem solving ability of the remo is the source of originality for most great works and achievements. Any great master, sage or genius would have to establish an exchange of creative ideas with the remo in some fashion.

The musicians Saint-Saens, Schumann, d'Indy and Mozart, and the writers Robert Louis Stevenson, Edgar Allan Poe, Voltaire, Dante, Tolstoy, etc., claim their achievements came from their dreams. A majority of mathematicians sampled in a study reported that they solved problems in their dreams.(59)

Dreams allow emotional problems to be combined with past experiences, then manipulated with various symbols. Thus, the rao may be symbolized as a driver, the remo as the car in a dream. These symbols are used for emotional expression to search for solutions.(34) As the remo worries with a dream about some conflict he searches the memory banks for other similar successful situations that can apply to resolve the problem.(43) Dreams have often been found to concentrate on a single conflict with the important elements reappearing as variations on the central theme, like a musical symphony.(24 & 85)

Your rational rao cannot begin to approach your remo's creative ability of simultaneously combining many different parts into new ideas. If you have a problem to solve, set up the circumstances of the situation, then give it over to your remo to solve over night. Your remo really enjoys being involved and contributing to the solution of problems. Positive recognition of your remo is appreciated, even when it's only showing an awareness of feelings. Your remo likes this attention, because you are embracing your remo, allowing it to be actively involved with you in your life.

MENTATIONS

When there is a problem to be solved, you want to solicit your remo's responses and viewpoint to discuss the pros and cons. If there is an internal problem or a conflict and your remo's desires don't agree with what you want to do, then a compromise should be mutually agreed upon.

You need to become aware of the reflective way your remo thinks. The remo does not think with logic or reasoning. You can observe your remo's thinking process by paying attention to your dreams and fantasies. During a dream the remo's meandering thinking process and muses is revealed without any influence from you. Some may have very fragmented dreams, while others may have well-integrated ones that tell a complete story, depending on the degree the status system has impaired the remo's development.

When you daydream, your remo's feelings and thoughts become conscious and drift in and out. After a little experience interacting with your remo, you will be able to distinguish when your ideas are originating in the feeling thoughts and flashes of insight of your remo's mind.

You will especially notice when you are tired, ill or exhausted, that your rao's intellectual influence is considerably weakened, so that the strength of your remo's "sentiments" will tend to predominate. That's why big men can become big babies or more child-like, depending on the maturity of their remo, when they have a bad case of the flu. Whether you become apprehensive, lethargic, abusive, fearful, superstitious, or remain the same will depend on the maturity and the nature of your remo.

AMELIORATION

If your remo has bad dreams and nightmares, you can teach it how to handle these night time problems. In a dream your remo is completely alone, and does not have the help and assistance of your rao, as your remo does in waking life. So your rao may have to show your remo how to fight back against the day's adverse incidents which your remo relives during a night time dream.

This is especially good for those who are afraid of a possible stroke or heart attack, or who suffer from hypertension. Most heart attacks occur during the heavy dreaming period in the early morning hours of sleep. It is at this time when daily stress or stress from the past can be re-experienced in dreams. Reliving these experiences can be overpowering, because the remo is alone without the protection of the rao's guidance and reasoning ability. Some are afraid to go to sleep at night, because of this.

You will need to discuss the things that happen in dreams that threaten your remo and resolve them in some manner. You should then practice the "stabilizing & integrative" responses using imagery, so your remo can use these behaviors as a reactive defense to these threats. You need to recall past disturbing events that you were unable to handle and practice the appropriate behavior you've learned from the emotional growth periods. You especially want to do this just before going to bed. And you should repeat the scenario with different circumstance and different people until your remo can response instantly with the proper behavioral defense.

Other techniques have been developed in a study of the Malaya Senoi by Stewart.(114) Since some fears are unfounded or imagined by your remo, you can combat them by using the same imaginary source that can cause the fears, "fighting fire with fire." For example, even an old lady walking down a dark alley can be Superwoman in her mind, and be able to conquer anything around the next corner, instead of being scared to death. This way, your remo is using fantasy to overcome threats by personifying them into something concrete that can be physically defeated within your mind.

CONFLICTS AND RESOLUTIONS

Some people may have a remo emotionally bound to some kind of authority, like a parent, cult or religion, so that the remo does not belong to the rao, but is guided and controlled by some other authority. That is, the ideas and beliefs of the rao do not count, if they are in conflict with the beliefs of this "superior" authority.

This disrupts the support the remo and the rao have for each other. Instead of the rao guiding with reason, this authority figure governs the remo, and therefore the rao. Usually no problems are created as long as the rao goes along, or agrees with this guidance for one's life. The trouble starts when the rao wants independence, and decides to break these established ties.

In a similar vein, sexual hang-ups may have developed, which you may want to overcome. Sexual hang-ups exist because of parents who instill a belief that sex is bad and dirty. Since the rao eventually finds out differently, then a conflict arises between the beliefs the remo was instilled with as a child and the rao's belief in the present reality. However, you can possibly overcome many sexual problems by communicating and resolving your sexual conflict with your remo.

Whether you have to pry your remo away from your parents or some religious cult to convert your remo to a belief that creates harmony, remember that your success depends on the efforts of the rao.

EXPERIMENTATION

You may want to experiment with many different types of relationships to find out what your remo enjoys, and what bothers or upsets your remo. Part of the pleasurable interactions you may like to encourage in your relationship with your remo could be a good-natured, light banter. Your rao and your remo can kid each other, or tease each other, in fun, for mistakes and blunders. The way you relate with others you care about will tend to be similar to your relationship with your remo.

The differences between the rao and the remo can make for very enjoyable company. The remo can come up with really enjoyable ways of imagining and expressing an idea, while the logical revelations of the rao can also be quite inspiring to the remo.

If an intimate relationship develops between the rao and the remo, then you will find that your moments alone with your remo can be quite rewarding. The remo can really surprise you with a naivete and gems that are precious and amusing.

However, any type of performance of a social nature requires the rao and remo to be united with a singleness of purpose. There is no way you can ever lose this unity, because we are biologically constructed to handle important situations by bringing all systems together for an effective performance. All concern is directed to the outer reality, ignoring the internal state of affairs. This temporarily eliminates internal conflicts by repressing or denying undesirable impulses, thoughts and feelings, so that one's actions can be most effective.

Therefore, you want to enjoy your inner relationship, at times when you are alone and have privacy, as a way to sustain, revitalize and rejuvenate yourself. When you are in the company of others, you have a need for the pleasure that only social stimulation and other people can give you.

SOBRIQUET

You need a nickname for your remo. You may want your remo to choose a nickname. However, you should be wary of adopting someone else's name because your remo admires him and desires to become like him. In order to develop yourself, the first step is to accept yourself, as you are, with all your faults. Choosing someone else as a model, by adopting his name does not encourage that attitude.

If you can't find a name that is suitable, there is a list of possible names (Appendix B) that you can use, to give you ideas for a name. However, the name you decide on doesn't necessarily have to be a permanent one. As you gradually evolve and develop your remo's emotional maturity by practicing the emotional growth behaviors, or as your remo expresses new attitudes, you can always adopt another nickname.

AFFINITY

You should allow yourself a period of time for some private seclusion, so that you can feel out and learn the remo's likes and dislikes. Developing your relationship is a learning situation, which calls for tolerance and self-acceptance. Your main objective is to love and enjoy yourself, and have fun with your "mate." The best thing you can do for yourself is to interact with your "mate," at least once a day. You can say, "Hi!" When you wake up in the morning, or say "Sweet dreams" when you go to bed at night.

Your remo needs "tender, loving care." Some may discover that feelings and expressions of care for each other, expressed, perhaps, with playful teasing, can make life more exciting, interesting, and relieve some of the tedium of everyday routine.

Finally, some may like the following vow that can reassure your closeness with your remo from the song "Morning Star/ Evening Star."

So I hereby
take myself
my soul doth take my heart
to honor love and cherish
till death do us part

I will, I will
accept myself
with hope and wonder
and I what I have joined together
let no one put asunder
- the end -

BEHAVIORS TO PRACTICE TO DEVELOP YOUR REMO'S MATURITY

This section is an abridged capsule review of the emotional behaviors needed to develop your remo's emotional maturity and social coping skills.

VEGETATIVE RESPONSE

The "vegetative" responses run on a continuum from a state of relaxation to a deep sleep. Generally, the "vegetative" response influences oral activity around the region of the mouth, so that the lips, tongue and jaws take on a loose slack appearance. When your lips relax, they protrude, thicken and hang loose so the lower teeth are exposed. The jaw slackens, drops and relaxes, permitting the corners of the mouth to come closer together. The tongue thickens, enlarges, and may even protrude slightly in some.

The eyes lose their sparkle and take on a dull untempered quality. Your breathing should become deep and rhythmical. If tense and stressed out, you want to transfer this negative energy and tension to the diaphragm located in the bread basket of your stomach. You should flare your nostrils as you contract your midriff, so that you inhale and exhale in deep forceful rhythmic breaths through your nose only. And you want to sniff the air by drawing the air past the deep back part of your throat with a force that pushes the air into the sinus cavities to activate the olfactory brain region. If your teeth are clenched you want to transfer that excess tension to a positive useful source in your diaphagm so you can breathe deeply.

Anxiety is often experienced with a choking sensation when tension is felt in the back of the throat, caused by contractions of the tongue muscles. Tight tongue muscles can be relaxed by gently letting the tongue protrude slightly, e.g. by wetting the lips with the tongue. You can also try alternately contracting the tongue muscles by making it as small as possible, and relaxing the tongue by making it as large as possible.

A gentle suckling motion, e.g., as when you kiss, will also help to relax the tongue muscles. Just as an infant sucks on a pacifier, you can create the same sucking sensation by enlarging the tongue so it fills the mouth. The suckling behavior also causes you to breathe in deeply and slowly to help you restore a slow relaxing rhythm. Keep your lips gently pressed together, while your upper and lower jaws are apart and relaxed, to create a suction on an enlarged tongue.

The energy of the "vegetative" response may be experienced best when you are extremely sleepy or tired, and when awaking in the early morning before your sleep is out. The heaviness of the "vegetative" response has what may be described as a "buzz" or "rumbling" feeling that can overcome you.

"Vegetative" responses can synchronize beta waves to control over reactions or unwanted excitation. It synchronizes cellular firing to create a sense of well-being and generate a relaxed casual feeling of self-contentment.

To re-establish your alpha rhythms, you should start out by taking a deep breath which is relaxing. Just hold it a couple of seconds and then let it all out. If you are really nervous, breathe out as if you are gently blowing out candles on a birthday cake. Relax by creating or imagining the heavy feeling you experience when arising from sleep.

You should try to practice this response as often as you can. Think ahead of all the possible difficult, stressful and tense social situations in which you might find yourself. Then practice this response to that situation in your imagination, so you can better establish this response when you find yourself in a real stressful situation.

DRY MOUTH

Stress also tends to produce a dry mouth. The stress you experience when interviewing for a job, when you have an important date with the opposite sex or with business people and when you have to speak before others can all cause the embarrassing condition of a dry mouth that interferes with your effectiveness.

However, you can overcome this speaking difficulty by activating the "synchronal" circuit, which can be very effective at producing copious amounts of salivary juices. The gentle suctioning action within your mouth is effective at making your mouth water. Although your mouth is closed you want your teeth to be apart and your lower jaw to be as relaxed as possible. You want to take deep rhythmic breaths drawing air past flared nostrils so that you can feel the air silently rush past the deep back part of your throat.

SNORING

Stressful social situations that occur during the day cause some to react with an inhibited tension that can suspend breathing momentarily or at least cause swallow breathing. As long as the rao is awake, the intake of air will be sufficient to sustain the individual. But when sleeping at night the remo's bad habit of inhibited emotional responses to social stress during the day are relived during dreams to create the threatening condition of apnea which causes snoring.

To stop snoring you need to practice the following exercise using the "vegetative" response with your imagination. You need to recall stressful situations, and react by transferring tension within the body to the diaphragm in order to take deep rhythmical breaths. If you have a wristwatch that chimes on the hour, you should use that as a signal to flare out your nostrils while taking deep breaths. You want to transfer the negative tension in your jaw, neck and shoulder muscles to be used as a positive source in your stomach and diaphragm muscles to breathe deeply.

By rehearsing this response to stress throughout the day, you'll find when you are actually in such a situation that you have the ability to breathe and relax. By continuing to practice this response after a month or so, your remo will have "locked-in" this response as an automatic behavior, which then can be transferred to the remo's nightly dreams about daily activities.

T M J

Those people who suffer with TMJ, often grind their teeth at night. The reason for this is that they have learned to clench their teeth during the day in response to stress. They should begin now to transfer that tension from their clamped jaw to the diaphragm in the pit of the stomach, while relaxing the oral region of the mouth with the "vegetative" response. The lips should pucker and protrude slightly while the jaw drops and loosens.

MORNING FATIGUE

Awakening tired and fatigued in the morning stems from the same bad habits of restrained breathing when reacting to stress through the day, instead of using your natural emotional abilities of breathing naturally while relaxing the mouth region. Review past situations that bothers you, and while using imagery, practice transferring the negative tension to your diaphragm muscles so you can breathe effectively.

Whether you snore, have TMJ or wake up tired, it's very important that you practice the breathing exercise of the "vegetative" response for approximately 5 minutes upon retiring. And you want to give instructions to your remo to continue employing those breathing techniques of transferring tension to the diaphragm while you sleep.

APPROACH RESPONSE

The "approach" response provides pleasure and a positive outlook on life, as an important defense to fight stress. The "approach" circuit is a behavior that orients you towards pleasure. To increase the quality of your life, your communications with your remo should be filled with fun and enjoyment. For example, in your mind's eye you can create an image of your remo and an image of your rao, so that your rao's image can smile and wink at your remo's image. In the same way you elicit pleasure and fun from a young tot, you can also elicit pleasure from your own remo.

When you give your remo a hug, or a wink and a grin, you are giving your remo some pleasure, and saying, "Hey! Things are not all that bad." This orientation towards pleasure helps to shift out of the displeasurable circuits in the brain into the pleasurable pathways. This can help you negate the negative apprehensions in life so you can develop a more constructive, positive approach. If you practice this attitude several times a day, your remo will soon start showing this positive attitude on its own.

The para-sympathetic division was activated when you relaxed your lips. Now you want to excite the sympathetic division by drawing your lips up thin so the upper and lower teeth are exposed in a smile. When you smile you redirect negative energy to the pleasure areas of the brain.

When out shopping you should have fun with the clerk; they enjoy the fun and humor of being kidded. Young kids you come in contact with casually are usually a kick, and up for a little fun. When driving you should let your remo dance to your favorite music in your mind's eye.

EXPECTANCY RESPONSE

The "expectancy" response is a circuit of the sensory nervous system and can be witnessed in an "orienting reflex" of a house cat when it directs all its senses and concentration towards some sound. The anticipation of the "expectancy" response provides a state of readiness.

In a state of low arousal, stimulation of sensory cells was found to create excessive excitation that was overwhelming. This was because a lack of awareness created a state that was unable to handle the stimulation. While in a keen state of awareness and attention, this same stimulation could be handled in stride with little noticeable excitatory effect.(70)

Being observant and paying attention to the details in the environment makes use of your energy of anticipation in an effective way. When you fail to use your natural abilities and behaviors by withdrawing or being too laid back, you have an excess of energy available that has no where to go except into the displeasurable circuits of the brain. So if you can't fight! Or flee! The energy can quickly flow into the anxiety and fear circuits of the brain.

When you don't make proper use of your anticipatory ability, the excess energy over stimulates you, while in a state of mind that cannot effectively handle it. And that's when displeasures such as irritability, agitation, anxiety and fear can result. The excess energy that creates excitation doesn't have to be displeasurable, it just has to be controlled and redirected into pleasurable channels by you.

But being laid back or retiring can be very maladaptive. The anticipation of the "expectancy" response, with attention and awareness of your surrounding, is an emotional behavior that can use energy in an adaptive way. If you're uptight about entering a new situation, and you try to be "cool" by being ultra relaxed and indifferent, then the lack of awareness, the lack of anticipation, inattentiveness or withdrawal from the environment will actually backfire on you. Thus playing the role of a wallflower because you're apprehensive and you want to blend into the surroundings and be unnoticed can cause you to become inhibited, shy and easily startled, to create agitation, anxiety and fear.

When under new or stressful social circumstances, the "expectancy" response allows you to be on the attack in a more assertive role. You want to open your eyes wide to be alert to details, you want to sniff the air, listen for sounds, etc. You want to use as many of your senses as you can. The alert readiness of the "expectancy" response that allows you to be more aware of your surroundings, should be used with an orientation towards pleasure. A state of pleasure can handle stress and excess energy with much greater ease.

ATTENTION TO DETAILS

The "expectancy" response can also strengthen the characteristic or trait known as an "attention to details." If this is a weak point you need to strengthen for your place of employment, studying for a test or just in your daily life, then you especially need to practice this behavior throughout the day. You need to practice and strengthen this behavior whether with people or when alone studying or doing your work on the job. This behavior is an aspect of the sensory nervous system where you take things in with your senses. You want to pay attention to the little things you see, hear and smell. And the more you can anticipate these details of life the more they will make an indelible impression on your senses.

CARE RESPONSE

The "care" response integrates the behaviors of the sensory nervous system and the autonomic nervous system. It ties together all the behaviors of the prior eight growth periods into more complex emotional expressions and versatility. The "care" response provides an emotional mobility rather than the acting or performance mobility.

The way to develop the integrative "care" pathways is to learn how to love. Once you can persuade your remo about the importance of loving, the ability to love can be developed between your rao and your remo.

You develop loving feelings by calling up pleasurable "vegetative" responses, while having a caring concern for the self. All types of love involve the para-sympathetic system with good warm viscera feelings. When you successfully create warm loving feelings for the self, you will experience a "buzz on" as your alpha brain waves are activated even through you are in a semi-excited or stimulated feeling state.

The pleasures of eating food and feeling love are closely related. Practice going hungry and then indulge yourself with food to enjoy the full intensity of the pleasurable feelings experienced as tension is released. The same can be said about sexual activity. The relaxing stimulation and pleasure of affectionate sex makes the subcortical circuitry come alive as the whole range of emotional scales can be played. Then a sharp awareness on your part makes mental impressions of the emotional experience. Your memories of these feelings permit them to be recalled and practiced later, so emotional learning can occur.

The integrative "care" pathways are there; they just have to be stimulated and activated by you. And the more often you are able to call up loving feelings for yourself, the more you are going to be able to love others.

When pleasure predominates, you can approach people. You will be able to get along with people, because the "approach" characteristics of pleasure provides the basis for enjoying people. If displeasure is dominant, then you lose this ability to enjoy people.

Humor is a good defense for this level of development to guard against anxiety. Humor acts to reduce anxiety by bringing pleasurable pathways into action. When you start to feel bad, angry or upset, humor can rechannel this negative energy to pleasurable areas that are better able to handle these uncomfortable feelings.

Humor can reduce the seriousness of a situation for the remo. At these times the rao needs to distract the remo's attention to something else just as you would a child. Being oriented towards pleasure, gives you other avenues of responses to divert the remo thoughts to something else. And humor lowers the "stakes" and allows the remo to save face by expressing concerns in a pleasurable way.

In other words, in a displeasurable situation, humor allows you to redirect excessive energies into the pleasurable pathways where it can be more easily handled. Being witty, clowning around, looking for the comical, and having fun with puns are humorous approaches that are pleasurably oriented.

READINESS RESPONSE

The anticipatory energy of the "expectancy" response creates a state of readiness, by orienting your senses towards a greater awareness of your surroundings. The keen, sharp, attentiveness of the "expectancy" response can be integrated with the relaxed "vegetative" response involving the lower jaw, mouth, tongue and lips.

Being accident prone is often caused by a lack of alert preparedness. By practicing the "readiness" response you can reduce mishaps and personal injuries. Anytime you're driving a car you should practice the "readiness" response. This allows you to be attentive and prepared for dangerous contingencies. Older people especially need to activate this the "readiness" response when driving. It can also revitalize their lives and make them feel young and energized.

INTEGRATING BEHAVIORS

You can practice periodically alternating the growth responses. For example, you can elicit the "approach" response to cheer up other people around you, just as you would cheer up your own remo, then switch to the "vegetative" response, to re-establish rhythmical breathing, then next you can pep things up with the "expectancy" response. Practice these behaviors as often as you can, and practice switching back and forth between behaviors.

When you walk into a new, challenging or different situation, you don't want to fixate on only one response, but all the circuitry responses you have at your disposal should be kept alive with different behavioral options.

The anticipatory energy of the "expectancy" response will provide a readiness to respond by orienting your senses to a greater awareness. This alert attentive readiness can be integrated with the relaxed "vegetative" response so the lower lip exposes the lower teeth, the lower jaw slackens, the tongue thickens, as you sniff the air taking deep rhymical breaths.

You want to integrate the "vegetative, approach and expectancy" responses. So an alert, attentive readiness can be integrated with a relaxed lower jaw, mouth and tongue, while contracting the upper lip in a sort of smile, that allows the lower jaw to drop and relax.

The easiest and quickest way to learn this integrative response is with a love of the self between your rao and your remo. You want to get an alpha "buzz on" with warm tingling feelings in your face and chest areas. When interacting with others a love of the self can give you an inner peace, so you can feel at home in almost any social situation.

You want to practice these behaviors as often as possible until all these behaviors can occur as one response. You want to integrate all the circuits together with feelings of love for the self first, and then if possible for another or others.

GOAL-DIRECTED BEHAVIOR

A strongly developed "goal-directed" circuit will encourage a strong love of variety, and a desire to experiment with all the different ways and methods of doing something to find the best way. This experimental attitude where everything reasonable has to be tried at least once, along with anticipation and imagination, allows the remo to be very innovative, inventive and original. More important than the "goal-directed" activities is the planning and organizing of activities ahead of time and ironing out the problems that might occur.

Many people become enthused over golf, because they have so many things to do when learning the game. Nothing can get the remo so impassioned as trying to do several things at the same time, as is needed in mastering a golf swing.

If you're cooking, you want to cook a dish in a new way. But instead of going to a cookbook, talk it over with your remo about the different ingredients you might add or substitute. Be daring! Let your remo come up with something unusual. You should study cookbooks to see new ways of combining ingredients from various dishes.

If you like to play some sport, suspend your desire for excellence for a while to experiment with new ways of performing a movement. Go to the library and refer to several books on a sport to give you ideas to apply during practice sessions. If you really want to develop the "goal-directed" circuit, the library is good aid to sharpen your investigative skills.

You should also experiment with various emotional behaviors and skills to develop your acting ability. Try to imitate behaviors you see in others, on TV, at the movies, etc. You should even try to do impressions of famous people to activate this "goal-directed" circuit. But most of all you want to experiment and express yourself in new and exciting ways. You want to improvise and express your own variation of the emotional behaviors of the various growth periods.

STABILIZING RESPONSE

The development of the "stabilizing" response provides the skill to control anxiety in the early stages. Objectivity is an important attitude of the "stabilizing" response that functions as a means to reduce or control displeasure. It represents an unemotional attitude that is neither pleasurable nor displeasurable, but resides near the center between them.

The memory recall process is primarily the same as the "stabilizing" response. The recall process makes your past experiences available, so you can apply them appropriately to the present situation.

The "stabilizing" response controls displeasure, because you learn not to care for situations, people, objects, etc., that cause displeasure. This in turn, reduces the amount of emotional arousal involved. Now, things that result in bad feelings can be looked at objectively by the remo to ascertain their value and determine whether these things are worth the price of caring.

The memory process of the "stabilizing" response is able to control emotional states that create distractions that disrupt the recall process. It nips excessive arousal in the bud to permit the absorption of ideas and materials that need to be learned. This allows you to listen, read and study for longer periods of time without interference, because the immediate need to gratify desires and impulses can be delayed by the inhibitory controls of the "stabilizing" (hippocampus) circuit.(42)

Things don't worry the remo so much at this stage. Instead of going over and over a hopeless problem, it learns not to care, and uses its energies more constructively. Instead of being jealous, the remo simply cares less about the person involved. This helps the remo to be objective, detached and to suspend emotional involvement to bring about more self-control.

The "stabilizing" response is most helpful in regards to bad memories of the past. Instead of becoming depressed or angry when recalling past displeasurable events, the remo learns not to care about what has happened in the past. Instead of letting past mistakes gnaw away, creating feelings of inadequacy and pulling the remo down, a "cool" indifference about these past events encourages a positive attitude and self-confidence to build.

The indifference of the "stabilizing" response allows a greater objectivity, thereby reducing the remo's prejudices. Inhibiting arousal at the early stages can create a desirable indifference. This allows you to postpone judgements until more facts are present to provide more impartiality and fairness to decisions. It reduces the problems that black and white appraisals tends to create. For example, instead of love-hate reactions, indifference can modify these extremes. And differences and conflicts between people can be discussed in a sensible manner without leading to over-reactions, heated arguments and bad feelings.

The "stabilizing" response gives you the confidence to "project" your feelings out towards others, as a kind of controlled energy, referred to as extroversion.

"Projection" is a kind of mental, emotional giving of the self that takes energy. Those who have an excess of energy can afford to be more generous than those who don't. Generosity develops now, because the inhibition of arousal keeps energies from being depleted, so it may be "projected" out with control.

Pleasure is also an important factor. Pleasure "projects" to permit you to be expansive and giving. And extroversion requires pleasure as an impetus for development.

Spontaneity is possible only if pleasure is dominant in a social situation. If displeasure predominates, then the "stabilizing" response requires you to be more premeditative in your behaviors instead of spontaneous.

The "stabilizing" response is activated by premeditated thought that innervates the memory process, and by inhibiting arousal in the early stages. The "stabilizing" response maintains a sense of readiness to sustain a state of equilibrium.

To maintain the flexibility of a state of equilibrium, then anticipation and premeditation are essential. That is, you can't just walk into a troubling situation and expect to control excessive excitation after it has already been initiated.

During the initial phase of developing the not caring attitude of the "stabilizing" response, you need to be aware of the remo's corresponding feeling state. The remo can acquire a new behavior by learning the emotional feeling involved with the behavioral attitude.

The "stabilizing" response keeps one centered in a state of equilibrium between pleasure and displeasure, that consists of an alertness, associated with a lack of emotional arousal during this memory recall process. The corresponding feeling state of the remo could perhaps be described as a mobile fluid state.

This fluid, emotional, searching movement by the remo that facilitates the memory recall process is similar to the problem solving process. During the "goal-directed" period, a rudimentary aspect of the "stabilizing" circuit was activated when problem solving was attempted. The next time you try to solve some absorbing problem, try to be aware of the sensations that occur within your mind and yourself via sensory feedback.

The carefree emotional state one feels when staring off into space by the rao, while the remo uses the memory banks of recall, would perhaps be a good description of the care free "stabilizing" response, except that the eyes are focused and actively used. There is a versatile energetic state internally that provides control. And the readiness of the "stabilizing" response can operate on a high energy level, while appearing to be "externally" relaxed.

When you find yourself starting to get anxious or uptight, then you want to activate your memory recall circuit. For example, you might want to recall some pertinent passage from this book, or recall similar situations or experiences from your past to elicit the not caring "stabilizing" response.

Another method to elicit the "stabilizing" response that can work, uses the facial muscles in the eyebrows of the forehead. Referring to a right handed person, when you are in a stressful situation and find you are getting nervous, your rao can raise the outside corner of your right eyebrow, while the inside corner near the bridge of the nose should be forced down. This can create the alert indifference of the "stabilizing" response.

Using your mental ability to activate the memory recall process along with this method will strengthen the "stabilizing" response even more. After your rao has become proficient with this method, you want your remo to learn this behavior by practicing with the left eyebrow.

When you experience more excitatory energy then you can handle, it can create a nervous feeling with facial tics, impatience, bouncing leg, tension, driving too fast, getting irritated with other drivers, etc. Now, when your induce the "stabilizing" response, you can eliminate or reduce the displeasurable energy to the level appropriate for the situation.

MOOD ELEVATOR

The "stabilizing" response also has the ability to arouse you when you are sleepy, morning, noon or night. Thus, when you are tired or fatigued, and you have to be "up" for a business meeting or social event, the "stabilizing" circuit can elevate your mood to prevent drowsiness, so you can be awake and aroused to the degree that you want.

After driving on the road for an extended time, when there is no safe place to pull over and sleep, you endanger your life and others when you start getting so sleepy you can hardly hold your eyes open. However, the "stabilizing" response has an exquisite ability to raise your level of arousal, so you can continue on your way fully alert!

LISTENING SKILLS

The "stabilizing" response adds a sense of emotional maturity to your life. When bored the person with a "child" remo can feel an inattentive restlessness or discontent that is hard to conceal. This impatience and internal tension could cause a friend, co-worker, employer, neighbor, spouse or family member to feel slighted or even insulted, because you don't appear to like their company. But with the "stabilizing" response, you can calm that internal tension and irritability while at the same time raise your arousal and attention level to become an excellent "listener." This higher level of self-control was something a person with a "child" remo was often incapable of accomplishing.

INTEGRATIVE RESPONSE

The "adult-child" remo is lively and spontaneous, because all the excitatory energy sources and their controls are brought together to provide great vitality and great self-control. You are now capable of cooking on all 12 burners at the same time.

The "goal-directed" circuit is the key behavior to innervate the "integrative" circuit, but during the "integration" period your "goal-directed" activities are related to social activities with people. The development of the "integration" circuit requires the stimulation and socialization that only other people can give.

The "integration" circuit can activate all three nervous system, the sensory, motor and autonomic, simultaneously. First, the autonomic system provides the "vegetative and approach" responses to help you relax and maintain a sense of self-contentment. Second, the sensory system provides an alert, exciting, sensual awareness of the environment with the "expectancy" response, along with some kind of "care" response. And third, the motor system, where muscular performance skills in speaking and facial expressions, is utilized at an optimal level of arousal via the "goal-directing & stabilizing" responses. The "integration" response is performed with a fluid emotional mobility, that allows a constant movement in all directions away from and back towards a feeling baseline of equilibrium. The "integration" response allows you to express all the many responses mentioned above as one response. But one moment the "vegetative" response can be more dominant over the others. In the next moment, the social situation may call for the "expectancy response to have more emphasis. Then, if you become overly excited let the "stabilizing" response have the most influence, etc.

An internal dramatization of social situations in thoughts, meditations or daydreams becomes an excellent abode to practice these different feeling responses and behaviors. Practice and experiment with as many of the emotional growth responses as possible. Learn to switch back and forth between behaviors with a fluid agility.

For example, using the problem solving aspect of the "goal-directed" circuit, think of as many responses as you can for the conditions of a social situation. Using your memory banks, recall the various behaviors to initiate the "stabilizing" response. You may also want the "approach" response to prevail over the other circuits to support and encourage other people. If you feel your energy getting low, your "vegetative" response have the most influence to recharge your batteries. Or if you would rather pep yourself up, then the "expectancy and stabilizing" responses can be combined to reign supreme.

Next, you want to create feelings of love for your self or others with the "care" response. Get a "buzz on" with feelings of warmth in your chest area and face with the slower alpha waves.

The main point is that as you practice and experiment with these behaviors, all your circuits and all your behaviors can come alive. And all these behaviors can be expressed as one response that can flow to emphasize one particular behavior as being more appropriate than another for the social situation at the moment.

SOCIALIZING RESPONSE

Any time you go out socializing or partying, you need to be in a mood that will allow you to enjoy yourself. A love of the self between your rao and remo is your most effective socializing response. But if that's a problem, then you want to integrate the mood elevating aspect of the "stabilizing" response with the "expectancy" response and the "vegetative" response. Combining these three social behaviors together as one response, using the "integrative" circuit, is referred to as the "socializing" response. The "socializing" response can give you great adaptive skills to deal with any kind of people or any kind of social situation.

CONCENTRATION PROBLEMS

Some people have bad study habits. They hate to study or read non-fiction books, because they clamp their jaws, grit their teeth, suspend their breathing or take minute swallow breaths. So after 10 or 15 minutes, there body has a build up of carbon dioxide to make them tried and fatigued with a need to take a nap. They're tired because they're not using their innate abilities of breathing naturally while relaxing the mouth region, involved with the "vegetative" response.

Learning is a problem solving exercise that should completely engross your remo. But an indifference attitude effectively excludes the remo's involvement. You need to try to find a hook to get you excited about a subject. And then you need to approach studying using your emotional coping skills. Ironically, the "socializing" response is the ideal behavior to employ when you want to absorb a new subject, even though you are alone.

THE ABILITY TO SLEEP

Once a full blown displeasurable reaction sets in, the "integration" circuit can provide control by integrating the "vegetative and stabilizing" responses for an extremely effective control of overwhelming displeasure. In addition, your ability at integrating these two responses determines your skill at going to sleep quickly and easily.

The primary sleep center is the "synchronal" circuit involved in the "vegetative" response. The secondary source is the "stabilizing" circuit. Low stimulation of the hippocampus ("stabilizing" circuit) depresses the arousal system to facilitate sleep by eliciting the behaviors that precede sleep such as yawning, stretching, etc. (56) You initiate the "stabilizing" circuit for sleep by forcing down the outside corners of both eyebrows.

The integration of the "vegetative" and "stabilizing" responses is referred to as the "sleep" response. With the development of the "sleep" response, you will increase your skill and ability to go to sleep easily whenever or where ever you want.

First, establish deep relaxed rhythmical breathing by sniffing the air. The "vegetative" deep breath is felt when air is taken in through the nose only, so that it rushes past the deep, back part of the throat. If you begin respiration by flaring your nostrils it will facilitate your breathing. Take a slow deep and expansive breath, so it is performed in a relaxed rhythmical manner.

If you have a lot of tension in your body, transfer the energy of the tension so it's concentrated in a downward pressure on the outer corners of your eyebrows, and on your diaphragm, located in the bread basket of your stomach region, allowing you to draw air in and push air out in deep forceful rhythmic breaths.

Next, relax and immobilize all your muscles. Your muscles should not only be relaxed, but try for a suggestive feeling state where you are not able to move a muscle without a strong exertion of effort. This produces a heavy feeling in the muscles that makes them relaxed but immobile. Also, there should be a thickening of the tongue and lips that makes them feel heavy, moist and immobile.

Third, you want to experience a cool or cold tingling or buzz sensation within your body. The cooler you are, the easier it is to sleep. The warmer you are the harder it is to sleep.

The "sleep" response has many responses you need to learn. You want to combine as many of these responses together as you can, so that eventually all of these behaviors will occur simultaneously as one response using the "integrative" response.

You should practice the "sleep" response as much as you can very day until these behaviors are soundly established or integrated. You should practice during the middle of the day when you have some privacy to take a little 5 or 10 minute catnap. And after this ability has been integrated by your remo, you should be able to shift into this response even when among people to take little micro-naps. These can revitalize you so much, you will find you will need one or two fewer hours of sleep each night!

OVERCOMING FEAR

Fear and anger creates a lot of negative energy. You need to know before hand how to cope with all this excess negative energy. There are four avenues of control. On a physical level this excessive negative energy can be both transferred and reduced. Negative tension can be transferred to the diaphragm to initiate deep breaths, to the lips as they pucker and protrude, to the nose as it flares out and to the outside corners of the eyebrow as they are pressed downward.

On the other hand, the amount of negative energy is reduced by acting out the behaviors of the "vegetative" response, such as a slacken jaw, deep rhythmic breaths, enlarged tongue, puckered lips, etc. These behaviors function like a Pavlovian response that can automatic reduces arousal.

At the mental level, this excessive negative energy can also be transferred and reduced. The "sleep" response which consist of the "stabilizing and vegetative" responses can both effectively reduce the energy level. The "vegetative" response does it by sychronizing cellular firing and the "stabilizing" circuit does it by inhibiting arousal in the neocortex. And to transfer negative energy at the mental level you employ the "expectancy" response. When you activate the "expectancy" response, the attentive awareness and readiness can divert a tremendous amount of energy away from the displeasurable pathway into the "expectancy" circuit.

When you combine the "expectancy" response with the "sleep" response, this will be referred to as the "soothing" response. So when you integrate the "expectancy and sleep" responses you both divert and lower the amount of negative energy and tension by deploying the "orienting" reflex of the "expectancy" response that you've seen in a cat, while depressing the outside corners of both eyebrows down using the "stabilizing" response. And you also want to redirect tension to the diaphragm so you take deep rhythmical breaths.

After you have integrated all the behaviors of the "sleep" response along with the "expectancy" response and they become an automatic response of your remo in the "soothing" response, you will always be able to quickly regain your composure no matter how overwhelming the crisis. You will always have the ability to pull in the reins and take a momentary break to calm yourself!

For example, if you're in a high anxiety state, and activate the "soothing" response, you can return to a state of normalcy in a remarkably short time! But be sure to redirect the negative tension from fear to the areas previously mentioned. It is important to restore deep rhythmical breathing by transferring the negative energy to your diaphragm muscles to inhale and exhale deeply and to a downward pressure on the outside corners of both eyebrows while also transferring energy to the "expectancy" response. Even if you are overwhelmed with fear, you can quickly pull out of a panic state to regain self control, when you employ the "soothing" response.

This is true for a fear of heights, fear of flying, claustrophobia or a fear of small places, like elevators, fear of crowds, bugs, animals, open places or anything. However, make sure you have mastered the "soothing" response first. Then imagine yourself in the fearful situation while practicing the "soothing" response before you actually put yourself in emotional jeopardy.

OVERCOMING ANGER

To control unjustified anger, the outlook is poor if a person doesn't want to adopt synergy. But if your rao, believes in synergy and your remo will go along, then your anger can be controlled and eventually eliminated.

First to control your anger, practice accepting and tolerating all kinds of people and behaviors. Next, integrate the "expectancy, vegetative and stabilizing" responses, so they can be expressed as the "soothing" response. You want to practice this response as often as you can to develop the emotional skills of your remo.

Then you change the remo's automatic responses that trigger angry reactions. Recall past irate episodes and employ the "soothing" response, as your remo's initial quick reaction. The more you practice this exercise, the faster you can eliminate anger as something you have to guard against. Spring past situations on your remo, so it can eventually react instinctively with the "soothing" response. Envision possible future troubles that might create a short fuse, and practice the "soothing" response, so the remo can develop more adaptable reactions.

If you are driving in a car, and someone is driving slowly or cuts you off, your first reaction should be the "soothing" response, instead of the futile attempt to control the behaviors of another driver and "lose" it. If someone cuts in line at a queue, you can use the "soothing" response, to correct them with a calm indifference, humor and/or the power of self-control, instead of getting hot under the collar and creating a scene with possible tragic consequences.

MAINTAINING YOUR DIET

If you have problems staying on a diet, the "soothing" response can give you the self-control you desire. The "care" response can produce great desires for food, while the "goal-directed" behaviors can produce great drives to obtain food, regardless of the obstacles. When these emotional states predominate, they create a restless discontent. But now you will find by employing the "soothing or socializing" response that you can lull that high strung state of irritability into an indifferent state of equilibrium.

The problem is the remo reacts automatically.   The remo doesn't think ahead about the consequences concerning daily activities like eating. Although your remo may want to lose weight, when caught up in your daily routine your remo's automatic habits kick in. If you're a little off guard you may find yourself snacking at certain key times of the day.

So the way to maintain a diet is to change your remo's established habits and develop new ones with the emotional controlling behavior of the "soothing or socializing" response. You have to prepare for these periods of weakness ahead of time. You need to think of all the situations that tempt you, and practice the calm indifference of the "soothing" response.

If you tend to snack during TV commercials, then you have to be prepared before hand to counteract your remo automatic actions. You need to picture yourself in this situation and even see yourself reacting to the sight of other people eating during a commercial, then you want to calm your desires by practicing the "soothing" response with a relax nonchalance.

If you're addicted to food this is not going to happen overnight. You need to organize your life around a sensible diet. You have to plan ahead, even for a week if you can. Plan out what time of day and what kind of food you want to eat. Make this a fun project using your "goal-directed" behaviors. Go to the library and investigate vegetarian cookbooks and diet books for ideas on creating a plan.

The big problem with dieting is when you lose fat you also lose muscle. So you need to use your "goal-directed" circuit to plan some daily exercise routine so it can become a habit with your remo. It's better to exercise with others, because it's more fun and it gives you a greater sense of obligation.

But the next time you get an urge to eat junk food is a good time to excite your memory banks by exercising your "stabilizing" response. Instead of eating sweets, start practicing your "soothing" response. You will simply be amazed at how effective it is at maintaining a state of balance equilibrium and self-control. Your daily accomplishments will give you a sense of pride and pleasure from the self-mastery you achieve.

CONTROLLING OTHER ADDICTIONS

People lose confidence in their ability to deal with all the daily difficulties in a status society. So they depend on whatever can get them through the day. The biggest problem in getting over any addiction whether food, tobacco, alcohol, etc. is not having a supportive group of people around you and a supportive remo within you. Your remo needs to feel emotionally security. You want to adopt synergy values between your rao and your remo, and you want to cultivate friends who are oriented towards pleasure and synergy.

Next, you want to develop your remo's emotional coping skills so you can have more self-control. The method used above to control the food you eat is the same technique you use to control any addiction. Just substitute your drug of choice for the food that is avoided to achieve weight control.

SEXUAL PROBLEMS

Great or anxious anticipation of the sex act can cause pre-ejaculation or impotence in men and a lack of lubricating readiness or frigidity in women. Now you have a cure for that problem! Using the "soothing" response to calm down the fearful antici-pation of sex can make you an effective sex partner.

The negative anticipation that caused so many emotional problems at an earlier stage of growth can now be used in an opposite way to rechannel energy to a positive source and control excitation. Anticipation used in conjunction with the "expect-ancy, stabilizing and vegetative" responses in the "soothing" response can create an about face to subdue and calm, instead of creating excessive excitement. Thus anticipation can work for you to reduce excitement and maintain a state of equilibrium.

First if you're uptight and can't relax, use the "soothing" response along with a light pleasurable banter to get in a relaxed mood. Now the anticipation of an exciting sexual adventure, can reduce arousal to keep you in a state of relaxed readiness. And when men use the "sleep" response during sex, they can greatly extend the sex act. As they approach an orgasmic state they can initiate the "sleep" response to cool down and prolong their pleasure and their partner's pleasure!

OVERCOMING DEPRESSION

If you're depressed and you don't know why, or if you're suffering because of a loss in self-esteem from the put downs and rejections that are so common in a status culture, then your depression stems from your remo punishing your self. When the remo gets angry, and the anger isn't expressed outwardly, then it is turned inwardly and experienced as depression. This anger is a result of a belief in status values, and is therefore, futile.

However, even though the remo may concur about the evilness of the status system and want to adopt synergy, the remo tends to react automatically from habit to status assaults on self-esteem. So you will have to teach the remo to react in a new way.

You need to relive those situations that caused you to be depressed, and have your remo respond with the "stabilizing" response of indifference. Within your mind the remo's first instant reaction to these devastating events should be the "stabilizing" response of a matter of fact indifference. When you activate the "stabilizing" circuit you short circuit the negative energy of displeasure and redirect it to a positive source. You are pulling your self up, by your own boot straps, out of displeasure into a state of indifference. The more you can practice this, the sooner you will defeat this scourge.

You may also want to imagine some future depressing scenario at work, with your spouse or friends, etc. to practice this response. If you practice this daily, after a month or so this response will "lock-in" as an automatic behavior of your remo.

If you've been put down, rejected, snubbed, insulted, etc., you need to realize these are the vile conditions of a status system. First, you should never stand and take such punishment from another. You need to let them know in no uncertain terms, that they do not have the freedom to treat or speak to you that way, if at all possible.

Next, if you were unable to stand up for your self, but believe in the values of synergy, then you should realize your esteem and worth is not dependent on others in a status system. The feeling of equality synergy engenders should gradually build feelings of self-confidence within you. You do not want to give anybody the right to evaluate you and determine your worth.

So if your remo agrees, you want to rehearse reacting to these status situations with the "stabilizing" response of indifference, instead of self-punishment. You should practice reacting to instances from your past over and over until it is an automatic response. And you should conjure up possible future or past situations out of the blue to surprise your remo to practice this new response.

If you have problems with depression you should plan ahead and visualize circumstances that can cause future problems. Thus, you might visualize responding to being fired from your job, getting a divorce, being rejected by a friend, etc. Remember your essence is not determined by the job you hold, being able to maintain a marriage, or someone else's opinion of your self, if you hold synergy's values.

If you want to be rid of depression, your rao has to take command and guide your remo towards synergy. During this period of training your rao has to raised your remo like you would a child. But this all depends on the communication breakthrough. If you don't have the courage to interact with your remo as an imaginary mate, then your chances of overcoming depression are considerably diminished.

APPENDIX A

AVOIDANCE
PERIOD
6 - 9 MONTHS

AVOIDANCE RESPONSE

The "avoidance" response develops a searching, expectant attitude of attention and curiosity. The need to avoid punishment has a power to motivate that is many times greater than the desire to approach pleasure. The "avoidance" response should be used to steer clear of those who are into the put downs and one-upmanship of status

The "avoidance" response is a behavior of the sensory system that is overly developed by most people under status. But if you want to understand your remo, and therefore, yourself, it pays to understand the behaviors that accompany each growth period. For example, this "avoidance" circuit develops again at approximately 10-1/2, 20-1/2, and 30-1/2 years of age in the remo's hemisphere, and again at approximately 5-1/2, 15-1/2, 25-1/2 and 35-1/2 years of age in the rao's hemisphere. Although the behaviors that manifest themselves will not always be the same, these will tend to be apprehensive and vulnerable periods in your life.

Sometimes, fearful reactions are seen now in a 6 month old infant, as what is unknown or unfamiliar can be a threat.(40) The "avoidance" response can operate as a rapid alarm system to be alert when danger threatens. This creates the excitation needed to arouse defensive flight reactions for the self-preservation of the individual.(54 & 45) When defensive flight reactions are combined with the "approach" reactions, fighting behavior can result.

The sensitivity of the "avoidance" response can often cause eagerness to turn to impatience. It can create feelings that range from curiosity, displeasure, foreboding, sadness, fear, to life-threatening terror.

The "avoidance" area appears to play an important function in selecting the right responses needed to get what is wanted, or to be more specific, to inhibit or avoid irrelevant responses that are not adaptive.(102)

In the six month old, an object's novelty, uncertainty or complexity may evoke a surprise response and hold his attention until familiarity is established.(116)

The baby now can be easily aroused and stimulated, so that she can play contentedly by herself needing very little to keep her entertained. With this spontaneous self-activity, she is becoming self-contained and often happier alone.(40) The baby is beginning to realize some autonomy, as she develops an ability to differentiate individuals, and she begins to narrow her interests to selected people familiar to her. This newly acquired ability to discriminate also makes her afraid of strangers.(99 & 129) Separation anxiety, an aspect of self-preservation, also develop, during this period.(11)

If emotional attachments are not established by infants during the "approach" period, before fear develops during this "avoidance" period, then the child will probably not be ready again to develop positive emotional relationships with his peers until after 3 years of age.(44)

AVOIDANCE CIRCUIT

The "avoidance" circuit is comprised of the basolateral division of the amygdala, the anterior, lateral, ventromedial nucleus, and lateral preoptic areas of the hypothalamus, and the globus pallidus. These areas are connected together via the ventral amygdalofugal and pallidohypothalamic fascicle nerve pathways.(see fig. 11)

There is much sensory inflow into the basolateral amygdalo-fugal from touch, auditory and visual stimulation, while there is little sensory inflow into the corticomedial amygdala. Also the golbus pallidus, along with the ventromedial nucleus area of the hypothalamus, seems to be developing the motor components of the "avoidance" response at this time.(106)

Meaningful noxious stimuli evoked a 40-45 cps rhythm within the basolateral amygdala that is not seen in the corticomedial amygdala nor in other parts of the limbric nervous system.(62) The basolateral area has important connections with the pituitary adrenal mechanism to influence a rapid alarm system, especially with ACTH secretions.(29, 54 & 51)

Stimulation of the basolateral area creates inhibition of all on-going activity and orients the movements of the eyes and head in a searching response, creating an expectant attitude of attention.(119 & 120) This is similar to a curiosity response, where an object's uncertainty may evoke a surprise response in the 6 month old, and hold his attention until he is used to it.(116) More intense stimulation of the basolateral amygdala gives rise to fear and defensive responses.(119 & 120)

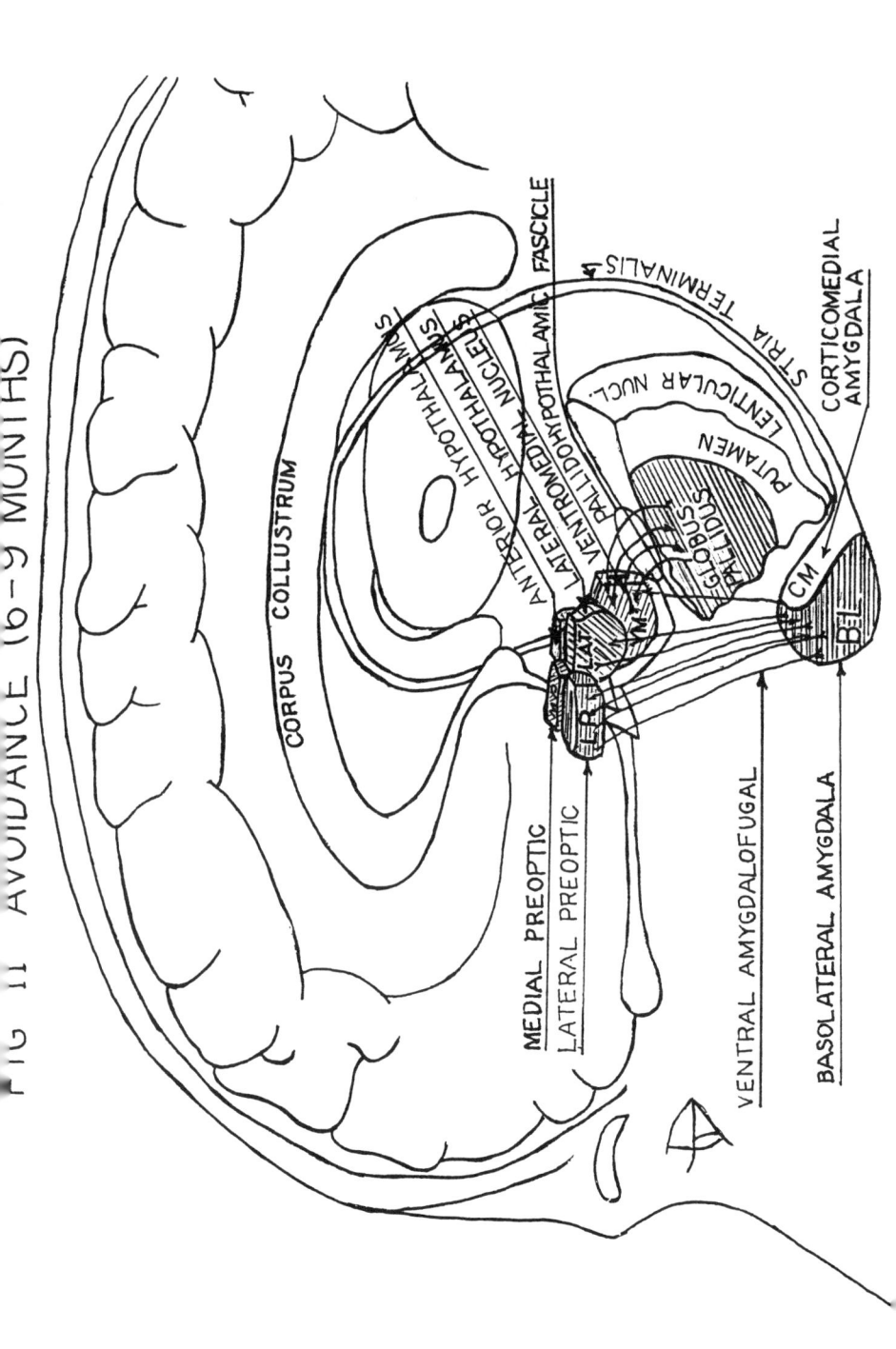

FIG 11 AVOIDANCE (6–9 MONTHS)

CORPUS COLLUSTRUM

ANTERIOR HYPOTHALAMUS

LATERAL HYPOTHALAMUS

VENTROMEDIAL NUCLEUS

LATEROMEDIAL HYPOTHALAMIC FASCICLE

STRIA TERMINALIS

LENTICULAR NUCL.

PUTAMEN

GLOBUS PALLIDUS

CM

BL

CORTICOMEDIAL AMYGDALA

MEDIAL PREOPTIC

LATERAL PREOPTIC

VENTRAL AMYGDALOFUGAL

BASOLATERAL AMYGDALA

The "avoidance" circuit has much to do with relevancy. It seems to be important in determining appropriate responses to rewards and punishments;(101) and this, in turn, has much to do with the role the basolateral plays in stimulus discrimination and generalization.(102 & 103)

Both divisions of the amygdala function as a self-preservation mechanism; the basolateral operates the avoidance or escape reactions, while the corticomedial division sets up social abilities with approach behavior, which can make self-preservation more effective in group situations. The corticomedial is comparatively much smaller than the basolateral in cats, but these two divisions are equal in rats.(128) This shows the functional importance of these areas in regard to the differences in behavior and temperament seen in these animals.

When the amygdala was removed in humans, there was a loss of the ability to shift attention and to respond emotionally. They became inert, with less zest and intensity of emotions, and were less capable of creative productivity.(1)

The ability to discriminate also creates a fear of strangers.(99 & 129) In self-stimulation studies, the basolateral area was found to be a punishing area of displeasure.(128 & 87) Displeasure experienced from this area is feelings of hunger, thirst, choking, suffocation, nausea, gagging, retching and the desire to defecate or urinate. Some secondary affects were feelings of foreboding, fear, terror, paranoia, sadness, wanting to be alone, strangeness and unreality.(113)

DISCRIMINATIVE PERIOD 9 - 12 MONTHS

INFANT STAGE

DISCRIMINATIVE BEHAVIOR

During the previous period an infant discriminated by avoiding that which is threatening. Now a different type of discrimination unfolds, as the ability to selectively screen out unnecessary information develops, so relevant input can be processed.

The ten month old infant has learned to inhibit some of his impatience, and wait for his meal. He concentrates when inspecting his toys; and his play shows more discrimination, as he may pretend to drink with a cup.(40)

He recognizes when an object that he is accustomed to is missing. More demanding and insistent, he is beginning to show a temper. He is becoming socially discriminating and more sensitive to events in his environment. He responds more to demonstration and teaching, as he imitates others, and learns social types of games by playing pat-a-cake, bye-bye, and peek-a-boo.(40)

In yourself, you want to develop and direct this ability to discriminate against social status hierarchies, especially when punishment such as gossip and disapproval are used against the harmless behaviors of others.

DISCRIMINATIVE CIRCUIT

The "discriminative" circuit consists primarily of the caudate nucleus with various connections to the hypothalamus, thalamus, globus pallious and putamen.(See Fig. 12) The caudate nucleus has reciprocal connections with the basolateral amygdala and the suppressor areas of the neocortex to influence an increased control over excitation, as its motor neurons operate to reduce sensory excitation when stimulated.(22, 23 & 31) The caudate nucleus provides the ability to process relevant information and selectively suppress that which is superfluous. This permits selective sensitivity that can heighten responsiveness to some specific interests, while reducing sensitivity to areas outside of these interests.

The caudate nucleus not only inhibits but has an excitatory aspect that can increase the curiosity derived from the basolateral amygdala to produce a very active exploratory drive.(15)

IG 12 DISCRIMINATIVE CIRCUIT (9-12 MONTHS)

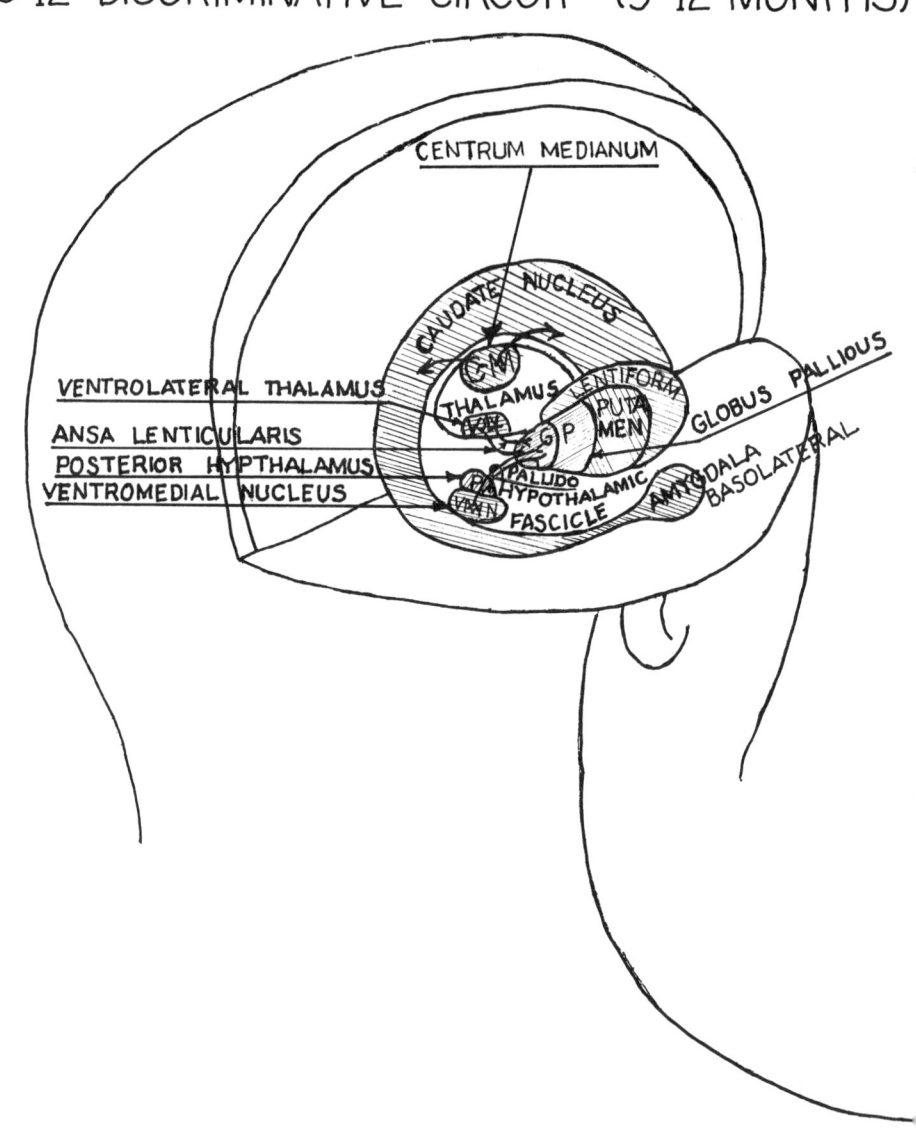

AFFECTIVE
PERIOD
12 - 15 MONTHS

INFANT-CHILD STAGE

AFFECTIVE RESPONSE

From 1 to 2 years of age is referred to as the infant-child stage of development. The "affective" response is similar to the "approach" response except it is concerned with emotional responses involved with higher, more complex motor control of the autonomic or viscera nervous system. The emotional ability to make better judgments improves, such as the judgment to like or dislike something, or to give motor direction to approach or avoid something.

The one year old has increased social needs and is starting to enjoy the social give and take of play with adults. Because of the social reciprocity involved, the one year old sometimes becomes a surprisingly good imitator, as he intently watches facial expressions. He likes an audience, and to be the center of attention. He enjoys applause and will repeat performances laughed at.(40)

The one year old engages in strong muscular activity and is starting to get into everything.(110) He is very active and likes to play with several objects rather than one.(40)

AFFECTIVE CIRCUIT

The "affective" circuit includes the cingulate area with pathways projecting from the mammillary bodies of the hypothalamus.   These pathways project via the mammillothalamic tract to the anterior thalamus, which in turn project thalamocortical fibers to the cingulate gyrus.(see Fig. 13) Also as part of the development of the extrapyramidal (gross) motor system, fibers are received and integrated at the ventral anterior thalamus from diffuse areas of the neocortex.   Involved in this gross motor activity is the development of the fields of Forel to interconnect the globus pallidus with the ventral anterior thalamus, and especially the zona incerta in this area in order to enhance timing behavior in motor movements.

The interpeduncular nucleus also seems to be developing now, as part of the "affective" circuit that projects fibers from the mammillothalamic tract down to the limbric midbrain area to unite the vegetative functions of the autonomic nervous system with the cingulate. The cingulate is considered to be very similar in function to the olfactory "synchronal" area only on a higher more complex level.(106 & 27)

Because the posterior cingulate facilitates vigorous motor activity, the one year old loves the excitement of being chased(68).   The cingulate influences the emotional memory,(5) so that the infant-child learns from past positive or negative experiences what is good and bad, and responds appropriately by approaching pleasure and avoiding displeasure.

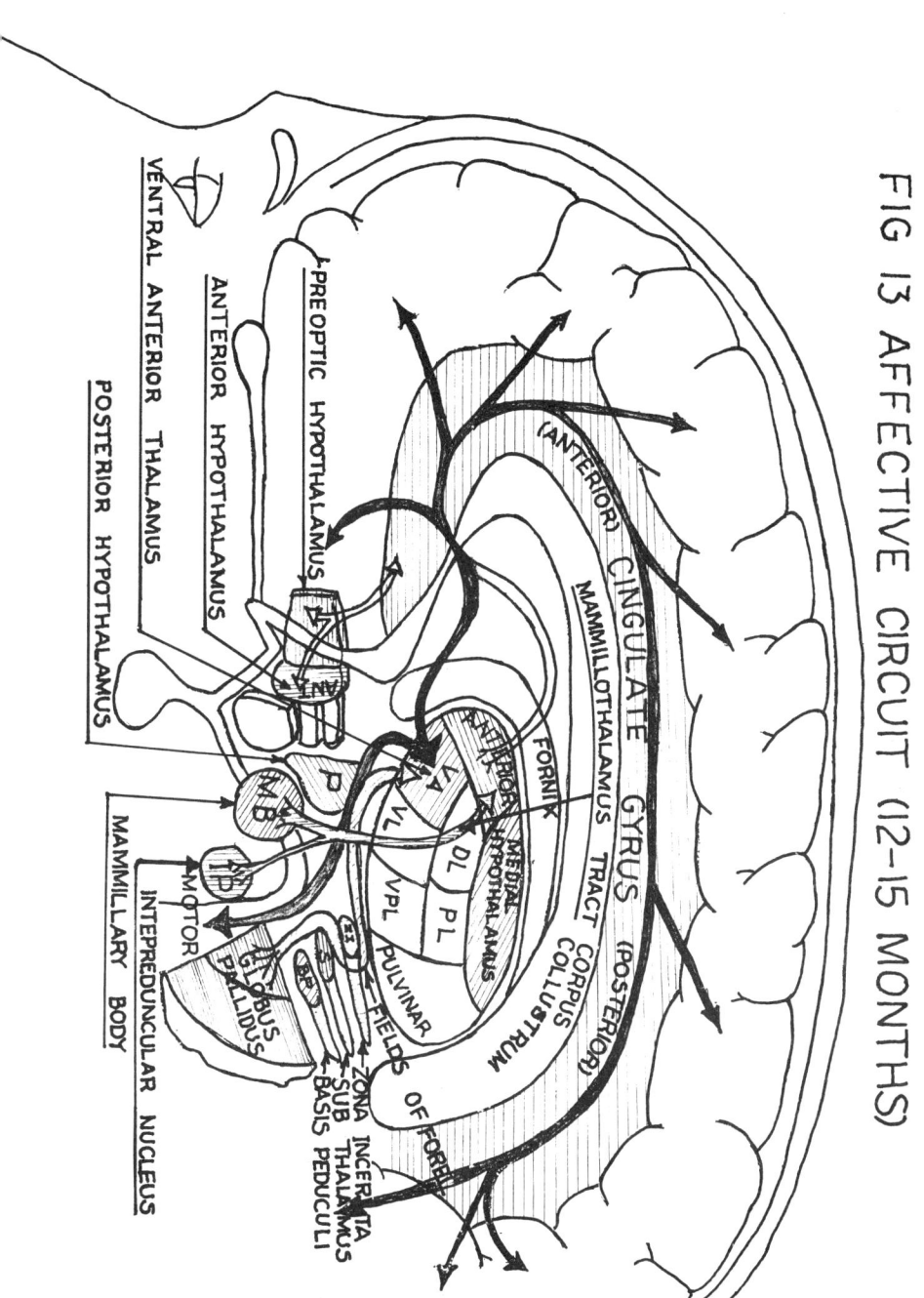

FIG 13 AFFECTIVE CIRCUIT (12-15 MONTHS)

Stimulation of the cingulate can produce such oral activities as chewing, licking, swallowing and vocalization, and some visceral reactions such as changes in blood pressure, gastric motility, pupillary dilatation, decrease in muscle tone, sleep, and other effects similar to vagus nerve stimulation.(106 & 126)

The cingulate area is where repression can occur on a higher level of control, as cingulate impulses are sent via the caudate to block thalamic activity causing a suppression of electrical activity of the neocortex.(69) Thus a traumatic shock can wipe out a specific memory from conscious recollection, but the emotional fear that was associated with it may remain.(5)

This "affective" circuit is also concerned with penile erection,(67) and vaginal lubrication. So the necessity for sociability in relation with early sexual activity develop together at this time.

IMAGERY PERIOD
15 - 18 MONTHS

INFANT-CHILD STAGE

IMAGERY RESPONSE

The "imagery" response is an aspect of the sensory nervous system. You can strengthen the "imagery" response by using your imagination to communicate by visualizing your remo. Using your imagination is an important part of the creative process. Your remo loves to visualize symbols to represent some idea; for example, someone climbing up a mountain can represent some hard to achieve goal to your remo.

A good way to develop this circuit is to communicate with your remo, using a close-up on which the remo will form a facial expression that will show how the remo feels at that moment. If you have trouble forming mental images, then you can study your reflexion in the mirror long and hard. Then close your eyes and try to recreate that image, and even try to sketch your image in a self-portrait. Or you can use the image of a person you really like, and use this image to communicate the feelings of your remo.

Now if the audio aspect of your imagination is weak or underdeveloped, then you need to strengthen the sounds in your mind's ear. The easiest way to develop this circuit is to play songs with words you like in you mind, but emphasize the words more than the melody.

Next try to encourage your remo to express ideas or feelings in words in a sing-song fashion, or even to some melody you like. It's always best to make a game of your communication efforts.

Using your imagination is an important part of your problem solving ability. You can practice a golf shot or basketball shot in your mind using your imagination, before you step up to take the shot. Or you can picture yourself at an important social event or business meeting, so you can practice what you want to say and how you want to say it within your mind.

The 15 month old child up until this time has formed no mental images of his surroundings. As a result he has lived exclusively in the present. Now there is an ability to form and retain an image that represents the beginning of symbolic thinking.(90)

The 15 month old watches and listens. He is very sensitive to visual and auditory cues which have social meaning. And the ability to speak and to understand is accelerating. His imagination creates expectations that cause him to be more demanding now. When he hears someone stirring, he stops what he is doing and changes to a position of alert anticipation. He is becoming very assertive and tends not to get on well with people. He is starting to want to be doing things for himself, asserting his independence.(40)

IMAGERY CIRCUIT

The "imagery" circuit refers to the pulvinar and lateral posterior nucleus of the thalamus and its corresponding association area in the temporal-parietal cortex. (See Fig. 14) The midline nuclei area of the thalamus provide a new awareness of the senses, as the diffuse and non-specific sensory feedback of internal and external cues, and non-specific exteroceptors seem to be developing now.

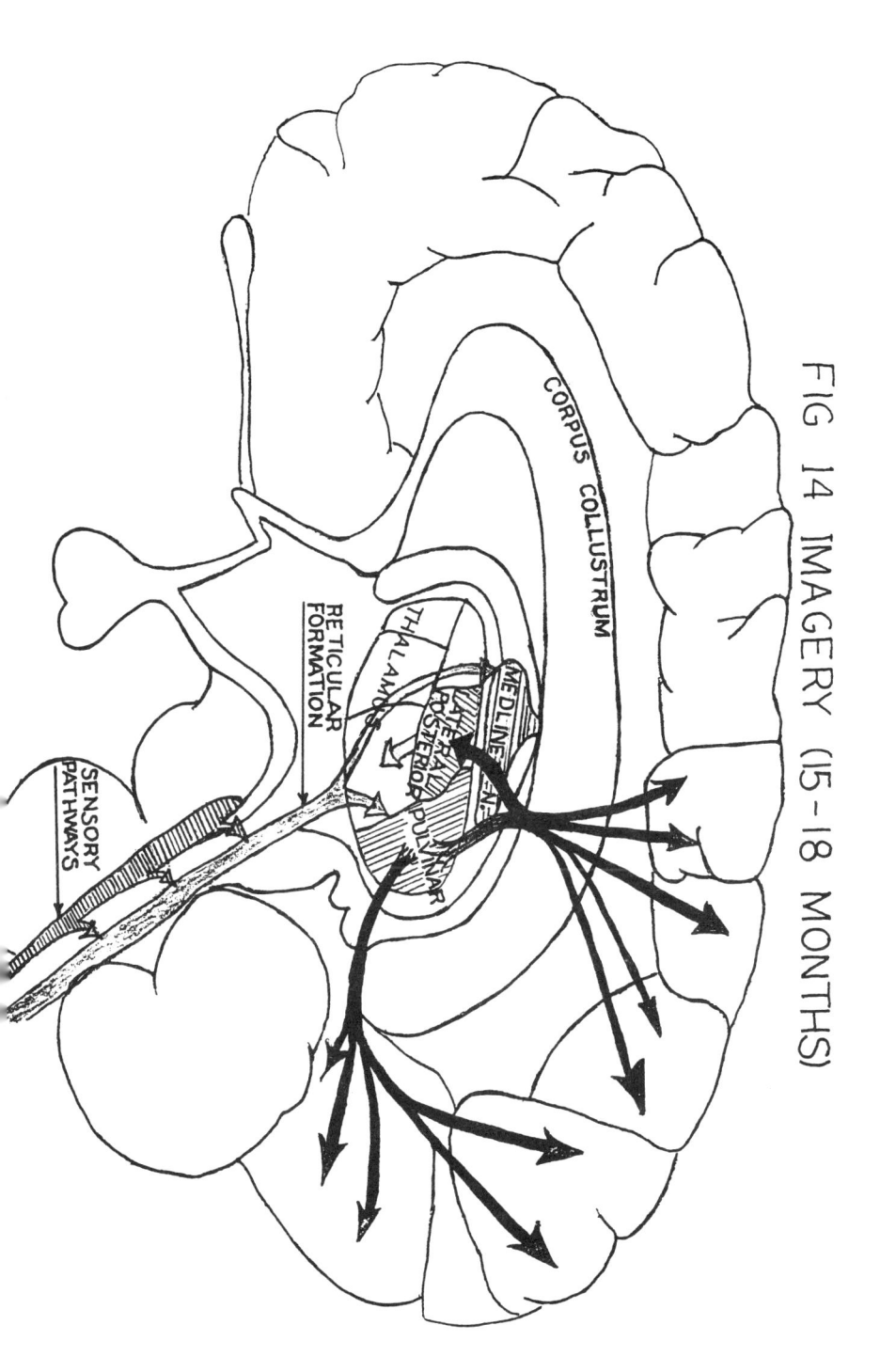

FIG 14 IMAGERY (15-18 MONTHS)

The area of the pulvinar thalamus has increased its relative size in man, because of its more elaborate integrating sensory function to provide one of the principle differences between man and animals. (63) The pulvinar thalamus borders the visual-auditory and somator-sensory cortex and is in an ideal position to influence and integrate sensory information.

The audio-visual and somatorsensory association function is one of recall, or of imagining similar things heard, seen or felt that leads to imagery of possible actions or consequences. This association mechanism of imagination is a diffuse system that permits a creative process to develop.

The ability of the pulvinar-parietal-temporatal areas to recall audio-visual sensation as imagery is combined and integrated with the affective memory of the cingulate area to provide the capacity for abstract thinking to develop.

ACTION PERIOD
18 - 21 MONTHS

INFANT-CHILD STAGE

The various behaviors of the motor nervous system are the components developing now. The information in this section was obtained from Gesell and Ilg.(40) The one and a half year old is a runabout, who is constantly getting into everything. He is impulsive, busy, self-contained and independent. He likes to chase and be chased, and he enjoys a little roughhousing now. Straining at the leash, he lugs, tugs, pulls, pushes and pounds. He would rather push his baby carriage now than ride in it.

The 18 month old endlessly shifts from one thing to another. He likes to go exploring, and discovers by moving about investigating in an exploratory manner. He refuses to be touched, to have his arm held, or be restrained by a playpen, as he needs room to run around.

His attention, like his body activity, is constantly shifting. So his attention span operates in brief quick strokes. The 18 month old finds it difficult to wait because he lives strictly in the present. Immersed in the here and now, he is blind to anything in the future. He accepts almost any stranger as a companion on excursions. After eating his afternoon meal, he goes right to sleep for a nap. When going to bed at night after an active day, he is easily quieted by being talked to.

He depends on an abundant non-verbal vocabulary of gestures to express himself. He manipulates things with competence and assurance. He completes a situation with a decisive manner that show an interest in conclusions.

He may treat other children as objects rather than people and poke, pull, push and pinch them as though they were objects for manipulation. Since people do not give him undue concern, he shows a high degree of self containment, and may play by himself for hours, quite contentedly. He enjoys turning the knob of the radio to play music to dance by, as he may sway his whole body keeping time with a musical rhythm.

If caught taking something he knows he shouldn't, he will run away and drop the object. He may become angry when things don't work out the way he thinks they should, sometimes going into a tantrum with violent crying, hitting, kicking and casting himself on the floor. When fatigued he has little desire to control his impulses and is apt to grab objects and go into a tantrum.

ACTION CIRCUIT

Gross motor integration seems to occur at the red nucleus and at the ventral lateral thalamus through which projections from the frontal lobe continue downward to lower motor areas.(See Fig. 15)

It seems that the subthalamus nucleus and the zona incerta motor areas are developing now. These motor areas along with the claustrum seem to play an important function in the rhythm and music ability that is becoming quite evident.

The proprioceptive aspect of the out going "specific" sensory ability seems to be developing. (The incoming "non-specific" sensory aspect developed during the last "imagery" period.) This proprioceptive feed-back provides a specific awareness within the muscle fibers of the body to give control for effective motor action. This information is integrated at the arcuate nucleus and the ventral posterior lateral nucleus of the thalamus that receive fibers from the trigeminal and medial lemniscus respectively, and project to the somesthetic gyrus of the parietal cortex.

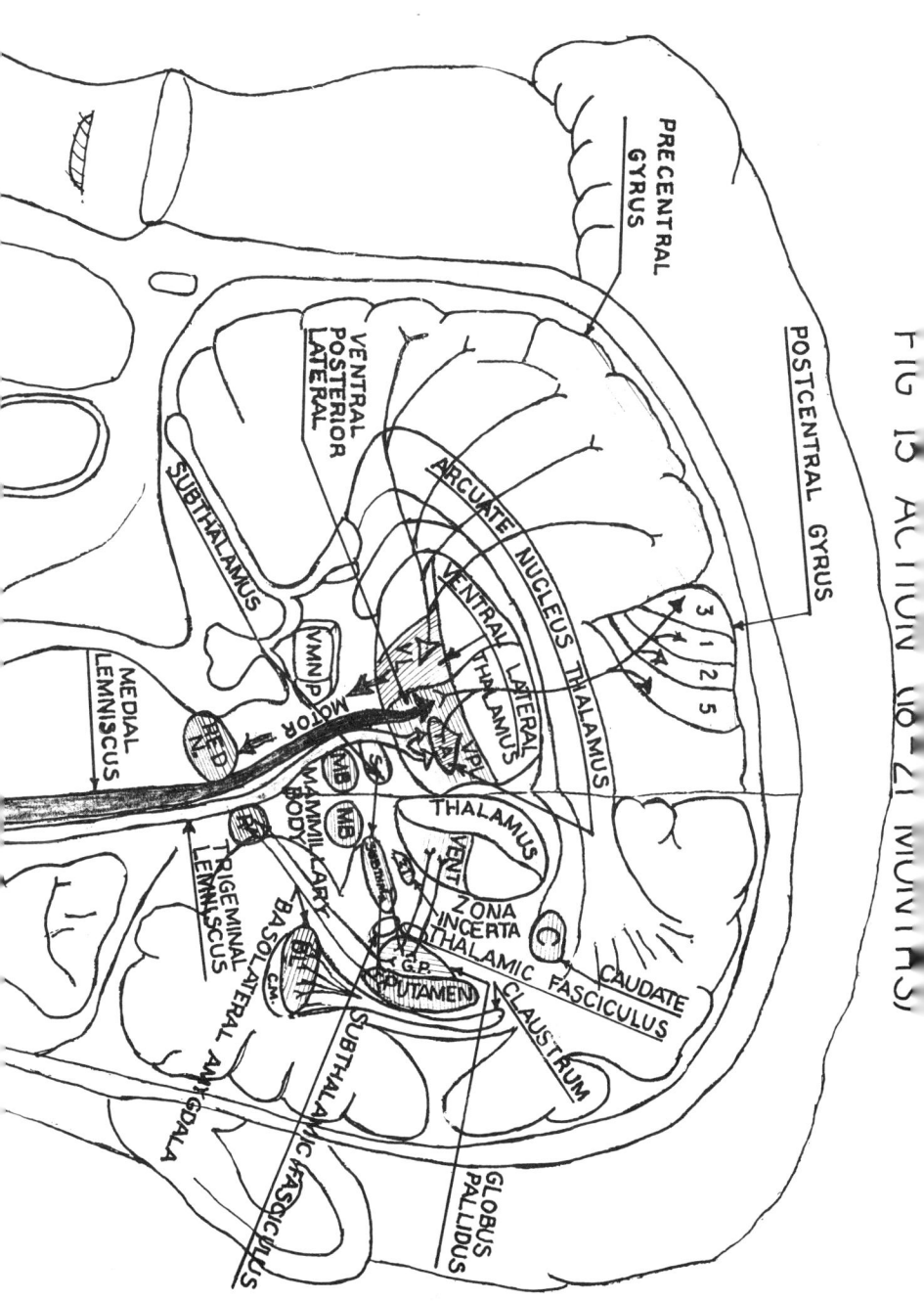

FIG 15 ACTION (18-21 MONTHS)

INTUITIVE PERIOD
3 - 1/ 2 TO 4 YEARS

JUVENILE STAGE

PROJECTION/ RECEPTION RESPONSE

We have an inner dynamic force that allow us to emit or "project" an inner vitality in the form of a kind of energy wave, that can be utilized to convey and receive thoughts.

The "juvenile" child seems to have the potential to develop a telepathic ability, but it will just be mentioned here briefly. Under status most of the sensitivities of the sensory nervous system are often a detriment. On the other hand, a lack of sensitivity permits the greatest protection from hurt, and provides the greatest potential for emotional survival.

Therefore sensitivity, goes undeveloped; to be aware of the critical thoughts of punitive minded status oriented people would only produce misery or violence. As a result, the sensitivity of a radar receptivity will gradually atrophy, because of the remo's dire need to avoid the punishment of displeasure.

This sensitivity is usually suppressed and discarded in order to survive in a status system. It is such a detriment under status that it would be a huge handicap. So instead of being cultivated, this intuitive ability withers away, gradually deteriorating until it is abandoned through disuse.

The 3-1/2 year old is very affectionate towards the parents, but may also be possessive of the parents, and jealous of younger siblings. There is an awkwardness and increased tension now, as seen in nail biting, eyeblinking, tremulous hands, temporary stuttering, and a need to seek assurance with "Do you love me?"(40)

The ability to "project" thoughts, and feeling to others, and the ability to receive directed thoughts and feelings from others, seems to come from the dentrate gyrus of the hippocampus. The dentrate gyrus is an adjoining sensory aspect of the hippocampus where many pathways converge from many different sensory modalities to provide integration for greater sensory acuity.

APPENDIX B
NAMES FOR REMO

Ace
Amigo
Aphrodite
April
Ayda

Babsie
Bae
Bammer
Beau
Bee Bee
Bell
Binky
Birdie
Blossom
Bo Bo
Bootsie
Bozo
Brandy
Broc
Buba
Bubbie
Bubbles
Bun
Bunny
Buster
Buzz(y)

Chip
Chiquita
Cho Cho
Chum
Cinnamon

Coco
Cookie
Cuddles
Cutsie

Daisy
Dede
Dee Da
Dixie
Dody
Doodler
Dove
Duckie
Dumplin

Egg
Elf
Eros
Ev

Fang
Flame
Flash
Foxy
Free
Froggy

Gingam
Gumba
Guy

Happy
Harmony
Harpy

Hawk
Heff
Holly
Hope
Hoppy

Jay
Jocko
Jude

Kid
Killer
King
Kitten
Kumquat

Lambchop
Lather
Lim
Lobo
Luv

Magna
Magnolia
Mate
Melissa
Midy
Mimi
Mojo
Mon Ami
Moose
Mosy
Muffy

Nibblet	Salt	Ulysses
Novena	Scamp	
	Scoop	Vada
Oaty	Scout	Vega
Owl	Scribe	Venus
	Shana	Vin
Pal	Sharpy	
Pan	Skeet	Waldo
Panda	Slugs	Waxy
Pard	Smokey	Wen
Parki	Smooch	Whiz
Pax	Snoopy	Wick
Peanut	Snoozy	Winkie
Penelope	Snuggles	Woofer
Penny	Sparrow	Woozle
Pepe	Sport	
Pepper	Spunky	Yum Yum
Perk(y)	Stormy	
Pijin	Sug	Zeno
Pip	Sugar	
Pogo	Sunny	
Poppy	Sunshine	
Princess	Swan	
Puddin		
Pudge	Tar	
Pug	Tasha	
Pumpkin	Teddy(bear)	
Pup	Thumper	
	Tigger	
Ragin	Tinkerbell	
Ram	Tonto	
Raven	Toots	
Rip	Torp(edo)	
Ro	Tuff(y)	
Robin	Tutu	
Rose	Tweety	
Rosebud	Twickle	
Roxy	Twiddle	
Ruff		

BIBLIOGRAPHY

1.   Andersen, R. Differences in the course of learning as measured by various memory tasks after amygdalectomy in man. In E. Hitchcock,L. Laitinen and K. Vaernet (Eds.). Psychosurgery. Springfield, Ill.:Charles C. Thomas, 1972, 177-183.

2.   Andersen, P., Eccles, J. C. and Lyning, Y.   Feedback inhibition via basket cells in the hippocampus. Journal Neurophysiol., 1964, 27:592-608.

3.   Anokhin, P.K. The multiple ascending influences of the subcortical centers on the cerebral cortex. Brain and Behavior.American Institute of Biological Sciences, Washington, 1961.

4.   Arieti, S. Special logic of schizophrenic and other types of autistic thought, in M. Zax and G. Stricker (ed.). Study of Abnormal Behavior. Macmillan, 1964, 167-183.

5.   Arnold, M.B.   Brain function in emotion. In P. Black (Ed.)Physiological Correlates of Emotion. Academic Press, 1970.

6.   Bass, H. Development of an adult's imaginary companion.Psychoanalytic Review. 1983, Vol. 79 (4), 519-533.

7.   Bennett, E.L. & Rosenzweig, M.R. Chemical alterations produced in brain by environment and training. In Lastho, A.(Ed.) 6 Handbook of Neurochemistry. NY: Plenum Press 1970, 173-201.

8.   Bennett, E.L., Diamond, I.T., Krech, D. and Roenzweig, M.R. Chemical and anatomical plasticity of the brain. Science, 1964, 46, 610-619.

9.   Bernstein, P. Run your own business: Worker owned plywood firms. Working Paper for a New Society. 1974, summer Vol. 2, No. 2,24-34.

10.   Blachly, P.H., Disher, W. & Roduner, G. Suicide by Physicians. Bulletin of Suicidology, Dec. 1-18, 1968.

11.   Bowlby, J. Separation anxiety. Int. Journal PSA., 1960, 41, 89-113.
12.   Braithwaite, J. Crime, Shame and Reintegration. Cambridge, N.Y.: Cambridge Univ. Press, 1989.
13.   Brooks, M. & Knowles, D. Parent's views of children's imaginary companions. Child Welfare, 1982, 61, 25-33.
14.   Bruner, J.S. On perceptual readiness. Psychological Review. 1957, 64, 123-152.
15.   Buchwald, N.A., Wuyers, E.J., Okuma, T. and Heuser, G. The caudate spindle. I: Electrophysiological Properties. EEG Clin. Neurophysiol. 1961, 13, 509-518.
16.   Cameron, P. Social stereotypes: three faces of happiness. Psychology Today. 1974, Aug. 63.
17.   Chatrian, G.E. & Chapman, W.R. Electrographic studies of the amygdaloid region with implanted electrodes in patients with temporal lobe epilepsy. In E. R. Ramey & D.S. O'Doherty(Eds.), Electrical Studies on the Unanaesthetized Brain. Hoeber, 1960.
18.   Cort'es, J.B. & Gatti, F.M. Physique & Motivation. Journal Consulting Psychology. 1966, 30, 408-414.
19.   Critchley, M. Speech and speech-loss in relation to duality of the brain, in V.B. Mountcastle (ed.) Interhemispheric Relations and cerebral dominance. Hopkins University Press, 1962, 208-213.
20.   Cushman, P. Relationship between narcotic addiction and crime. Federal Probation. 1974, Vol. 38, No. 3, 38-43.
21.   Cushman, P. Why the self is empty. American Psychologist. 1990, May 599-609.
22.   Dafny, N. and Feldman, S. Effects of caudate nucleus stimulation. Electroencephalog. Clin. Neurophysiol. 1967, 23, 546-557.
23.   Dafny, N. and Feldman, S. Responsiveness of posterior hypothelamic neurons to striatal and peripheral stimuli. Exp. Neurol. 1968, 21, 397-412.
24.   Dement, W.C. & Wolpert, E. A. Relationships in the manifest content of dreams occurring on the same night. Journal of Nervous Mental Disorder. 1958, 126, 568-577.
25.   Dey, F.L., Fisher, C., Berry, C.M. and Ranson, S.W. Disturbances in reproductive functions caused by hypothalamic lesions in female guinea pigs. American Journal of Physiology, 1940, 129, 39-46.

26.   Eccles, J.C. The Understanding of the Brain. McGraw-Hill, 1973.

27.   Edinger, L. The anatomy of the central nervous system of man and of vertebrates in general. F.A. Davis, 1899.

28.   Edwards, R. Death by Unemployment. New Statesman. Vol. 106:6, Nov. 25, 1983.

29.   Endroczi, E. Lissak, K. and Kovacs, S. The inhibitory influence of archicortical structures on pituitary-adrenal function. Acta Physiol. Acad. Sci. Hung., 1959,16,17-22.

30.   Farmer, R.D. and Harvey, P.G. Alienated youth. Social Science and Medicine. 1974, April vol. 8, No. 4, 191-194.

31.   Feldman, S. and Dafny, N. Modification of single cell responses in the posterior hypothalamus to sensory stimuli by caudate and globus pallidus stimulation. Brain Res. 1968, 10, 402-417.

32.   Fernandez De Molina, A. and Hunsperger, R.W. Central representation of affective reactions in forebrain and brain stem. Journal of Physiology. 1959, 145, 251-265.

33.   Fraiberg, S. On the sleep disturbances of early childhood. The Psychoanalytic Study Of The Child. International Universities Press, 1950, 285-309.

34.   French, T.M. The integration of behavior, Vol. 2, The integrative Process in Dreams. Universituy of Chicago Press, 1954.

35.   Gazzaniga, M.S. The split brain in man. Scientific American.1967, 217, 2, 24-29.

36.   Gazzaniga, M.S. & Freedman, N. Observations of visual processes following posterior callosal section. Neurology. 1973, 23, 1126-1130.

37.   Gazzaniga, M.S. & Sperry, R.W. Simultaneous double discrimination following brain bisection. Psychonomic Science. 1966, 4, 262-263.

38.   Gellhorn, E. & Loofbourrow, G. Emotions & Emotional Disorders. Harper & Row, 1963.

39.   Geschwind, N. & Kaplan, E. A human cerebral deconnection syndrome. Neurology. 1962, 12, 675.

40.   Gesell, A.L. and Ilg, F.L. Child Development: an introduction to the study of human growth. Harper and Brothers, 1949.

41.   Giambra, L.M. Daydreaming across the life span. International Journal of Aging and Human Dev. 1974, 5, 116-135.

42.   Grossman, S.P. A textbook of Physiological Psychology. JohnWiley and Sons, 1967.

43.   Hall, C.S. Diagnosing Personality by the analysis of dreams. Journal of Abnormal Social Psychology. 1947, 42, 68-79.

44.   Harlow, H.G. and Harlow, M.K. Developmental aspect of emotional behavior. In P. Black (Ed.) Physiological Correlates of Emotion. Academic Press, 1970.

45.   Hayward, J.N. and Smith, W.K. Influence of limbric system on neurohypophysis. Arch. Neurol. 1963, 9, 171-177.

46.   Herrick, C.J. The functions of the olfactory parts of the cerebral cortex. Proc. Nat. Acad. Sci. 1933, 19, 17-14.

47.   Hess, W.R. Das Zwischenhien, Basel. Schwabe 1949.

48.   Janet, P. Symposium on the subconscious. Journal of Abnormal and Social Psychology. 1907-08, Vol.2, 61-62.

49.   Jasper, H.H., Proctor, L.D., Knighton, R.S., Noshay, W.C. and Costello, R.T. (Eds.) The Reticular Formation of the Brain. Boston: Little Brown, 1958.

50.   Kanner, L. and Lesser, L. Early infantile Autism. Pediatric Clinics of N. America, 1958, 5(3), 711-730.

51.   Kawakami, M., Seto, K., Tevasawa, E. and Yoshida, K. Mechanisms in the limbric system controlling reproductive functions of the ovary with special reference to the positive feedback of progestin to the hippocampus. Progressive Brain Res. 1967, 27, 69-102.

52.   Kipnis, D. Technology And Power. Springer Verlag. N.Y., pg. 45-46, 1990.

53.   Knapp, P. Emotional aspects of hearing loss, Phychosomatic Med., 10, 203, 1968.

54.   Knigge, K.M. Adrenocórtical Response to stress in rats with lesions in hippocampus and amygdala. Proceedings of the Society for Experimental Biology and Medicine. 1961, 108, 18-21.

55.   Knobloch, H. and Pasamanick, B. Gesell and Amatruda's Developmental Diagnosis. Harper and Row, 1974.

56.   Koella, W.P. The central nervous control of sleep. In W. Haymaker, E. Anderson and W. Nauta (Ed.), The Hypothalamus. Charles C. Thomas, 1969, 622-644.

57.   Kohn, A. No Contest: The Case Against Competition. Houghton Mifflin, ppbk, 1992.

58.   Korsakoff, S.S. Etude Me'dico-psychologique sur une forme des maladies de la me'moire. Revue de Philosophie, 1889, 28, 501-530.

59.   Krippner, S. & Hughes, W. Dreams and human potential. Journal of Humanistic Psychology. 1970,10,1-12.

60.   Lawler, E. & Seashore, S. Labor takeovers. Human Behavior. 1975,Dec. Vol.4, No. 12, 70.

61.   Lenneberg, E. Biological Foundations of Language. Wiley, N.Y.1967.

62.   Lesse, H. Rhinencephalic eletrophysiological activity during emotional behavior in cats. In L.J. West and M. Greenblatt (Eds.), Explorations in the Physiology of Emotions. A.P.A. Psychiat. Res. Reports, 1960, 12, 224.

63.   Lindsley, D.B. The role of nonspecific reticulo-thalamo-cortical systems in emotion. In P. Black (Ed.) Physiological Correlates of Emotion. Academic Press, 1970.

64.   Livingston, R.B. Central control of receptors and sensory transmission systems. In Handbook of Physiology. Vol. I., J. Gield. (Eds.) Baltimore: Williams and Wilkins, 1959.

65.   Maccoby, E.E. Selective auditory attention in children. In L.P. Lipsitt and C.C. Spiker (Eds.) Advances in Child Dev. and Behavior. Vol. III N.Y.: Academic Press, 1967.

66.   Maclean, P.D. The hypothalamus and emotional behavior. In W. Haymaker, E.Anderson & W. Nauta (Ed.) The Hypothalamus 1969, 659-679.

67.   Maclean, P.D. and Ploug, D.W. Cerebral representation of penile erection. Journal Neurophysiol., 1962, 25, 30-55.

68.   McCleary, R.A. and Moore, R.Y. Subcortical Mechanisms of Behavior. Basic Books, 1965.

69.   McCulloch, W.S. Some connections of the frontal lobe established by Physiological Neuronography. Res. Publ. Ass. Nerv. Ment. Dis., 1948, 27, 95-105.

70.   Mclennan, H. and Greystone, P. The electrical activity of the amygdala and its relationship to that of the olfactory bulb. Canad. Journal Physiol. Pharmacol., 1965, 43, 1009-1017.

71.   Magoun, H.W. The Waking Brain. Thomas Books, 1969.

72.   Manosevitz, M., Prentice,N.M. & Wilson, R. Individual family correlates of imaginary companion in preschool children. Developmental Psychology, 1973, Vol.8, No. 1, 72-79.

73.   Margules, D.L. and Olds, J. Identical feeding and re-warding systems in the lateral hypothalamus of rats. Science, 135, 374-375.

74.   Maslow, A. H. & Honigmann, J.J. Synergy: Some notes of Ruth Benedict. American Anthropologist, 1970, Vol.72, No. 1, 320-333.

75.   Meissner, W.W. Learning and memory in the Korsakoff Syndrome. International Journal of Neuropsychiatry, 1968, 4(1), 6-20.

76.   Miller, W.H. Manifest anxiety in visually impaired adolescents. Education of the Visually Handicapped. 1970, (Oct.), Vol. 11(3), 91-95.

77.   Moos, R.H., Dopell, B.S., Melges, F.T., Yalom, I.D., Lunde, D.T., Clayton, R.B. and Hamburg, D.A. Fluctuations in symptoms and moods during the menstrual cycle. Journal of Psychosomatic Research, 1969, 13, 37-44.

78.   Moriarty, T. A Nation of willing Victims. Psychology Today. 1975, April, Vol. 8, No. 11, 43-50.

79.   Muhl, A.M. Automatic Writing as an indicator of the fundamental factors underlying the personality. Journal of abnormal and social psychology. 1922-23, Vol. 17, 162-183.

80.   Muhl, A.M. In the use of automatic writing in determining conflicts an early childhood impressions. Journal of Abnormal and Social Psychology. 1923-24, Vol. 18, 1-32.

81.   Nauta, W.J.H. Hypothalamic regulation of sleep in rats: an experimental study. Journal Neurophysiol. 1946, 9, 285-316.

82.   Nauta, W. and Haymaker, W. Hypothalamic nuclei and fiber connections. In the hypothalamus. W. Haymaker, E. Anderson and W. Nauta (Ed.), Thomas Books, 1969, 136-209.

83.   Nelson, L. & Kagan, S. Competition: The star-spangled scramble. Psychology Today. 1972, Sept. 53.

84.   Obler, L. & Fein, D. The Exceptional Brain. Guilford Press. N.Y. 1988.

85.   Offendrantz, W. & Rechtschaffen, A. Clinical studies of sequential dreams. Archives of General Psychiatry. 1963, 8, 497-508.

86.   Olds, J. Differential effects of drive and drugs on self-stimulation at brain sites. In Electrical Stimulation of the Brain. D.E. Sheer (ED) Austin: Univ. of Texas Press, 1961.

87.   Olds, M.E. and Olds, J. Approach-avoidance analysis of rat diencephalon. Journal Comp. Neurol., 1963, 120, 259-295.
88.   Orbach, J., Milner, B. and Rasmussen, T. Learning and retention in monkeys after amygdala hippocampal resection. Arch. Neurol., 1960, 3, 230-251.
89.   Ornstein, R.E. The Psychology of Consciousness. Viking, 1973.
90.   Piaget, J. The Construction of Reality in the Child. Trans. by M. Cook. N.Y. Basic Books, 1954.
91.   Pickenhain, L. and Klingberg, F. Hippocampal slow wave activity as a correlate of basic behavioral mechanisms in the rat. Progressive Brain Res., 1967, 27, 218-227.
92.   Pinter, R., Fusfeld, I. & Brunscwig, L. Personality tests of deaf adults, Journal of Genetic Psychology. 1937, V.51, 305.
93.   Pribram, K.H. Languages Of The Brain. Prentice-Hall, 1971, 28-43.
94.   Redford, W. The Trusting Heart. Random House, 1989.
95.   Rose, K. & Rosnow, I. Physicians who kill themselves. Archives of General Psychiatry, 29, 800-805, 1973.
96.   Rothfield, L. and Harman, P. On the relation of the hippocampal-fornix system to the control of rage responses in cats. Journal Comp. Neurol., 1954, 101, 265-282.
97.   Rushton, J.P. Race differences in behavior: a review and evoluntionary analysis. Personality and individual differences. 1988, Vol. 9(6), 1009-1024.
98.   Samples, R.E. Learning with the whole brain. Human Behavior. 1975, Vol. 4, 16-23.
99.   Schaffer, H.R. and Emerson, P.E. The development of social attachments in infancy. Monographs of the Society for Research in Child Development, 1964, Serial No.94, 29.
100.   Schneck, J.M. Automatic writing during hypnoanalysis. Journal of General Psychology. 1952, 46, 233-241.
101.   Schwartzbaum, J.S. Changes in reinforcing properties of stimuli following ablation of the amygdaloid complex in monkey. Journal of Comparative and Physiological Psychology. 1960, 53, 388-395.
102.   Schwartzbaum, J.S. Discrimination behavior after amygdalectomy in monkeys. Journal of Comparative and Physiological Psychology. 1965, 60, 314-319.

103.   Schwartzbaum, J.S.   Discrimination behavior after amygdalectomy in monkeys. Journal of comparative and Physiological Psychology, 1965, 60, 314-319.

104.   Simpson, D.A.   The efferent fibers of the hippocampus in the monkey. Journal Neurol. Neurosurg. Psychiat., 1952, 15, 79.

105.   Singer, J.S. Child's world of make believe: experimental studies of imaginative play. Academic Press, 1973.

106.   Smythies, J.R. Brain mechanisms and behavior. Academic Press, 1970.

107.   Sokolov, E.N.   Higher nervous functions: the orienting reflex. Annual Review of Physiology. Stanford, Calif.: Annual Reviews,1963, 544-580.

108.   Sperry, R.W. Hemisphere deconnection and unity of conscious awareness. American Psychologist, 1968, 23,723-733.

109.   Sperry, R.W. Perception in the absence of the neocortical commissures. Perception And Its Disorders, Res. Publ. 1970, Vol. 48.

110.   Spock, B.   Baby and Child Care. Pocket books, 1968.

111.   Steppacher, R. & Mawner, J. Suicide in Male and Female Physicians. Journal of the American Medical Association, 228, 223-228, 1974.

112.   Sterman, M.B. and Clemente, C.D.   Forebrain inhibiting mechanisms; cortical synchronization induced by basal forebrain stimuation. Exp. Neurol., 1962, 6, 91-117.

113.   Stevens, J.R., Glaser, G.H. and Maclean, P.D. The influence of sodium amytal on the recollection of seizure states. Tran. Amer. Neurol. Assoc. 1954, 79(1), 40-95.

114.   Stewart, K. Dream theory in Malaya. Altered States of Consciousness. Tart, C.T. (ed.). Wiley, 1969.

115.   Straus, M.A. Beating the Devil Out of Them: Corporal Punishment in American families. Lexington Books, 1994.

116.   Sutton-Smith, B.   Child Psychology. Appleton Century Crofts,1973.

117.   Teitelbaum, H. and Milner, P. Activity changes following partial hippocampal lesions in rats. Journal Comp. Physiol. Psychol., 1963, 56, 284-289.

118.   Ullmann, L.P. and Krasner, L.A.   Psychological Approach To Abnormal Behavior. Prentice-Hall, 1969.

119.   Ursin, H. and Kaada, B.R. Subcortical structures medi-
        ating attention response induced by amygdala stimulation.
        Exp. Neurol. 1960, 2, 109-122.
120.   Ursin, H. and Kaada, B.R. Functional localization within
        the amygdaloid complex in the cat. EEG Clin. Neurophysiol.
        1969, 12, 1-20.
121.   Ustinov, P. Dear Me. Middlesex, England. Penguin, 1977.
122.   Vanderloos, H. Improperly oriented cells in the cortex
        and its bearing on growth and cell proliferation. Bulletin of
        Johns Hopkins Hospital, 1965, 117, 228-250.
123.   Victor, M., Angevine, J.B., Mancall, E.L. and Fisher, C.M.
        Memory loss with lesions of hippocampal formation. Arch.
        Neurol.,1961, 5, 244-263.
124.   Vostrosky, C.A. Study of imaginary play companions.
        Education, 1985, 15, 383-397.
125.   Walter, W.G., Cooper, R.A., Aldridge, V.J., Mccallum,
        W.C. and Winter, A.L. Contingent negative variation: an
        electric sign of sensori-motor assoc. and expectancy in the
        brain. Nature, 1964, 203, 380-384.
126.   Ward, A.A. The cingular gyrus: area 24. Journal
        Neurophysiol., 1948, 11, 13-23.
127.   Winton, C.A. Legally blind young adult. University of
        Calif., Berkely. Dissertation Abstracts International. 1971
        (Jan), Vol. 31.
128.   Wurtz, R.H. and Olds, J. Amygdaloid stimulation and
        operant reinforcement in the rat. Journal Comp. Physiol.
        Psychol. 1963, 56, 941-949.
129.   Yarrow, L.J. Separation from parents during childhood.
        Review of Child Development research, Vol. I. Russell Sage
        Foundation,1954.
130.   Zaidel, E. & Sperry, R. The right has something to say
        after all. Psychology Today. 1975, Dec. V.9, 7, 121.

GLOSSARY

ACCEPTANCE CHAIN: different levels of acceptance that link those at various ranks in a vertical social status structure.

ACCEPTANCE, CONDITIONAL: an attitude where you are not disapproved of, if you do what is right, if you do what is expected, and if you are successful in what you attempt to do.

ADULT-CHILD STAGE: the remo's level of emotional development from four to five years of age.

AFFINITY: close connection and relationship.

ALPHA WAVES: a relaxed tranquil state when brain cell waves fire at a semi-synchronize frequency rate of 8-12 cycles per second (cps).

AMELIORATION: to improve, to make better.

APATHY: a listless condition with a lack of interest and a lack of emotion.

APNEA: when breathing is temporary stopped.

APPROACH RESPONSE: provides a pleasurable positive outlook on life using the sympathetic nervous system.

AUTOMATIC BEHAVIORS: an act repeated so often that it becomes a habit that's performed by your remo.

AUTONOMIC NERVOUS SYSTEM: consist of the sympathetic and para-sympathetic divisions that control the motor functions of the heart, lungs, intestines, glands, and other internal organs.

AXONS: part of the brain's nerve cell through which impulses travel away from the cell body.

BETA WAVES: an excited or highly active state when brain cell waves randomly fire at an irregular frequency rate of 20-25 cycles per second (cps).

BOUTON: a terminal club-shaped enlargement of a nerve fiber lying in contact with the body of dendrites of another neuron.

CARE RESPONSE: first develops from two to two and half years of age and integrates all the prior growth periods to provide integrity, conscientiousness, problem solving ability and an ability to love the self.

CHILD STAGE: the remo's level of development from two to three years of age.

COLLATERALS: a small side branch of an axon or nerve.

COLLOQUY: a conversation

CORPUS CALLOSUM: a large mass of neural fibers connecting the rao's hemisphere with the remo's hemisphere, so communicate can take place.

DENDRITES: the branching part of the brain's nerve cell that carries impulses toward the cell body.

DIAPHRAGM: a muscle between the chest cavity and the abdominal cavity that helps push air out of the lungs.

EIGHT STAGES OF DEVELOPMENT: each stage is a five year period involving 12 limbric circuits; the eight stages occur between birth and 40 years of age, the remo develops during the first half of each decade, while the rao develops in the second half.

EMANATIONS: something or someone who comes forth, or to send forth.

EQUILIBRIUM: a state of balance that results in mental and emotional stability and poise.

EXPECTANCY RESPONSE: a keen state of awareness, attention and readiness as witnessed in an "orienting reflex" of a house cat.

FAMILIAL STAGE: growth in the remo's hemisphere from 30 to 35 years of age, involving 12 subcortical circuits and periods that solidify with connections in the top associative autonomic layer of the neocortex.

GENERALIST: an ability of the remo to provide a comprehensive overview, to see the whole picture; and workers who are trained to take part in almost any aspect of a business.

GLIA: the connective tissues or membranes that support and bind together branched cells of the neocortex.

GROWTH PERIODS: twelve circuits in the subcortical limbric area that represent behaviors that develop during a five year stage of development; each growth stage locks into one of six layers of the neocortex in the rao's or remo's hemisphere.

HYPOTHALAMUS: a nuclear group that acts as the lower central organizing seat of the subcortical limbric nervous system, that the remo appears to operate from to dominate its hemisphere of the brain.

ID: a source of psychic energy and instinctual drives dominated by the pleasure principle and irrational wishing.

IMPULSIVE STAGE: growth in the remo's hemisphere from 20 to 25 years of age, involving 12 subcortical circuits and periods that lock-in with connections in the second motor layer of the neocortex.

INFANT-CHILD STAGE: the development of the remo from one to two years of age.

INFANT STAGE: the development of the remo from birth to one year of age.

INTEGRATIVE RESPONSE: the integration of the sensory, motor and autonomic nervous systems by integrating all eleven of the prior emotional growth circuits at the adult-child stage.

INTUITIVE STAGE: growth in the remo's hemisphere from birth to 5 years of age, involving 12 subcortical circuits and periods that solidify with connections in the bottom three layer of the neocortex.

JUVENILE STAGE: the remo's level of development from three to four years of age.

LIBIDO: a source of psychic energy that consist of positive, pleasurable and loving instincts.

LIMBRIC NERVOUS SYSTEM: the neural circuits and nuclei that operate below the grey matter of the neocortex.

LOCK-IN: when one of the twelve emotional behavioral circuits changes from malleable, pliant and mobile neurons to so-lidify into permanent neural pathways.

MALLEABLE STAGE: growth in the rao's hemisphere from 5 to 10 years of age, involving 12 subcortical circuits that solidify with connections in the bottom three layer of the neocortex.

MENTATIONS: the process of using the mind and thought.

MOTOR NERVOUS SYSTEM: nerve fibers that carry impulses from the central nervous system (brain and spinal cord) to muscles producing motion.

MULTIFORMITY: the acceptance and encouragement of all behaviors except harmful behaviors.

NEOCORTEX: six layers of the grey matter of the brain under the cranium of the skull and above the limbric nervous system.

NEURON: consist of a nerve cell body and all its processes, including an axon and one or more dendrites.

NEUROSIS: mental/emotional disorders characterized by anxiety, compulsions, phobias, depression, dissociations, etc. that occur from a breakdown of behavioral defenses when the remo has been stopped in growth at the child stage.

OLFACTORY REGION: primarily concerned with the sense of smell, but also has an emotional function that acts on the viscera to influence bodily attitudes and affective moods by producing gross visceral approach and avoidance reactions; it can also impair consciousness with tired or sleepy feelings.

PARA-SYMPATHETIC NERVOUS SYSTEM: a division of the autonomic nervous system that slows the body down for repair; a restorative function that operates to revitalize the body from cellular breakdown; also an energy response that acts in a preservatory function of sleeping, drinking, eating and eliminating.

PAVLOVIAN RESPONSE: a conditioned reflex in which the response (e.g., secretion of saliva in a dog) is occasioned by a secondary stimulus (e.g., the ringing of a bell) repeatedly associated with the primary stimulus (e.g., the sight of meat).

POLITICAL STAGE: growth in the rao's hemisphere from 35 to 40 years of age, involving 12 subcortical circuits and periods that solidify with connections in the top associative autonomic layer of the neocortex.

PRODUCTIVE STAGE: growth in the rao's hemisphere from 25 to 30 years of age, involving 12 subcortical circuits and periods that solidify with connections in the second motor layer of the neocortex.

PROLIX: using more words than are necessary.

PYRRHIC VICTORY: a victory that is too costly.

RAO: normally the left hemisphere of the brain in the right-handed person and represents the conscious thinking discriminating self; also recognized by terms like the ego, the conscious self, the adult ego and yang.

READINESS RESPONSE: the integration of the "vegetative and expectancy" responses as an aspect of the "care" growth period.

REMO: normally the right hemisphere of the brain in the right-handed person and represents the subconscious child within you; also recognized by terms like the unconscious, the conscience, the id, the libido, yin, the parent ego, the imaginary companion and what is known as your "heart" and "soul."

SENSITIVITY STAGE: growth in the remo's hemisphere from 10 to 15 years of age, involving 12 subcortical circuits and periods that lock-in with connections in the third sensory layer of the neocortex.

SENSORY NERVOUS SYSTEM: nerve fibers that carry impulses from the eyes, ears, nose, mouth and skin to the central nervous system (brain and spinal cord)

SENSUOUS STAGE: growth in the rao's hemisphere from 15 to 20 years of age, involving 12 subcortical circuits and periods that solidify with connections in the third sensory layer of the neocortex.

SIBLING: brother or sister; having one parent in common.

SLEEP RESPONSE: the integration of the "vegetative" response with the mood depressing aspect of the "stabilizing" response to allow one to go to sleep quickly and easily, anytime or anywhere.

SOBRIQUET: a nickname.

SOCIALIZING RESPONSE: the integration of the mood elevating aspect of the "stabilizing" response with the "readiness" response.

SOOTHING RESPONSE: the integration of the "sleep" response with the "expectancy" response to serve as a control over anger and fear.

SPECIALIST; an ability of the rao to provide the concentrated attention needed for fine details; and workers who are trained to be an expert in a specific area of a business.

STABILIZING RESPONSE: a memory response with a mood elevating and mood reducing aspect that provides the ability to moderate the "care" response with an impartial indifference, and has an ability to inhibit displeasures such as anxiety and anger in the early stages.

STATUS: a social system that has a vertical structure with the shape of a pyramid; those at the top are entitled to acceptance from all those who are below, and those on the bottom are entitled to no acceptance from those above; and this competition for acceptance is what causes the social problems between people.

SUBLIMINAL SELF: represents the remo who can operates below the level of consciousness.

SYCHRONAL (PERIOD) CIRCUIT: represents the emotional behaviors of the olfactory region of the brain that develop in the first three months of each growth period.

SYMPATHETIC NERVOUS SYSTEM: a division of the autonomic nervous system that's experienced as an excited or active state when beta brain waves dominate.

SYNAPSE: the point of contact between neurons where impulses are transmitted.

SYNERGY: a social system that has a horizontal or flat social structure where all behaviors and people are accepted except harmful behaviors and people; there is an orientation towards pleasure where punishment is restricted to harmful behaviors and people.

THALAMUS: a nuclear group that acts as the higher central organizing seat of the subcortical limbic nervous system, that the rao appears to operate from to dominate its hemisphere of the brain.

THETA WAVES: a drowsy sleep state when brain waves fire at a synchronize frequency rate of 4-6 cycles per second (cps).

TMJ: temporomandibular joint syndrome with spasm of the chewing muscles due to clenching or grinding the teeth.

VEGETATIVE RESPONSE: runs on a continuum from a state of relaxation to a deep sleep, and influences oral activity around the region of the mouth, so that the lips, tongue and jaws take on a relaxed loose appearance.

YANG: in Chinese philosophy, an active, positive, masculine force; and a source of light and heat.

INDEX

Order Form

Postal Orders: Synergy Press, Marvin Kistler,
  P. O. Box 41457, St. Petersburg, Fl. 33743-1457
(813) 545-1560

Please send me:

☐ Copies of **The Stranger Within**, by Marvin Kistler
Cost $29.95 (Please add $2.00 postage & handling for one
book, $0.50 for each additional book. Fla. residents add
6.50% sales tax.)

Name: _____

Address: _____

City/State/Zip: _____